# a year of good eating

Nigel Slater is the author of a collection of bestselling books and presenter of BBC One's *Eating Together*. He has been food columnist for the *Observer* for over twenty years. His books include the classics *Appetite* and *The Kitchen Diaries I* and *II*, the critically acclaimed two-volume *Tender* and the bestselling *Eat*. His award-winning memoir *Toast – the story of a boy's hunger* won six major awards and is now a BBC film starring Helena Bonham Carter and Freddie Highmore. His writing has won the National Book Award, the Glenfiddich Trophy, the André Simon Memorial Prize and the British Biography of the Year. He was the winner of the Guild of Food Writers' Award for his BBC One series *Simple Suppers*.

Also by Nigel Slater:
*Eat*
*The Kitchen Diaries II*
*Tender Volumes I and II*
*Eating for England*
*The Kitchen Diaries I*
*Toast – the story of a boy's hunger*
*Appetite*
*Nigel Slater's Real Food*
*Real Cooking*
*The 30-Minute Cook*
*Real Fast Food*

# A YEAR OF GOOD EATING

## the kitchen diaries III

## Nigel Slater

Photography by Jonathan Lovekin

FOURTH ESTATE · London

First published in Great Britain by
Fourth Estate
a division of HarperCollinsPublishers
The News Building
1 London Bridge Street
London
SE1 9GF

www.4thestate.co.uk

A catalogue record for this book is available from
the British Library

ISBN 978-0-00-753680-1

Typeset by GS Typesetting
Printed in Germany by
Mohn Media Mohndruck GmbH

*For James*

# Acknowledgements

I am eternally indebted to Louise Haines for encouraging me to put pen to paper, and to still be there, twenty-four years later. Louise, thank you for everything.

My thanks too go to:

Allan Jenkins, Ruaridh Nicoll, Gareth Grundy and to everyone at the *Observer*. I feel truly blessed to work with each and every one of you.

My literary agent Araminta Whitley and everyone at LAW, and to my television agent Rosemary Scoular and the team at United Agents. Thank you for your guidance, expertise and insight.

Everyone at 4th Estate, especially Michelle Kane, Georgia Mason, Chris Gurney, Julian Humphries, and to Annie Lee, David Pearson, Gary Simpson and Louise Tucker. Without whom the book would never have reached the page so beautifully. Thanks, as always, to Jonathan Lovekin and to Jenny Zarins.

Danny Cohen, Charlotte Moore and Alison Kirkham at BBC1 for their support and encouragement.

My collaborators at Sloe Films for their brilliance: James Thompson, Emma Boswell, Katya Nelhams-Wright, Sarah Myland, John Collins, Conor Connolly, Robbie Johnson, Sam Jones, Natalie Thomson and Pete Lawrence.

A big shout-out to Rob Watson and Sam Jackson at ph9 for doing sterling work for nigelslater.com. To Pascal Barry and Joe Lovelock at Studio Lovelock. To Dalton Wong and George Ashwell at Twenty Two Training and to Richard Stepney at Fourth Floor. You are all heroes.

To all my followers on Twitter and Instagram whose words and pictures are such a joy.

But most of all, thank you to James Thompson, business and creative partner, producer, collaborator and best friend. For your inspiration, dedication, endless enthusiasm and, above all, your friendship, I can never thank you enough.

My love and gratitude to you all.

A note on the type

Monotype Haarlemmer was originally designed
by Jan van Krimpen (1892–1958), but never finished.
Working from van Krimpen's original drawings,
Frank E. Blokland completed the family for
the Dutch Type Library in 2002.

ITC Johnston was designed by Richard Dawson
and Dave Farey in 1999 and is based on Edward
Johnston's lettering for The Underground Group,
London (introduced in 1916 and still in use today).

# Contents

# Introduction

We are not here for long.
So let's at least make ourselves something good to eat.

A lovingly kneaded loaf; a casserole of beef, garlic, thyme, stock and onions you have left to its own devices in a slow oven; a salad that crunches and crackles with young, spring leaves and sprouted seeds. A sandwich maybe, its hot filling of roast pork and crackling peeking tantalisingly from between two pieces of bread. A fool. A tart. A sticky rib. The possibilities are infinite.

I have been cooking, on an almost daily basis, for five decades. I have eaten the great, the good and things I rather wish I hadn't. As a cook, and indeed as a cookery writer, I have got things right, wrong and somewhere in between. But what never changes is my curiosity and my appetite. That, and the endless delight I get from giving people, loved ones, friends, complete strangers, something good to eat.

Just as with music or literature, there are the classics of which I never tire, yet the excitement of finding new works never dims. For me, it is the same with food. You know how it is. There are old favourites you make over and over, recipes that become part of the rhythm of your life, and then there is the stuff of fresh thinking, cooking that is spontaneous and spirited.

What has always mattered to me is that we enjoy not just the end result, but the hands-on craft along the way, the act of making ourselves and others a meal. Cooking has, for this cook at least, never been purely about the end result. It is the small, joyous details of cooking that have made it a lifelong pleasure.

# The recipes

I enjoy my work more with each passing year. And never more so than when I hear or say the words 'What shall we have to eat?' The point in my working day when food is no longer something on the page or the screen, but becomes something on a plate.

Between the pages of this, the third volume of my kitchen diaries, is a collection of good things I have eaten over the last few years. Recipes, moments and ideas I would like to share with you.

Does the world need more recipes? I like to think so. Cooking doesn't stand still, at least not for anyone with spirit, an appetite and a continuing sense of wonder. No one is exactly re-inventing the wheel in cookery nowadays, no matter what they might think, but there is still much fun to be had.

A cookery book can open a door to a world of delicious possibilities. As I hope this one will. Discovering a new way with a familiar ingredient; a reworking of an old friend; a twist, a turn, a whim or even just a simple reminder. The recipes are here to follow word for word or simply to spark your imagination, as you wish.

There are new things here: sausage fried with sauerkraut and mushrooms; the cheese, gherkins and ham of an alpine raclette turned into a tart; steak braised with sake; chicken cooked with haricot beans and lemon; friands of candied orange and bitter chocolate. There is a curry with a pungent coriander herb paste for the adventurous, and a bergamot water ice whose citrus notes will make anyone's eyes sparkle.

There are chapters you may simply want to read before you go to sleep at night – the pork bone soup simmered for three hours, for instance; and others you may want to make immediately – the grilled chicken with miso and yuzu, or perhaps the ice cream with burnt butter and toasted almonds.

There are recipes to pounce upon gleefully: tender maple biscuits that are the very essence of autumn; a salad of warm roast chicken and ripe melon for a summer lunch; grilled asparagus with an almost soupy lemon mash; gnocchi cooked with cream and dolcelatte for a winter's night and langoustines in butter with Parmesan-flecked juices to lick, hot and salty, from your fingers.

I have included recipes for those who love to cook and feel the ingredients in their hands (tartlets of figs and red onions poised somewhere between sweet and savoury, or a blackberry shortbread almost too crumbly to lift). But at least half of them are written for those who need simple, useful recipes for the end of a working day.

## The grace of understatement

But there is something else. With this book comes something of a plea for both good food and a love of cooking to be just part and parcel of our everyday lives. Thoughtful, considered, always delicious, but something to be quietly enjoyed rather than put on a pedestal. (The very notion of someone being a 'foodie' makes me shudder.)

I worry that the competitive element currently prevalent in food and cooking is scaring people, particularly new cooks, away from getting stuck in. There is, I believe, too much pressure on us to 'perform', to reach for perfection, instead of simply treating the art of making something to eat as the lifelong joy it should be.

I like to think I have an attitude to cooking and eating built on foundations of good taste and pleasure rather than of veneration and worship. Yes, I like eating the good stuff and I cook from scratch pretty much every day of my life, but I can't help thinking good food should be something we take in our stride, a life-enriching punctuation to our day, rather than something to be fetishised. And if I read once more that someone is a 'passionate cook' I think I'll eat my oven gloves.

## A healthy attitude to eating

I am concerned about the current victimisation of food. The apparent need to divide the contents of our plates into heroes and villains. The current villains are sugar and gluten, though it used to be fat, and before that it was salt (and before that it was carbs and . . . oh, I've lost track). It is worth remembering that today's devil will probably be tomorrow's angel and vice versa.

We risk having the life sucked out of our eating by allowing ourselves to be shamed over our food choices. If this escalates, historians may look back on this generation as one in which society's decision about what to eat was driven by guilt and shame rather than by good taste or pleasure. Well, not on my watch.

Yes, I eat cake, and ice cream and meat. I eat biscuits and bread and drink alcohol too. What is more, I eat it all without a shred of guilt. And yet, I like to think my eating is mindful rather than mindless. I care deeply about where my food has come from, its long-term effect on me and the planet. That said, I eat what you might call 'just enough' rather than too much.

My rule of thumb – just don't eat too much of any one thing.

## Eat something new

Most of us have our favourite meals (I have eaten fishcakes with hollandaise sauce on the side at every Friday breakfast for a decade). These are dishes we love and like to cook or eat regularly. Yet there are so many fine things out there. We would be foolish not to try everything at least once. If I hadn't, I would still be living on the diet of lamb chops and peas I survived on as a child.

In this book there is a plethora of vegetables, grains and fish dishes that my parents' generation wouldn't have known. Spelt with cherries and ham, a pizza with hempseed and rocket, salmon with oatmeal, a kedgeree of pearl barley and chickpeas cooked with mussels, to name but a few. One or two of the ingredients in here are things I have only myself discovered in the last few years – freekeh, the delicious roasted wheat, for instance, or spelt or miso. For the open-minded, cooking moves on, and mostly in a good way. I want us to celebrate that.

## Short eats

Amongst my diary entries are four seasonal sections devoted to simple, everyday eating. Written in the short, crisp style of the ideas in my previous book, *Eat*, this is the sort of cooking most of us could consider ourselves capable of attempting on a weekday.

There is grilled fish, the occasional steak or cutlet, but the backbone of these suggestions is vegetables, grains and beans. The results are sustaining, yet very few start with 'peel and chop an onion'. There is no marinating, proving or pastry-making either. Just great, fast food for every day. The recipes illuminate the seasonal, the cheap and the quick, the subjects at the very heart of modern everyday eating. Think of them as achievable, contemporary home cooking, straightforward and without a list of ingredients as long as your arm.

These recipes are not written in stone. Each and every idea welcomes additions, omissions and substitutions. They are to be interpreted as you wish. I bring you suggestions, not rules.

I think of good eating as something to enrich our daily lives, be it a dish of slow-roast ribs with creamed cauliflower or a bowl of saffron-hued dal. Simple cooking that results in something unfussy, unshowy, understated. Something to bring pleasure to our own lives and to those of others.

Nigel Slater, London
September 2015
www.nigelslater.com

Twitter: @nigelslater
Instagram: @thenigelslater

# JANUARY

## Rising

### New Year's Day

The kitchen is never silent. Even now, at 5 a.m. and still dark, there is the sound of muffled footsteps on the paving stones outside, of drunken revellers weaving their way home. At the back of the house, the constant drip of water, as regular as a ticking clock on a mantelpiece, falling into the paved courtyard outside the kitchen window. And then it starts, a favourite sound – like that of a crackling wood fire or snowfall in a forest – the patter of steady rain.

The year starts gently in this kitchen, just as it always has, with baking and a pan of soup on the stove. The kitchen table is unusually tidy. A pot of mistletoe. A single candle burning in a glass jar that once held goose fat. A tiny cup of coffee. Toast crumbs.

Instead of a loaf, I decide to make a pile of crispbread, thin and freckled with flour. I have never been particularly happy with my crispbread recipe. A little hard. Too heavy. Too sweet. Rather than the ritual baking of a loaf, I will celebrate the first day of the New Year with the rustle of a new and better crispbread.

Late last year, in Gothenburg, I found sheets of bread finer than vellum that shattered over the table as you snapped them. Sheets of crispbread speckled with blue poppy seeds and black nigella, rough with flax or linseed or gently puckered with dots and ridges, like Braille on a medicine bottle. Bread so fragile it shattered like sheets of ice.

You can make flatbreads without yeast, but I like the notion of yeast rising, of new life in the kitchen on the first day of the New Year. Eccentric, daft even, but to me it just feels right.

# Poppy seed crispbread

rye flour – 100g
plain spelt flour – 100g
oat bran – 50g
easy bake dried yeast – 7g
(a heaped teaspoon)

sea salt – half a teaspoon
honey – 3 teaspoons
warm water – 150ml
poppy seeds

Put the flours and bran into the bowl of a food mixer, tip in the yeast and salt, then turn once or twice to stir evenly through the flour. Dissolve the honey in the warm water, then pour most of it into the flour, the paddle turning slowly. The dough needs to be soft but not sticky, so you may not need all the liquid. Leave the mixer going for a good three or four minutes, till the dough comes cleanly away from the sides of the bowl. Turn off the machine, remove the bowl, and leave the dough in a warm place, covered with a cloth, for about half an hour. Set the oven at 200°C/Gas 6.

Lightly flour the work surface – I like to use a large wooden board – tip the dough on to it, then tear off pieces the size of a golf ball. Roll each piece out to roughly the size of a side plate and the thickness of a ten pence piece, laying each one on a baking sheet. With two baking sheets on the go I can bake eight at a time. Sprinkle lightly with poppy seeds, pressing them down into the surface with your hand. Bake for twelve minutes, then transfer to a cooling rack and leave for several minutes to crisp even further. They will keep in good condition in a tin for a few days. Makes 12.

# Goose fat and flat-roasties

There is a chicken in the fridge, small, plump and heavy for its size. I like to roast meat in its own juices, but today I spread the bird, generously, with goose fat. It seems wrong to mix one bird's fat with another, but in truth, no less appropriate than the cow's butter, bacon or olive oil I could have chosen. Duck or goose fat, snow-white and left over from Christmas, brings much savour to a roast chicken and to the potatoes that will accompany it.

I keep some sort of fat in the fridge, a block of butter, tightly wrapped; a jar of Ibérico lard, the sort that comes in a jar from a Spanish food shop, for the times I don't want to use olive oil.

The roast potatoes I like best are those with a little more crust than usual. The ones left in the roasting tin, whose edges, crisped to the point of shattering, are almost translucent. The potatoes you have returned to the oven while the roast rests, the ones that are blessed with a second chance to crisp up in a higher heat.

The best potato is the one you have taken the trouble to peel and parboil before you tip it, soft and slightly bruised around the edges, into the hot fat in the roasting tin. The fat that is already mixed with the juices from the roast, the seasoning and the occasional bay leaf. Dropped into the roasting tin, the potato already soft and partly cooked, its edges a little rough and floury and the fat hot and well seasoned, the roast potato couldn't have a better start.

Today, I let the potatoes, Maris Pipers, parboil for too long. They collapse into the water. As I drain them, they resemble a half-hearted mash, the odd lump poking up through its almost puréed friends. There is no question of starting again. Not enough time.

Rather than hurl them into the bin, I persevere, spooning the lumpy half-mash into the sizzling fat and butter around the roasting chicken. I scatter thyme leaves amongst the potatoes. A couple of pinches of salt. A screw or two of the peppermill.

Twenty-five minutes later, in an oven at 180°C/Gas 4, the potatoes have crisped to perfection. More golden crust than fluffy interior, everything I want a roast potato to be.

## Goose fat chicken, garlic roast potatoes

*For the chicken:*
a plump chicken
goose fat or butter – 75g

*For the potatoes:*
floury, white-fleshed
  potatoes – 650g
thyme – a few sprigs
garlic – 3 cloves

Set the oven at 200°C/Gas 6. Place the chicken in a roasting tin, smear it all over generously with goose fat, season with salt and black pepper, then roast for ten minutes before turning the heat down to 180°C/Gas 4 (the bird will need about an hour in the oven). From time to time, baste the bird with the fat and juices.

Peel the potatoes, then cut them into large chunks and cook them in boiling, generously salted water for about twenty to twenty-five minutes, maybe longer, depending on the variety. Watch their progress carefully, and let them cook to the point where they are on the verge of collapse, longer than you might do for serving them as boiled potatoes. When tested with the point of a knife, they should almost start to break up.

Drain the potatoes very carefully – you want them to be battered and broken, some in small pieces, all their edges bruised. Add the cooked potatoes, thyme and garlic to the roasting tin about thirty-five minutes from the time the bird is due to be done.

Remove the chicken from the oven and leave to rest for fifteen minutes before carving. Turn the heat up to 200°C/Gas 6 and return the potatoes to the oven to crisp even further. Carve the chicken, scatter a little sea salt over the potatoes and serve. For 4.

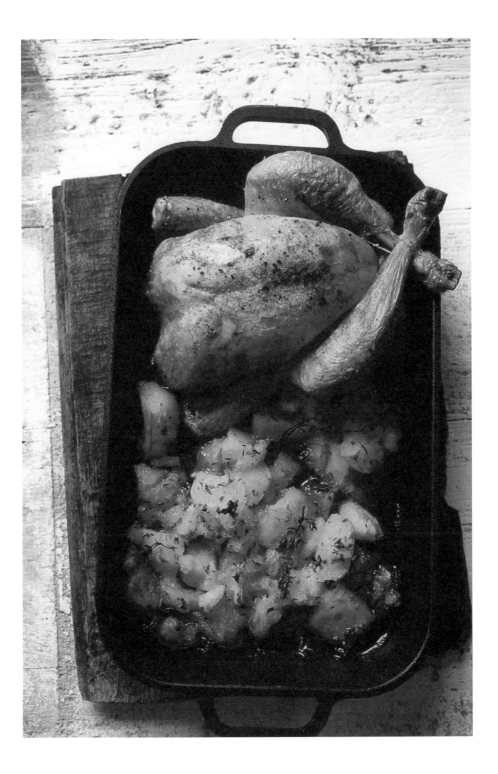

# A new breakfast

When James first suggested the notion of putting bacon in granola I was sceptical. I know that bacon works with dried fruits (think devils on horseback) and is a fine breakfast when eaten with soft, warm oatcakes, but somehow I couldn't feel it. It sounded too much like putting a sausage in your porridge.

Well, I was wrong. The crisp bacon (it really must be crisp) tumbled with the warm oats and dried fruits, then stirred through with crème fraîche, had me wolfing a second helping.

A curious one this, and not for the unadventurous, but it is a fine thing indeed to come down to on a freezing Sunday morning or, perhaps even better, on your way back from a night out.

## Bacon granola

smoked streaky bacon –
6 rashers
butter – 40g
rolled oats – 100g
whole almonds – 50g

pumpkin seeds – 50g
hemp seeds – 2 tablespoons
dried cranberries – a handful
crème fraîche – 4
tablespoons

Cut the bacon into small chunks the size of a postage stamp. Put the butter into a shallow pan, add the bacon and cook till crisp and golden, then tip in the oats, almonds, pumpkin seeds, hemp seeds and dried cranberries. Leave them to warm over a moderate heat, stirring from time to time so the nuts don't burn.

When the oats are golden and smell warm and sweet, spoon into a bowl, then stir in the créme fraîche. I like to stir only once or twice. Enough for 4.

# A winter's tart

The ancient idea of melting a large wedge of cheese in front of an open hearth, then, as it softens and melts, scraping the flowing cheese on to bread, is a notion I find almost too delicious to contemplate.

The modern version, where raclette cheese is left to melt over hot potatoes or is melted on a tabletop burner, stands to remind us just how good simple food can be. Once you add a few accompaniments in the shape of knobbly green cornichons and a slice or two cut from a decent fat-speckled salami or, more traditionally, slices of air-dried mountain ham, you have a fine dinner indeed.

Tonight, with that warming image in mind, I knock up a slim, crisp tart, complete with a scattering of sliced cornichons, shredded salami and a few mildly hot, soft green peppercorns. Brought to the table with a bowl of crisp and spiky frisée salad, it keeps out the cold for yet another winter's night.

## Raclette tart

*For the pastry:*
plain flour – 200g
butter – 100g
an egg yolk
milk – a little

*For the filling:*
egg yolks – 2

crème fraîche – 200ml
cornichons – 12
salami – 50g, thinly sliced
green peppercorns –
  2 teaspoons
thyme leaves – a good pinch
raclette, thinly sliced – 350g

You will need a shallow tart tin with a removable base, about 22cm in diameter.

Make the pastry: put the flour into a large mixing bowl with a pinch of salt. Cut the butter into cubes and rub in with your fingertips until the mixture resembles soft fresh breadcrumbs (a matter of seconds in a food processor). Add the egg yolk, mix a little more, then add enough milk – a couple of tablespoons – to bring the dough to a soft, rollable consistency.

Using a little flour on a wooden board, roll the pastry out and use it to line the tart tin. Line with baking parchment or greaseproof paper and fill with baking beans. Set aside for twenty to thirty minutes in the fridge to rest. This will stop it shrinking during baking. Set the oven at 200°C/Gas 6 and place a metal baking sheet in the oven.

When the pastry case has rested, bake on the hot baking sheet for twenty minutes. Remove the case from the oven, carefully lift out the paper and baking beans, then return to the oven for five minutes, until dry to the touch. Lower the heat to 180°C/Gas 4.

Put the egg yolks into a mixing bowl and stir in the crème fraîche and a little salt and black pepper. Slice the cornichons in half lengthways, shred the salami, rinse the green peppercorns and chop the thyme leaves.

Place the slices of cheese neatly in the base of the tart case. Scatter over the shredded salami, green peppercorns, thyme leaves and cornichons, then pour over the crème fraîche and egg mixture. Carefully take to the oven, place on the heated tray, and bake for twenty-five to thirty minutes, until the filling is lightly set and pale gold. Leave to cool a little before serving. For 6.

# Sometimes, you just want pie

January 12

## Peri peri chicken pie

chicken thighs – 8
red onions – 3
medium-hot red chillies – 2
oregano leaves – 10g
garlic – 4 cloves
red wine vinegar –
  2 tablespoons
olive oil – 2 tablespoons
Worcestershire sauce –
  1 tablespoon

celery seeds – 2 tablespoons
the juice of a lime
plain flour – 2 tablespoons
large tomatoes – 5

*For the crust:*
puff pastry – 325g
a little beaten egg

Remove the skin from the chicken thighs, then cut the meat from the bones and into large chunks. Peel and thinly slice the onions.

Put the chillies, oregano, garlic, vinegar, oil, Worcestershire sauce, celery seeds and lime juice into a processor and blitz. Scrape out the peri peri seasoning into a large pan over a moderate heat, and as it starts to sizzle, stir in the onions. Cook over a moderate heat for a few minutes, stirring from time to time, then add the chicken pieces.

Continue cooking for seven or eight minutes, then scatter over the flour and cook for two minutes more. Roughly chop the tomatoes, add them to the pan with some salt, and continue cooking for about twenty minutes, stirring occasionally. Set the oven at 200°C/Gas 6.

Roll out the pastry to cover the top of a large, deep pie dish, leaving enough for an overhang. Tip the chicken filling into the pie dish, then lay the pastry over the surface and brush lightly with beaten egg. Bake for thirty-five to forty minutes, till golden. Serves 4–6.

# A frost of sugar and citrus

## January 14

A perfect day. Frost on the hedges. Air that bites rather than merely nips. A sky the colour of milk.

We make madeleines. Tiny, three-bite sponge cakes the shape of a scallop shell, the only item of French pâtisserie that has ever really interested me. (Gâteaux have never really been my thing. Nor those camp little macarons.) My madeleines get ground almonds and lemon zest.

The citrus element of the traditional recipe is so subtle as to be barely detectable, so we make a syrup and soak the little cakes in it, spooning the lemony lotion over as the cakes cool. I decide to ice them. A crisp, wafer-thin layer of lemon icing, thin as frost and patchy, like lace. James decides to put black pepper in.

So we sit and drink lemon verbena tea on a bone-white winter afternoon, eating tiny French cakes, soft and damp with citrus, sweet with snow-white icing, the occasional tingle of black pepper.

## Lemon and black pepper madeleines

butter – 100g
caster sugar – 100g
the finely grated zest of
  a lemon
eggs – 2
self-raising flour – 50g
ground almonds – 45g

*For the syrup:*
caster sugar – 70g
water – 80ml
the juice of half a lemon

*For the icing:*
icing sugar – 80g
lemon juice – 3 tablespoons
black pepper – 3 grinds

Put the butter, cut into small pieces, into the bowl of a food mixer, add the caster sugar and beat till light and creamy. This will always take longer than you might think, so allow a good eight to ten minutes at a moderate speed.

Set the oven at 230°C/Gas 8. If your madeleine tins aren't non-stick, brush them lightly with butter and dust with flour. (I find buttering non-stick moulds tends to make the cakes stick. So much for belt and braces.)

Fold in the grated lemon zest, then add the eggs, lightly beaten, a little at a time. Should the mixture show any sign of curdling, fold in a spoonful of flour. Gently fold in the flour and ground almonds, then divide between the tins and bake for eight minutes.

Make the syrup: put the sugar and water into a saucepan and bring to the boil. Stir gently and occasionally, until the sugar has dissolved. Stir in the lemon juice, then set aside. Remove the madeleines from the oven and put them on a cooling rack over a tray. Spoon the lemon syrup over the warm madeleines.

To make the icing, sift the icing sugar into a bowl to remove any lumps, then stir in the lemon juice and three good grinds of coarse black pepper. Spoon the icing over the cakes. As it starts to set, grind over a little more pepper and leave to set. Makes 12.

# Do not disturb

Yes, we had the playful bruléed livers and the cod's curd with bee pollen at A Fuego Negro; the legendary garlic prawns on their lip-piercing wooden skewers at Goiz Argi; the black and mysterious squid in its ink at Ganbara and the dark, marbled Ibérico at La Cepa. Later, we wolfed rabbit with fat nibs of young garlic, sliced anchovies in oil and lemon; fragile tartlets of shredded artichoke with parsley and tiny pixie-hat peppers filled to the brim with creamed cod. We drank endless glasses of fizzy ice-cold Txakoli and sampled more Ribera than I would care to admit, as I suspect do most on a pintxo crawl through the cobbled streets of San Sebastián.

It was a dish of braised pig's cheeks, eaten just before our last bar of the evening closed, that I wanted to bring home to my own kitchen. Dark as night, soft enough to require no knife, and served in a shallow bowl with smooth, almost soupy, mashed potato, it left me wondering where all our own pig's cheeks go. (Answer, mince.) Yes, even the most well-stocked butcher may need a few days' warning, but once you have them in your clutches they are easy to prepare.

Pig's cheeks respond best to slow cooking in a hearty liquid, imbued perhaps with softened onions, a few sweet root vegetables, a bunch of thyme or bay and a generous depth of red wine, cider or stout. A dinner of braised cheeks takes barely fifteen minutes to prepare. The bulk of the work is done by the oven, where the plump cushions of meat must sit submerged in rich liquor for a couple of hours or more. Do not disturb.

The dish is one of those where you let the gravy from the pan lap the edges of some sort of creamy starch on your plate: a sloppy butter-rich mash of potato, say, or creamed parsnip; a heap of noodles you have tossed in crème fraîche, or perhaps some spoonfuls of plain and

simple risotto. If you take the boiled potato route, keep them floury, and crush them into the cheeky gravy with the tines of your fork.

## Pig's cheeks with apples and cider

A pile of cream-rich mashed potato is a fine thing on which to lay your pig's cheeks, but a mash made from celeriac and kale is my choice at this time of year.

| | |
|---|---|
| olive oil – 3 tablespoons | apples, a sharp variety – 3 |
| pig's cheeks – 6 | chicken stock – 500ml |
| (about 600g) | cider – 500ml |
| red onions – 3 | |

Warm the oil in a flameproof baking dish over a moderate heat. Dust the pig's cheeks with salt and pepper, then brown them lightly on all sides in the oil. While the cheeks are browning, peel the onions, quarter them, then slice them thickly. Remove the cheeks from the pan to a plate, then add the onions to the pan and let them soften. Set the oven at 160°C/Gas 3. Once the onions are tender and translucent, return the cheeks to the pan, cut the apples into quarters, removing the cores as you go, then add them to the pan together with the stock and the cider. Bring the liquid to the boil, then immediately lower the heat, season with salt and pepper, cover with a lid, and transfer to the oven.

Bake the cheeks, occasionally turning them in their cooking liquor, for three hours. Remove from the oven and allow the cheeks to rest in a warm place. Place the baking dish over a moderate heat and let the sauce reduce in volume a little, until it is thick enough to coat the cheeks. Return the cheeks to the sauce, check the seasoning, and serve with the kale colcannon on the following page. Serves 3.

# Kale colcannon

a large celeriac          butter – a thick slice
kale – 100g

Peel and trim the celeriac, then cut it into large pieces. Cook in boiling water, or steam, till tender enough to crush with a fork. Trim the kale and remove any tough stalks. Cut or tear the leaves into small pieces, cook in boiling, lightly salted water for two or three minutes, till tender, then drain.

Drain the celeriac thoroughly, then crush with a vegetable masher or in a food mixer with a paddle attachment. Add a little butter if you wish. Fold in the drained kale, season and serve.

# A bright, piercing pink chutney for a grey day

What seemed like a proud victory in autumn, serried rows of tightly stoppered jars sporting handwritten labels, can become a bit of a millstone by New Year. There are only so many people who will welcome a jar of your carefully stirred homemade chutney.

I have never been a big chutney-maker. More my style is to make small amounts of several types throughout the year. An ever-changing parade of bright, glittering preserves which are more about celebrating the season than holding it prisoner.

It comes as no surprise that rhubarb, so blisteringly good in a crumble, is less popular than it could be. It is a fruit (or vegetable to the pedant) that requires cooking – in a pie, a tart or a jam. You need to put some work in. Rhubarb's inherent acidity affords it a place in the chutney-maker's lexicon.

This cold afternoon, under a sky the colour of dishwater, I make several ribs of exceptionally red rhubarb into a punchy chutney, not to keep, but primarily to sit alongside a grilled pork chop. A fruity smack across the cheeks for the glorious pork fat.

# Pork chop, rhubarb chutney

Not a 'keeping chutney' but a fresh, brightly hued tracklement that is meant to be eaten straight away, though it will store in a cool place for a few days.

red onions – 2
granulated sugar – 200g
white wine vinegar – 250ml
small hot chillies – 4
star anise – 2 whole
black mustard seeds –
   1 tablespoon

coriander seeds – 1 teaspoon
a small orange
rhubarb – 300g
pomegranate seeds – 200g
pork chops – 2 (300g each)

Peel the onions, then roughly chop them. Put them into a stainless steel or other non-reactive pan with the sugar and vinegar and bring to the boil.

Add the whole chillies, the star anise, mustard seeds and coriander seeds, lightly crushed, and leave to simmer over a moderate heat.

While the onions continue to soften, remove the zest from the orange in short lengths, then cut each into fine strips, as thin as you can make them. Stir into the onions and continue to cook for about fifteen minutes, until the mixture has thickened.

Cut the rhubarb into pieces the size of a wine cork, add to the onion mixture and continue cooking for about ten minutes, until it has softened but not completely collapsed. Stir the pomegranate seeds into the chutney and set aside.

Snip into the rim of fat around the pork chops with a knife or kitchen scissors – it will help the fat to crisp as it cooks. Oil and season the chops, then grill on both sides till lightly cooked and the fat is golden. Serve with some of the chutney. For 2, with extra chutney.

# Rattle and putter

There's a steamed pudding on the stove, a porky version of the traditional steak and kidney. You can't hear a cake baking, but you can certainly hear a pudding steaming. The soft rattle and putter as it cooks, the sound of deep comfort and joy or a mild dose of tinnitus depending on your outlook, is a subtle reminder that dinner, and a rib-sticking one at that, is on its way.

And what a dinner. A vast bowl of meat and fat and gravy to be shared is a fine thing, but then there is something rather sweet about having a tiny one, all to oneself. A large pud (made in a 1-litre basin, it will feed four generously) is good-natured, keeping in perfect condition for half an hour after it's ready. Individual ones probably will keep well too, the water underneath switched off, the pan still covered with its lid.

Turning a steak and kidney out on to a plate, to stand proud as a hat, has always filled me with terror. I braved it the first time I made tonight's pudding and it worked a treat, standing up in textbook style. Alas, there was no one there but me to witness it. But then a steamed pudding is much easier to serve straight from the bowl, brought swaddled in a tea towel, like the little baby Jesus, to the table.

There are pitfalls. Using too much suet can render your crust as heavy as a wet duvet; allowing the water to creep under the foil will turn your pastry into a bloated sponge. Leaving the pan to boil dry will result in a cracked dish. Other than that, steamed pudding, sweet or savoury, is a doddle. Only observing the pained cries of the food police, those sad, empty enemies of good eating, can stop us.

# Steamed bacon and sausage pudding

*For the filling:*
an onion, medium-sized
smoked pancetta – 75g
olive oil – 2 tablespoons
chestnut mushrooms – 75g
sausages – 4 large
plain flour – 2 tablespoons
beef stock – 1 litre
Dijon mustard – 2 teaspoons
dry Marsala or sherry –
  3 tablespoons
Worcestershire sauce –
  2 teaspoons

parsley, chopped –
  3 tablespoons

*For the parsley pastry:*
self-raising flour – 275g
suet – 135g
parsley, chopped –
  2 tablespoons
water – 100ml
butter – a little

You will need a heatproof pudding basin that will hold 1 litre, plus a circle of greaseproof paper large enough to cover the top with a 3cm overhang and a single pleat down the middle. You will also need string and foil.

To make the filling, peel and roughly chop the onion and cut the pancetta into bite-sized cubes or strips. Warm the oil in a large, deep pan over a moderate heat and cook the onion and pancetta till pale gold.

Thickly slice the mushrooms, slice each sausage into four or five pieces, and stir them both into the onions and pancetta. Continue cooking for five minutes, stirring from time to time. Scatter the flour over the surface, stir and continue cooking for a couple of minutes, then heat and pour in the stock and bring to the boil. Season with salt and black pepper.

Lower the heat and let the filling simmer for about fifteen to twenty minutes, until it has reduced in volume by about half. Stir in the mustard, Marsala, Worcestershire sauce and parsley, then leave to cool a little.

To make the pastry, put the flour and suet into a mixing bowl, add the chopped parsley and tumble the ingredients together. Pour in the water, pulling the dough together with your hand or a wooden spoon to a soft but rollable consistency.

Lightly dust a wooden board with flour, then break off two-thirds of the dough and roll it into a disc large enough to line the 1-litre pudding basin. Lightly butter the inside of the basin – it will help to prevent the pastry sticking and will give it a good colour too. Line the inside of the basin with the pastry, pushing it into the base and up the sides, with a little overhanging at the rim. Roll the remaining piece of dough out to fit the top of the basin.

Ladle the filling into the lined basin. Dampen the edges of the pastry, then lay the pastry lid on top. Firmly press the lid and sides of the pastry together, then trim as necessary. Cover with the greaseproof paper. Tie it securely with string then wrap foil over the top of the basin, scrunching it to secure. Lower into a very large saucepan and fill with enough hot water to come halfway up the sides of the basin. Cover with a lid.

Let the pudding steam for two hours, regularly topping up with water. Serve straight from the basin. For 4.

# Food for a windy night

This old house with its endless stairs, drab colours and creaking boards has an aura that some visitors find faintly spooky, and never more so than on a bone-cold winter's night. When a gale blows, the wind rattles down the chimneys like a tube train coming into a station, with gusts and thumps and the occasional bang that, at 3 a.m., sets your heart pounding in your chest.

And yes, it is a cold house and sometimes we need seriously warming food on the table. Tonight, the coldest this year, dinner takes on a new significance. Not just a hot meal to fatten and fill, but something that will warm our very souls.

That Alpine dish of tartiflette, whose layers of potatoes, onions, smoked bacon and Reblochon cheese help to thaw out skiers and snowboarders alike, is possibly the most insulating dish ever invented. It's named after the Savoyard word for potatoes, and I find no dish that warms quite so successfully.

I increase the amount of cheese according to how cold the weather is. Traditionally the dish is all about Reblochon, whose pale milky curds melt into a velvety blanket, and whose flavour softens upon heating, but other good melting cheeses can be added too. Just don't tell the purists otherwise they'll bore you to death.

It's a winter favourite in my kitchen, and this year I swap half the potatoes in my tartiflette for Jerusalem artichokes. The knobbly tubers add a break from the mounds of potato, a welcome earthiness and another way to use these under-valued root vegetables. Wonderful, even if, a day later, we have to rechristen it 'fartiflette'.

# Artichoke 'tartiflette'

A crisp salad involving frisée, watercress and perhaps Belgian chicory would be just the thing with which to mop your plate.

| | |
|---|---|
| floury potatoes – 600g | red onions, sliced – 2 |
| Jerusalem artichokes – 400g | garlic – 2 cloves |
| smoked lardons or pancetta | Reblochon – 500g |
| – 250g | crème fraîche – 450ml |
| olive oil – a little | Parmesan – a little (optional) |

Peel the potatoes and artichokes, then steam or boil them in deep, salted water until they are tender. They will take roughly the same time, so you can cook them together if you wish. Drain them and cut each one into thick slices. Don't worry if they crumble a little. Cut the pancetta into short, thick pieces. Heat the oven to 180°C/Gas 4.

Warm the olive oil in a shallow pan, add the lardons or pancetta and leave to cook over a moderate heat with the occasional stir, till the fat is golden. Using a draining spoon, transfer the pancetta to a plate, leaving behind the oil and fat. Peel the onions, then slice thickly. Add the onions and crushed garlic to the oil and pancetta fat and let them cook for a good ten minutes, until they are pale gold and soft.

Put the sliced potatoes and artichokes into the pan and continue cooking for three or four minutes, shaking the pan occasionally, till the potatoes have coloured lightly here and there. Stir in the cooked pancetta.

Cut the Reblochon into thick slices. Spoon a layer of the potato, onion and pancetta into a baking dish, add a few slices of Reblochon, then more of the potato mixture. Finish with the remaining Reblochon, spoonfuls of the crème fraîche and, if you wish, a fine grating of Parmesan.

Bake the tartiflette for about forty minutes, till bubbling. Serves 4.

# Comfort(able) food

I have begun posting pictures on Instagram. Hardly photographs at all really, just snaps from my phone. The postings have neither rhyme nor reason and can be anything from a dish I have just put on the table for dinner to a view from a railway carriage in deepest Norway or the sun piercing my bedroom blinds. One of the more popular postings was 'every wallet I have ever owned' (apart from the one that was 'lifted' of course). Neither are they particularly 'insta' either, and are often pictures from my archive.

Being a newbie to this particular form of social media (I only took to Twitter years after everyone else), I am always surprised and delighted when someone 'likes' one of my photographs. Today, after posting a picture of last night's dinner, I am somewhat shocked by the number of people to whom it appeals. But looking again at the tangle of sauerkraut, browned onions, soured cream and sausage I can see their point. It really does look good.

This is often the way. The food you throw together without a second's thought often looks more delicious than the food you have arranged oh so artistically on a plate. It's the same with flowers in a jug or throwing on any old thing in the morning and realising you look better than when you spend ages getting ready to go out.

I guess this is why, for me at least, the informal dinner at home will always win over the dinner party. The best things (clothes, flower arrangements, dinners, etc.) are invariably those that are the most relaxed. Those that have an impromptu, unconsidered feel to them. Food which, like us, feels comfortable in its own skin.

# Polish sausage, sauerkraut, onions and soured cream

The famous Polish sausage cooked with potatoes, onions and sauerkraut.

floury potatoes, medium-sized, such as Maris Piper – 350g
an onion, medium to large
chestnut mushrooms – 200g
kiełbasa or similar sausages – 200g

olive or groundnut oil – 2–3 tablespoons
sauerkraut, rinsed – 200g
dill, chopped – 2 tablespoons
soured cream – 2 heaped tablespoons

Peel the potatoes, cut them into quarters, then boil them in deep, salted water till tender to the point of a knife. Drain the potatoes, then slice them thickly.

Peel and finely chop the onion. Slice the mushrooms and cut the sausages into thick pieces. Warm a tablespoon of oil in a large shallow pan, add the onion and let it soften over a moderate heat for five minutes, then add the sliced mushrooms and kiełbasa, and, if necessary, a little more oil. Continue cooking till the mushrooms are starting to turn golden brown. Add the potatoes to the pan, crushing them lightly as you go.

Spoon the sauerkraut into the pan, tucking it amongst the mushrooms and onions. Season with salt, pepper and the chopped dill, then add the soured cream in spoonfuls. Do not be tempted to stir the cream in. Serves 2.

# The less travelled root

The last time I found salsify, those long, mud-encrusted roots, in the market I scrubbed them, cut them into pieces the size of a cork, and cooked them in a little water, butter, lemon juice and tarragon. We ate them as a dish on their own, rather than cooking them around the Sunday roast as I had intended, and jolly good they were too. The trace of oysters I had been promised was nowhere to be tasted, but there was a definite note of Jerusalem artichoke (no, not that note) and a pleasing gentleness.

You won't find the long roots of salsify or its sister the black-skinned scorzonera in many shops, but I am sensing a renewed interest in them. Difficult to grow successfully for yourself unless you have very fine soil, they appear, mostly from Holland, with a little of the fine, dusty soil they like to grow in, and often packed in waxed paper. They need peeling and must be dropped immediately into water into which you have squeezed a generous splash of lemon juice. They discolour quickly.

The best use for salsify I have come across is the blissful parcels Jeremy Lee makes at Quo Vadis in Soho, where the blanched roots are smothered in Parmesan and rolled in filo pastry. But they don't exactly mind being baked in cream and Parmesan either.

Salsify's pale ivory flesh, and the way it makes a velvety purée when boiled and mashed with butter and a little cream, reminds me of artichokes. There's soup of course (follow any Jerusalem artichoke soup recipe, and don't forget the lemon), but they make a cracking good roast too, either with garlic cloves and lemon or tucked around beef or pork as it spits and pops in the oven.

# Salsify, toasted dill crumbs

A rather cute little side dish, the salsify soft and tender within its herb crust.

| | |
|---|---|
| a lemon | mild, smoked paprika – |
| salsify – 250g | 1 teaspoon |
| fresh white breadcrumbs | eggs – 2 |
| – 200g | oil, for frying |
| dill – a handful | lemon, to serve |

Grate the zest from the lemon and set aside.

Wash, trim and peel the salsify and drop them into a bowl of generously acidulated water. (Use the juice of the zested lemon with about 500ml of cold water.) Cut each root into four pieces, then steam or boil for ten minutes or so, till tender.

Mix the breadcrumbs with the chopped dill, salt and pepper, the reserved lemon zest and the paprika. Break the eggs into a shallow bowl and beat lightly. Tip the crumbs into a shallow bowl or on to a plate.

Roll the steamed salsify first in the beaten egg and then in the crumbs. Warm a shallow layer of oil in a frying pan over a moderate heat, and fry the crumbed salsify till the crumbs are pale gold and crisp. Serve hot, with lemon. For 2 as a side dish.

# Fishcakes for winter

You could measure my life in fishcakes. Those golden patties of crumbled fish and mashed potatoes, of herbs and crumbs, spices and spinach, flattened into patties and fried till crisp. Over the years there have been old-fashioned cakes of cod with calming parsley sauce, chilli-hot balls of prawn and lemon grass and flat cakes of spiced brown crab. I have rolled them in breadcrumbs, polenta or salt and pepper flecked flour and offered them up with sauces of spinach, tomato, parsley or chilli.

But the cakes I like best are those made with smoked fish. (I particularly remember one made from kippers that made a somewhat splendid Sunday breakfast.) Mackerel, smoked on the bone till its blue and silver skin has turned a rich burnished gold, makes a fine addition to a fishcake. The smoky flavours and soft textures within seem particularly right for autumn and winter eating.

Horseradish, the traditional accompaniment of smoked eel, works well with smoked mackerel too, and I grated some into today's fishcakes along with coarsely shredded beetroot for sweetness. If ever there was a fishcake for a cold evening, this sweet, smoky version is it.

A lighter, more vegetable-heavy version can be made with salmon and courgettes (see page 303).

On the side, a little sauce of yoghurt perhaps, flecked with dill and parsley, or a dipping sauce of lemon, orange and lime juice mixed with a little olive oil, or perhaps a small bowl of mayonnaise into which you have folded chopped tarragon, capers and a squeeze of lemon juice.

# Smoked mackerel fishcakes

I prefer to use whole smoked mackerel for this, the flesh being more moist and thicker than the pre-packed fillets. But they have plenty of flavour too and come a close second.

floury potatoes – 500g
butter – 50g, plus a little
   for frying
chives, chopped –
   4 tablespoons

cooked beetroot – 150g
a whole smoked mackerel
horseradish root – 30g
oil, for frying

Peel the potatoes, cut them into large chunks and cook them in boiling, generously salted water till tender. Depending on the variety of the potato, I start testing for doneness after twenty minutes. Drain the potatoes thoroughly and tip into the bowl of a food mixer fitted with a flat beater attachment. Beat the potatoes to a smooth fluffy mash with the butter, then add the chopped chives.

Coarsely grate the cooked beetroot and squeeze out any excess juice; you need the beetroot to be fairly dry.

Slice the mackerel in half lengthways, removing the skin as you go, then remove the flesh from the bones in large flakes. Add the mackerel flesh to the potatoes, checking carefully for bones as you do so. Fold in the beetroot briefly, mixing just enough to incorporate the beets without making the mixture pink.

Finely grate the horseradish root into the fishcake mix, season with black pepper, then shape into six small fishcakes and set aside in the fridge for thirty minutes.

Warm a thin layer of oil in a non-stick frying pan, then add the butter and let it melt. Carefully lower the fishcakes into the pan and let them cook for about six to eight minutes, until they have formed a golden crust on the underside. Do not move them during this initial cooking. Once they have formed a crust, carefully turn each one over and cook the other side. Lift out with a palette knife or fish slice and serve. For 3.

# FEBRUARY

## A new pot

### February 4

People imagine I have a vast *batterie de cuisine* at my fingertips. Nothing could be further from the truth. I cook today with much the same few pieces of cookware I have for the last thirty years. Yes, occasionally a new pan might catch my eye, a non-stick frying pan may need replacing or something may just vanish, only to turn up, inexplicably, months later. But generally, there is little in my kitchen that hasn't been there for a decade or more.

The whole point of a cast-iron or pottery casserole is its advanced state of patination, the result of a lifetime's stews and hotpots, bean-bakes and cassoulets. I have only had two, perhaps three, in my entire life. They have, through prolonged contact with haricot and butter beans, duck fat and sausages, onions and swedes, cider and red wine, and clove upon clove of garlic, become glazed with a sort of invisible seasoning. Everything I cook in them seems to be blessed by some unseen, deeply benign force.

My love of the repaired, the revived and the recycled is boundless. Nothing makes me happier than giving an unloved pot or pan a new home. Today I stumble upon a piece of studio pottery from the 1950s, a Bernard Leach casserole complete with its lid. Like much studio pottery it is pleasingly rough to the touch, with a smooth celadon interior. The pot, deep and round – you could call it tubby – begs for beans, woody herbs and wine.

Of course you can bring a fine stew to tenderness in any pot. It could be stainless steel, tin-lined copper or heatproof china. Your beans can bake in cast-iron or crock or ovenproof glass, like the old

Pyrex in which my dad would leave sausage and beans in the bottom oven of the Aga for when I came home from school.

This 'new' pot has clearly not seen fifty years of kitchen action. There are stains on the lid, and the odd hairline crack in the glaze, but it appears to have seen few long spells in the oven. I can't help wondering where it has been and what its story is. The soft grey of the Cornish coast, and glazed inside with the colour of the sea on a winter's day, the pot is one that appears in Bernard Leach's first catalogue of standard ware from his St Ives studio, as shown in Josie Walter's delightful book *Pots in the Kitchen*. Whatever secrets it may hold, the plump, weighty casserole gets a welcome in my kitchen, where I hope it won't mind if I put it straight to work, as I'm sure was Mr Leach's intention.

## Aubergine 'cassoulet'

The true cassoulet, that magnificent recipe of beans, duck, pork and sausages, is something I might make once a decade. Tonight, I make a version with aubergines, haricot beans and thyme, a very different dish, but made in the same spirit, to warm and sustain on a cold and wet February day.

| | |
|---|---|
| aubergines – 2 | tomato purée – a little |
| olive oil | haricot beans – two 400g tins |
| onions – 2 | vegetable stock – 250ml |
| garlic – 3 cloves | |
| tomatoes – 250g | *For the crust:* |
| bay leaves – 2 | white bread – 120g |
| thyme – 4 sprigs | thyme leaves – 1 tablespoon |
| rosemary – 3 sprigs | olive oil |

Discard the stems of the aubergines, then slice each one in half lengthways, then in half again. Warm 3 or 4 tablespoons of oil in a deep, heavy-based casserole and fry the aubergines till they are soft and nicely golden brown on their cut sides. Remove from the pan and set aside.

Peel the onions, roughly chop them, then let them cook in the same pan, adding more oil if necessary, for about ten to fifteen minutes, till soft and pale honey-coloured. Peel and thinly slice the garlic, and stir into the onion as it cooks. Set the oven at 200°C/Gas 6.

Roughly chop the tomatoes and add to the onions, together with the bay leaves, and the whole sprigs of thyme and rosemary. Stir in the tomato purée and continue cooking for a good five minutes, then tip in the haricot beans, drained and rinsed, the browned aubergines, a generous seasoning of salt and black pepper and the vegetable stock. Partially cover with a lid and leave to simmer for ten minutes.

Reduce the bread to coarse crumbs in a food processor. Add the thyme leaves, process briefly, then scatter over the surface of the beans and aubergine mixture.

Shake enough olive oil over the crumbs to lightly saturate them, then bake for twenty-five to thirty minutes, till the crumb crust is crisp and the cassoulet is bubbling around the edges. Serves 4–6.

# A short rib feast

There has been a row of short ribs marinating in the fridge for a couple of days now, the meat and wide bones sitting patiently in a dark and interesting pool of soy sauce, apple juice, honey and aniseed. I will bake them slowly, till the meat can be pulled effortlessly from its bones, and the marinade has reduced to an intensely flavoured syrup. The sort of recipe that leaves your lips tingling, your fingers sticky and your plate licked clean.

This is the latest of the many rib recipes I have worked on over the years and the countless number I have eaten, from the almost black ribs made with pomegranate molasses and lemon, to those with anise and soy, or honey and garlic. Others have come with the gloss of chilli or black bean, whilst still more have landed on my plate that have slow cooked, long marinated or dry roasted. There have been smoked ribs and those barbecued outdoors or grilled inside. Pork ribs and beef ribs, short ribs and long, ribs with their fat and others with nowt. Particularly memorable are the sweet little pork ribs the size of my index finger and fat, flat beef ones whose meat literally fell off of its own accord.

It should be said that rather too many rib recipes I have come across have been simply sweet and hot. I want more. For the last few weeks I have been tinkering with one that brings together my favourite elements of a dense but not overly sticky sauce and the lingering notes of anise. Sweet but not treacly, aromatic rather than hot, tender but far from suck-thru'-a-straw soft. And just maybe for once, beef rather than my usual pork. These are the ribs I have been working on, and the latest batch is about to go into the oven.

But what to eat with them? Well, I have never felt that rice was right, even though a mound of snow-white basmati is more than appropriate for cleaning the sweet, fiery gunge from your plate.

A tangle of plain, wide noodles can be good too, especially if you toss them in the sauce from the ribs, using them to wipe your dish. For a change I experimented with a thick mash of vegetables and was very happy with it. Potatoes were an obvious choice but too heavy. Cauliflower, steamed, creamed and seasoned with a fresh green herb oil, was just about perfect. Mashed swede or sweet potato are worth exploring too.

A plate of ribs is not for the faint-hearted eater. This is the sort of food you won't really enjoy unless you are prepared to roll up your sleeves and get sticky. Start with a knife and fork by all means, but rest them as soon as you have the larger pieces of meat off the bones. It's time to get dirty.

## Slow-roast ribs with honey, anise and creamed cauliflower

I find the easiest way to deal with these is to get the butcher to cut two lengths of short ribs, with four ribs in each piece. A zip-lock or plastic click-seal freezer bag is ideal for marinating.

| | |
|---|---|
| light soy sauce – 100ml | garlic – 2 large cloves |
| unfiltered apple juice – 150ml | black peppercorns – 10 |
| water – 500ml | star anise – 3 |
| honey – 150ml | bone-in beef short ribs – 8, |
| roasted sesame oil – 1 tablespoon | cut into two 4-rib lengths |

Put the soy sauce into a saucepan, then pour in the apple juice, water, honey and sesame oil. Bring to the boil and stir till the honey has dissolved. Flatten the garlic cloves with a heavy weight or the flat side of a knife, then add to the marinade with the whole peppercorns and star anise. Turn off the heat and leave to cool.

Put the ribs into a large plastic food bag, pour in the cooled marinade and seal the bag. Refrigerate for anywhere between twenty-four and forty-eight hours. Turn the bag occasionally to ensure the meat is evenly marinated.

Set the oven at 160°C/Gas 3. Tip the ribs and their marinade into a roasting tin and roast for two to two-and-a-half hours, turning once or twice during cooking. Cover with foil if they appear to be cooking too quickly. Remove a little, but by no means all the fat from the surface with a spoon. The meat should be tender enough to pull away from the bones with a fork.

Serve the ribs with the sauce and the cauliflower and chive purée below. For 4.

## Cauliflower and chive purée

cauliflower – 1kg              chives – a 25g bunch
butter – 100g                  olive oil – 6 tablespoons

Break the cauliflower into large florets, steam or cook them in boiling, lightly salted water till tender to the point of a knife, then drain. Put the hot, drained cauliflower into a food processor, blitz, then add the butter, cut into cubes. Keep the machine running till you have a thoroughly smooth purée, then transfer to a warm serving bowl.

Roughly chop the chives, put them into the rinsed bowl of the food processor, then pour in the olive oil and blitz to a fine, emerald-green purée.

Lightly stir the chive oil into the cauliflower purée and serve. For 4–6.

# Grey sky. Citrus snow.

## February 10

A hauntingly beautiful winter afternoon. Brown bark against pale grey skies. The sort of day you need a bergamot lemon in the house.

Round, deep orange-yellow, with a pronounced nipple, it appears that the bergamot lemon, sometimes called the bergamot orange, is the daughter of the sweet lime and the bitter orange. No other citrus comes near it for the magical scent of its zest. Light but complex, it has a touch of pink grapefruit, lime and juniper about it, of Italian lemon blossom.

From February to March, when I have a small supply (they are expensive) in the house, I occasionally pierce the zest of one with a fingernail, to release an almost invisible spray of juice into the cold winter air. The bergamot lemon is a difficult treasure to find. I get mine from the market in Bermondsey on a Saturday, but they turn up elsewhere occasionally. The top notes of the fruit are difficult to capture in a mousse or even the most barely cooked curd, but you can harness them in the frozen crystals of a sorbet. They are, it must be said, for serious lemon aficionados only.


## Seriously lemon lemon sorbet

You can of course use the common or garden lemon for this.

caster sugar – 100g  
water – 200ml  
bergamot lemon juice – 400ml  
(8–10 lemons)

Make the sugar syrup. Put the sugar and water into a saucepan and warm over a moderate to high heat until the sugar has dissolved. There is no need to boil this down to a thick syrup, just make sure

there is no undissolved sugar left. Leave to cool, then chill in the fridge. To bring the temperature down quickly, put the saucepan into a sink full of cold water and leave till cool, then chill as usual. You won't need all of this mixture, but it is best to make this amount so you can sweeten your sorbet to taste.

Pour the lemon juice into 100ml of the sugar syrup. It will be seriously sharp and refreshing. If you can't handle this, add more sugar syrup to taste. Either pour the mixture into an ice cream maker or freeze by hand. If you are taking the latter option, pour the mixture into a freezer box and freeze for three or four hours, till ice crystals are forming around the edge. Beat them into the liquid centre till you have a sort of lemon slush, freeze again for a couple of hours, then once again beat the mixture and freeze again. This beating will help the structure of the sorbet, and stop it freezing into a solid block, though the texture will be far from that of sorbet made in a machine.

Once the sorbet is frozen, leave it to soften slightly before serving. I like mine in rough snowy lumps rather than neat scoops. For 4.

# A fabulous little pasta recipe

February 11

You don't find a lot of dill in pasta recipes. With its aniseed soul, dill is to Scandinavian cooking what tarragon is to French and fennel and basil are to Italian. It has an affinity with fish, particularly the oily-fleshed salmon and herring, loves rubbing shoulders with potatoes and turns up in a few Mediterranean pilafs and grain dishes, but rarely meets up with this particular starch.

And yet, dill is my first choice to toss with cream, grated cheese and ribbons of fettucine or tagliatelle. Even more than basil. (The rustling sound you can hear is millions of Italians turning in their graves.) Add bacon to that, crisp and cut into small pieces, and you have what might just be my favourite pasta dish of all.

## Pasta with dill and bacon

| | |
|---|---|
| dill – 25g | smoked streaky bacon – 180g |
| grated Parmesan – 125g | garlic – 2 large cloves |
| double cream – 250ml | fettucine – 250g |

Put the dill and grated Parmesan into a food processor. Blitz to coarse crumbs, then tip into a saucepan. Pour in the cream and bring gently to the boil, stirring until the Parmesan has melted. Just as the cream starts to boil, remove from the heat, cover with a lid and leave to infuse for ten minutes.

Dice the bacon, then cook till crisp in a non-stick frying pan. Add the garlic, finely sliced. Continue cooking till the garlic is nicely toasted.

Cook the fettucine in salted, boiling water till al dente, then drain. Toss with the bacon and the dill and Parmesan cream. I like to reserve a few bits of crisp bacon for the top. Serves 2.

# A sense of order

February 12

I regard time spent looking for things – the scissors, the Sellotape, my passport, that-key-thingy-you-need-to-bleed-the-radiators – as time wasted. The fifteen minutes spent searching for the cream of tartar I 'know' is somewhere in the cupboard is time I will never get back. Hence my slight obsession with storage jars.

The sight of an ordered cupboard or larder is pleasing but it has more to it than simply looking attractive. Having everything clearly displayed in stoppered jars means you can instantly locate the ingredient you need, and reduces waste by keeping things dry and fresh. The money you spend on kitting yourself out with glass jars is paid for time and again by the reduction in waste.

There is a shelf in the larder for lentils, beans, grains and rice. Stocked with glass jars of every dry good from basmati and sesame seeds to pearl barley and arborio, it is a little shelf of calm. A still life in shades of oatmeal, it is a constant reminder, if ever I need one, that there is never really 'nothing in the house to eat'.

Today I raid one of the jars for mograbia, the large pearl form of couscous that looks like (and is) little beads of starch. Like gnocchi, it needs cooking in a deep pan of salted, boiling water.

## Mograbia with chorizo and tomato

| | |
|---|---|
| mograbia – 200g | tomatoes – 400g |
| chorizo sausages – 4 | bay leaves – 2 |

Put a large pan of deep water on to boil. Salt it generously, as you would for pasta, then add the mograbia and boil for about twenty

minutes, or until the couscous is tender. Check it regularly. I like mine to retain a slight bite.

Thickly slice the chorizo sausages, then let them sizzle in a deep-sided frying pan for about ten minutes, till golden brown, tossing them round the pan so they brown evenly. Roughly chop the tomatoes, put them in with the chorizo, season generously with black pepper, add a little salt and the bay leaves, then leave them to simmer for about fifteen minutes, till thick and slushy. Stir from time to time, to stop the mixture sticking.

Drain the mograbia, then fold into the tomato and chorizo. Check the seasoning and serve. For 2.

# Sticking together

## February 13

The older I get the more I like clean, bright flavours. The fresh, astringent notes of ginger, lemon, pomegranate and passion fruit. The bite of yuzu and vinegar. The cool, ice-crisp notes of mint and lime, white grapefruit and soy. The sort of flavours that quicken your heart rate rather than slow your pulse.

And yet, there is much pleasure to be found in the occasional wodge of claggy cheesecake. A cake to slow your pace. Cream cheese, Nutella, chocolate. The sort of stuff that lands on both plate and palate with a dull thud.

Cloying foods have a comfort-blanket quality. Tahini, the sesame paste the colour of a Cotswold barn, has enough 'cloy and clag' to glue anyone's lips together. Peanut butter is the sweet version, a paste to coat your mouth like a melted Milky Bar. Dulce de leche, the creamy caramel spread found sandwiched between the short-cake and chocolate of a millionaire's shortbread, is at the decadent end. KitKat the other. (Less so if, like me, you keep your KitKats in the fridge.)

So, a recipe for the mother of all cheesecakes, a gift to those of us who understand the need for an occasional slice of rib-sticking cake. A nutty, chocolatey, cream-cheese-laden slice of heaven. For those who understand.

## Chocolate peanut butter cheesecake

This is a very softly set, gooey cheesecake, so don't expect to get neat slices from it. It is possibly the richest thing you could ever eat, so serve it in small amounts. It is essential to keep it in the fridge overnight, so start the day before.

*For the base:*
butter – 75g
dark chocolate digestives – 175g
salted roasted peanuts – 100g

*For the filling:*
dark chocolate – 100g
full-fat cream cheese – 450g
eggs – 4
an extra egg yolk
caster sugar – 120g
vanilla extract – a teaspoon
crunchy peanut butter – 100g

You will need a 20cm springform cake tin.

Melt the butter in a small pan. Blitz the digestive biscuits in a food processor or put them into a plastic bag and bash them to large crumbs with a rolling pin. Tip the crumbs into the melted butter. Process the peanuts to a coarse powder in the food processor, then stir them into the mixture. Tip the mixture into the cake tin and smooth flat, but without compacting the crumbs. Place in the fridge to set.

Set the oven at 160°C/Gas 3. Break the chocolate into small pieces, then melt it in a bowl over a pan of simmering water. Do not stir, but push any unmelted chocolate down into the liquid chocolate with a spoon. The less you stir, the less likely it is to 'seize'. Put the cream cheese, eggs, egg yolk, caster sugar and vanilla into the bowl of a food mixer and beat slowly till thoroughly mixed.

Wrap the base of the cake tin in two layers of kitchen foil so no water can get in as it cooks. Pour the cream cheese filling on to the biscuit base. Pour the melted chocolate on next, then spoonfuls of peanut butter at regular intervals. Using a skewer or the handle of a spoon, swirl the chocolate and peanut butter throughout the cream cheese mixture.

Put the cake tin into a roasting tin and pour in hot water to come halfway up the sides of the tin. Bake in the oven for fifty-five to sixty minutes. The cake should still wobble in the centre. Leave it in a little longer if necessary, covering with foil to stop the top colouring.

Remove the cake from the oven and let it cool in the roasting tin of water. Transfer to the fridge and leave overnight or for at least seven hours. Serves at least 8.

# Breakfast for superheroes

## February 15

It is Sunday morning. There has to be breakfast. In fact Sunday is probably the only day there actually 'has' to be breakfast. The other days we sometimes tend to bypass the first meal of the day, acting like we have a train to catch, even if we don't. Today there could be porridge, croissants or sourdough toast and jam, or perhaps a bacon sandwich. Some will plump for muesli, yoghurt or a smoothie. There must be someone, somewhere, who still has a kipper of a Sunday morning.

Then there is the full English, whose gargantuan proportions I am less fond of than I probably should be. Today we pile the best bits of the weekend breakfast, sausage, black pudding, bacon, mushrooms, into a roasting tin full of batter. I resist the temptation to add a tomato, which would almost certainly produce too much liquid, or beans, which would just look disgusting.

The result, a sort of toad-in-the-morning, is truly wonderful. The sort of heroic breakfast you need the morning after the night before.

## Sunday breakfast toad-in-the-hole

eggs – 2
plain flour – 125g
milk – 150ml
grain mustard – 1 tablespoon
good herby sausages – 350g

oil or dripping – a little
back bacon rashers – 200g
chestnut mushrooms – 100g
black pudding – 200g

Make a batter by lightly beating together the eggs, flour, milk, grain mustard and a little salt and pepper. When the batter is smooth, set aside.

Tear or cut the sausages into large chunks. Warm a little oil or dripping in a frying pan, then add the sausages and let them brown lightly on all sides. Slice the bacon rashers into short lengths and add to the sausages as they cook to a pale gold. Set the oven at 230°C/ Gas 8.

Lift the sausage and bacon out and set aside, then add the chestnut mushrooms, cut into quarters, to the pan. Fry till the mushrooms are soft and tender, then crumble the black pudding over them. Continue cooking for a couple of minutes, then add to the bacon and sausage.

Tip the bacon, sausage, mushrooms and black pudding into a roasting tin or baking dish with a couple of tablespoons of oil or dripping, then heat in the preheated oven till the fat is almost smoking. Pour the batter over the breakfast ingredients in the pan and slide straight back into the oven. Let the batter bake for ten minutes, then turn the heat down to 180°C/Gas 4 and continue cooking for a further twenty minutes, till risen and puffed up. Serves 4.

Note: The essential point when making any batter pudding is to get the fat truly hot and sizzling before you pour the batter in. The fat should be hot enough that the mixture crackles and pops loudly when it goes in, so a crust is formed almost immediately.

# Basting

A giant, velvet-gilled field mushroom, the size of a small saucer, sits quietly sizzling in a pan of oil and butter, and I am spooning the cooking juices over it, generously, tenderly, almost hypnotically, as if it were a steak.

It is a perfect moment, peaceful and life-enhancing, after a chaotic day that has had me trying to do several things at once, none of them particularly well. I am determined to rescue the day. Sometimes making something to eat can do that.

The best bit is that the pan previously contained a few fat chicken wings that I had fried, slowly over a low heat, destined for a sort of soupy, soothing chicken dinner. They have left their sticky film on the pan, and together with a clove or two of smoked garlic have made the base for the most mellow, intense juices with which to baste a couple of mushrooms.

And there we have it, basting. Slowly, carefully, taking up the flavours and sweet juices from a pan and spooning them over your dinner. The simplest of cooking procedures and yet one of the most worthwhile. Rarely has such a simple exercise put my day to rights. If only things were always so easy.

## Chicken wings with barley

chicken wings – 8 large
olive oil – a little
chicken stock – 1 litre
thin leeks – 4 or 5
pearl barley – 150g
butter – a thick slice

smoked garlic – 2 cloves
large flat mushrooms – 2
parsley, chopped – a small
 handful
tarragon, chopped –
 1 tablespoon

Season the chicken wings and brown them in a little olive oil in a shallow, non-stick pan. Transfer the wings to a deeper, heavy pan over a moderate heat and pour in three-quarters of the chicken stock.

Chop the leeks into pieces the length of a wine cork, add them to the chicken, tip in the pearl barley and return to the boil. Lower the heat and simmer for twenty minutes, or until the barley is tender.

Take the original shallow pan, add the rest of the stock and stir over a moderate heat till some of the sticky film left by the chicken has dissolved. Tip the contents into the simmering chicken.

Add a little more fresh oil and the butter to the frying pan, then add the flattened cloves of smoked garlic and the mushrooms. Spoon the butter and oil over the mushrooms, then cover with a lid. Lower the heat and continue cooking for a good ten to fifteen minutes, turning once, basting often, till tender and soft.

Add a couple of tablespoons of parsley and one of tarragon to the barley and correct the seasoning. Serve the leeks and barley alongside the mushrooms. For 2.

# Eating the unfashionable

I am happier in the East End than in the West. Increasingly, it is kitchens in Hackney, Shoreditch and Dalston that tempt. Shops too. I am more comfortable there, and not just because of its rough edges or that it is close to home. Whisper it, we often seem to have a better time there than elsewhere.

The kitchens in the East End are often short-lived. The kitchen teams are more transient. The energy moves on. Ingredients tend to be picked up, explored and then dropped. The culinary version of speed-dating. Right now, if you can smoke it, pickle it or salt it then you'll find it on the menu. Tomorrow of course will bring something new. There is barely an entrail, meat or fish, that hasn't had its fifteen minutes on the menu here. Pig's head croquettes and grilled chicken hearts. Oh yes please. Chocolate made from vintage cocoa beans. Craft beers with names that sound like shades from a Farrow & Ball paint chart. Bring it on.

Of course, all of this inevitably leads to casualties. One minute we are wading through a sea of cod's cheeks and black pudding croquettes, the next they are banished to restaurant Siberia. And so it is with the poor lamb shank. It seems like only yesterday that no menu was complete without slow-cooked shank meat falling off its thick bone into a mess of soft onions and gravy. Now, no menu would be seen dead wearing one. Pity then, that they are so goddamn delicious.

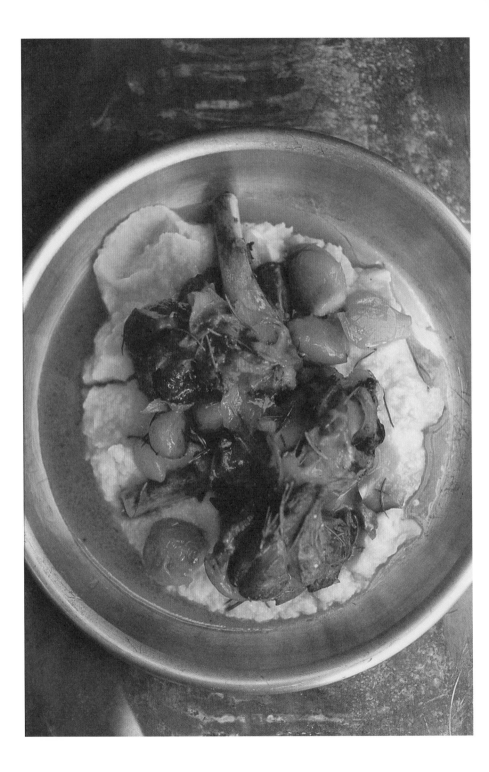

# Lamb with beer and shallots

The smaller lamb shanks are just enough for one per person. The tenderness of lamb shanks varies rather more than one might like, so cook them for longer than I suggest if the meat proves less than effortless to pull from the bone.

small lamb shanks – 2
groundnut or olive oil –
  2 tablespoons
small-medium shallots – 8
wheat beer – 500ml
rosemary – 6 sprigs
bay leaves – 3

honey – 1 tablespoon
Dijon mustard – 1 tablespoon

*For the parsnip mash:*
parsnips – 600g
butter – 30g
double cream – 100ml

Lightly season the lamb shanks, then brown them as evenly as you can in the oil in a deep pan set over a moderate heat. Peel and trim the shallots, keeping them whole, and add them to the lamb. When the shallots are lightly coloured, pour in the beer, then tuck the rosemary sprigs amongst the lamb, add the bay leaves, partially cover with a lid, and simmer for an hour and a half.

To make the mash, peel and roughly chop the parsnips, then boil them in deep, lightly salted water or steam them till tender to the point of a knife. Drain the parsnips, let them sit briefly to lose all their steam (wet parsnips will give a wet mash). Warm the butter and cream in a small pan, finely crush the parsnips with a vegetable masher, then stir in the butter and cream to give a soft, velvety mash.

Remove the shanks from the pan, cover with foil and set aside to rest. Dissolve the honey and mustard in the juices from the lamb, check the seasoning, then reduce slightly over a fierce heat.

Serve the parsnip mash on plates or in shallow bowls, place a shank on each, and spoon over the cooking liquor. Serve with spoons as well as knives and forks. For 2.

# A toast for the mackerel

## February 28

This book chronicles what I have eaten, but focuses on those recipes I feel will be of most use to others, hence the main dishes and baking. It is rare that a starter appears on my table – I just don't do them at home really – but here is a useful recipe for a first course, a light lunch, a snack, or something to eat with drinks.

## Mackerel toasts

Mackerel's oily quality makes it a good fish for pickling or sousing. This can be done with raw fish over a couple of days, or, more instantly, using fish that has been lightly cooked. These are served with soured cream on thin, crisp toasts.

mackerel fillets – 4
  (2 medium fish)
a little olive oil
red wine vinegar – 125ml
malt vinegar – 2 tablespoons
garlic – 2 cloves
water – 125ml
black peppercorns – 1 teaspoon
star anise – 3
celery seeds – 1 tablespoon

light muscovado sugar –
  2 teaspoons
lemon zest – 3 short strips

*To serve:*
very thin slices of French
  stick – 12
soured cream – 100ml
frisée leaves

Cut each mackerel fillet into three, place them on a grill pan, and brush generously with oil. Cook the mackerel under a hot grill for a few minutes, until golden.

Make the marinade: pour the vinegars into a non-reactive saucepan. Peel and very finely slice the garlic, then add to the vinegar with the water, 2 teaspoons of sea salt and a teaspoon of black peppercorns, the star anise and celery seeds, light muscovado sugar and strips of lemon zest. Bring to the boil, then pour over the hot, grilled mackerel and set aside to cool.

When the mackerel has cooled a little (you can serve it cold if you prefer), toast the bread – it should be very thin and crisp, like Melba toast – then add a spoonful of soured cream, a few frisée leaves and the fish. Makes 12.

# MARCH

## Making pizza

I have my ball of dough, soft and floury to the touch, kneaded with love and energy and ready to roll into the thinnest pieces I can manage. All I need now is something interesting, suitably spring-like, to sit on top.

There are as many options for finishing a homemade pizza as there are cooks. Give me fried garlic mushrooms with melting mozzarella, spicy sausage with smoked cheese, or perhaps crème fraîche and basil with grilled aubergine and thyme. Or what about a layer of pesto with grilled courgettes and Parmesan, or an assembly of marinated artichokes, the chargrilled sort from the deli counter, with green olives and flat-leaf parsley?

I like the idea of slices of sausage on my pizza. Not breakfast sausage, which somehow feels plain wrong, but thickly sliced Milano salami or maybe chorizo. Better still, I think, is the sausage I used this week, a chubby salsiccia, spiced with black pepper, fennel and chilli, which you can often pick up at an Italian delicatessen.

Friends seem to like a mozzarella-topped pizza crowned with a golden egg yolk and scattered with peppery rocket. A small version maybe, where you could need as many as two or even three per person. The idea is that the egg is added at the last minute, then cooked for barely a minute or two, so that when cut the yolks ooze into the molten mozzarella.

Other thoughts: onions, sliced and softened by slow cooking in olive oil, fillets of anchovy and rashers of smoked bacon. Or perhaps morcilla, the soft Spanish black pudding, pancetta and Manchego, or thinly sliced air-dried ham with black olives and rosemary.

# Basic pizza dough

plain flour – 500g                    warm water – approx. 300ml
easy bake dried yeast – a 7g sachet

Put the flour into a large, warm mixing bowl. Add the yeast and a good pinch of sea salt, then pour in most of the warm water. Mix to a soft dough, by hand or using a food mixer fitted with a dough hook, adding more liquid if your dough seems too tight.

Flour a work surface generously, then turn out the dough and knead till it feels smooth and elastic. A good ten minutes of firm kneading is necessary if you are doing it by hand, five or so if you are using a machine and dough hook.

Put the dough into its bowl, cover it with a tea towel or clingfilm and leave in a warm place for about an hour, until it has almost doubled in size. Generously flour your board, then roll out the dough to your desired size and thickness.

# Hemp seed pizzas with egg and rocket

Small, seed-studded pizzas that rely on being eaten straight away. The egg yolks cook in a minute or so, but will be only worth eating if you get them on the table immediately.

the dough above – 250g              egg yolks – 4
hemp seeds – 1 tablespoon           rocket leaves – a couple of
mozzarella – two 150g balls         handfuls
olive oil

Set the oven at 230°C/Gas 8. Knead the dough, scattering the hemp seeds over as you go, and continue until they are incorporated. Break the dough into four equal pieces and roll each one out to form a disc

roughly 20cm in diameter. Place them on a baking sheet. Thickly slice the mozzarella and divide between them. Trickle a little olive oil over the surface.

Bake the pizzas for ten to fifteen minutes, till the edges are crisp and the cheese has melted. Slide them out of the oven and place one egg yolk on each pizza, then return them to the oven for one or two minutes, till the egg has just set.

Slide the pizzas on to plates, scatter over the rocket leaves and eat immediately. Makes 4 small pizzas.

# A better batter – a trip to Japan

Go when they are busy. That way, you will be led not to the counter with its wide copper pan of crackling oil and bowl of frothing batter, but to a holding area, where your shoes will be removed and you will be nannied with roasted buckwheat tea on a tray by the fire. You will shuffle in your socks across the tatami to admire the jewel box garden with its silent carpet of emerald moss, stone lanterns and becalming Koi carp.

The day I arrive for lunch, I am ushered in from the spring rain under a wagasa – the bamboo and oil-paper parasol more often seen protecting a geisha's porcelain skin from the sun's rays. Bowl of tea in hand, I sit watching raindrops falling into the garden stream while the kettle, encrusted with verdigris, putters away in the hearth.

Beckoned through, I squeeze into a packed counter, and am brought more tea and a hot towel. There is a menu of sorts. The difference seems to be the number of morsels you will be offered, spitting and popping, from the cauldron of oil under the counter. There will be fish. Three long, pale pink prawns with the tips of their tails exposed; whitebait fried as if caught leaping into the fryer, and squares of white fish so delicate as to be nigh on impossible to pick up with chopsticks without crushing them.

Most of all there will be vegetables. Sweet potato, aubergines, halved, sliced and pressed into a fan, and wedges of kabocha, the firm-textured pumpkin with flesh the colour of a marigold. There will be shiitake mushrooms cut into fat juicy nuggets, lotus roots with their Emmental-like holes and asparagus as thick as a stick of spring rhubarb. Eating in March means I get fiddlehead ferns too, caught as they shyly unfurl, and fukinoto, the opening buds of the Japanese butterbur, all held in batter as fragile as a butterfly's wing.

And what batter. This is not the golden, crunchy armour of our beloved fish and chip supper. This batter is so light as to be barely present, a hit-and-miss type of coating, where patches of colour – a glimmer of silver skin, a flash of sage green or brilliant orange pumpkin – peep through. It will be almost white.

And here's the thing. As a cook, I realise how much of my time I have wasted trying to beat my batter into smoothness. This is lumpy, with unmixed flour encrusted round the edges of the steel bowl, and is stirred with a single wooden stick, not beaten with a balloon whisk. A piece of potato, a mushroom, a cube of fish, is dunked in, removed instantly, then dropped into the fat. It fizzes lightly rather than disappears under a froth of bubbles like mine at home.

The vegetables and fish cook just below the surface of the oil, allowing any loose batter to come to the surface and float above them. The chef removes, scrupulously, almost obsessively, every speck of loose batter, the freckles of burnt flour and water that will taint the oil. What we called batter bits and bought by the little greasy bag from the chip shop for sixpence when I was a kid. At all times, the oil is kept clean and bright. The temperature is set lower than that at which we fry our fish. The frying food fizzes rather than explodes, hisses rather than spits. As they meet their maker, the prawns and fiddleheads, lotus roots and shiitake, seem to sigh rather than scream.

I am offered each rustling morsel individually. A single prawn, a quartered mushroom, a point of peeled asparagus at a time. They come to rest on a folded rectangle of paper, giving each a few seconds to cool and settle before I reach out with my chopsticks. Lifted from the paper, each piece of tempura leaves barely a trace of oil, the merest shadow of evidence.

The seasoning of each piece is, I suppose, up to me. But as ever with eating in Japan, there are rules. Flakes of sea salt and lemon for the fish. A dusting of chilli spice mix for the aubergine and the mushroom. The fern, the root vegetables and the squash are given a dip in a bowl of vinegar and grated radish. A dip as brief as the blink of an eye.

There is no milk in tempura coating, as befits a culture not given to large doses of lactose. Just flour, eggs and water, lightly beaten so the batter stays lumpy. The dipping of each piece of fish or vegetable is brief and individual. The frying is done in batches of two or three pieces only. Lifted from the oil after just a minute or two, the batter is pale, patchy and blistered. It is batter, but only just.

## Tempura vegetables

I can't stress enough that the water should be ice cold. I have made the batter with iced, chilled and lukewarm, and the iced version was lighter by far.

plain flour – 80g
cornflour – 20g
ice-cold water – 175ml
pumpkin – 200g, peeled and
   seeded
sweet potato – 150g

beetroot – 2 small
large mushrooms – 100g
a handful of kale leaves
vegetable oil for deep-frying
an egg white

Put the plain flour and cornflour into a wide mixing bowl and mix briefly together. Pour in the ice-cold water, then beat, lightly, almost half-heartedly, with a whisk or wooden spoon. Care is needed not to overbeat, or to be tempted to bash out the lumps. Strangely, lumps will not affect the finished result. Set aside for a good hour.

Cut the pumpkin into thin slices, about the thickness of two one-pound coins placed on top of one another. Peel the sweet potato and slice into thin rounds. Do the same with the beetroot. Cut the mushrooms into thick slices. Rinse and dry the kale leaves.

Get the oil hot in a deep pan, leaving enough room for it to bubble up when you put the vegetables in. I can't emphasise this enough.

Beat the egg white with a whisk until it is lightly foaming. You don't need to beat till it stands in peaks, just till it thickens into a soft mound. Tenderly fold the beaten egg white into the batter. With the

oil hot and ready (it should be at 180°C), dip the vegetables, a few pieces at a time, into the batter and then lower into the oil using a metal spider or a pair of tongs.

Fry the vegetables only until they are tender. The batter should remain pale and barely coloured. Some will fall off, but the batter should be thin and transparent. Lift the vegetables out of the hot oil, drain very briefly and serve with the dipping sauce below.

## Dipping sauce

Dashi stock is now available to buy from many larger supermarkets as well as Japanese food shops.

| | |
|---|---|
| dashi stock – 100ml | ginger, freshly grated – |
| mirin – 50ml | 3 teaspoons |
| caster sugar – 2 teaspoons | daikon radish, very finely |
| soy sauce – 2 teaspoons | grated – 2 tablespoons |

Pour the dashi into a small saucepan and place over a moderate heat. Stir in the mirin and sugar and bring to the boil. As soon as the sugar has dissolved, remove from the heat, stir in the soy sauce and leave to cool. Serve in small bowls, with the grated ginger and daikon served separately. Add the ginger and daikon to the dipping sauce and stir before using.

# An extraordinary dinner

We drive across the wooden bridge, the river glistening under the full moon. The restaurant is identifiable by its white paper lanterns. The kitchen is visible from the road. A low, glowing light, chefs in white moving slowly. Steam. Bamboo steaming baskets. A giant kettle on a low boil. Cheery hellos. Laughter. Seats at the counter.

A scrubbed chopping board on which are placed four firefly squid, each the size of a toggle on a duffle coat, two on the right, two on the left. A tiny white porcelain dish of finely mashed ginger is set between them. Each squid is sliced into six. Two round dishes, so hot you can feel the searing heat coming from them, are placed in front of us; the squid are instantly scooped up on the blade of a long thin cook's knife, and slid, in two swift movements, into the hot dishes. A crackle. A hiss and a spit. Then a spoonful of wet rice, heavy with stock, and the ginger paste. 'Mix, quickly. Eat. Now!' The instructions are both precise and scary. The pink squid and rice bubble and hiss as we stir them. 'Eat, eat,' the men in white urge, laughing. Too hot, surely. We do as we are told and no, not too hot, but wonderful. Soft rice, the essence of the squid, a nip of heat.

A rough pottery plate of coarse salt is placed on the counter, on which the chef places a single stick of grey charcoal as thick as a baby's arm. A lump of yellowtail, pierced on a skewer, then pressed on to the hot coals, first on one side, then on the other. A puff of white smoke. Maybe three, then turned again. The outside of the fish colours a little, amber and grey. Away from the heat, the fish is sliced thinly. Just two pieces each. A dot of wasabi the size of a caper is placed on each piece. The flesh is raw, cold, pearlescent pink and yellow. The skin hot, and toasted crisp. There are no words of thanks, no congratulations. Just a long, thoughtful sigh. Why can't all food be like this?

Two rectangular dishes the size of a soap dish, yellow and crackled from years of service, are placed in front of us. In each is a layer of fish custard, so barely set it will, later, almost fall from our spoons like the finest silken tofu. On top, white lumps, the size of small scallops, are brought over from the grill. Two in each dish. The grilled livers of the puffa fish. Then, a spoonful of sesame sauce, the colour of honey. One of the two or three most extraordinary, awesome things I have ever eaten. I photograph it, knowing instantly this would be a difficult dish to tweet. I can imagine the comments. The words, slimy, quivering, worse. Yes, the textures would be difficult for some to understand. A little rectangular dish of all that wobbles and oozes, for many a glimpse of hell, but for me, four mouthfuls of food I will never, ever forget. If heaven was edible, I have just eaten it.

Then a three-hundred-year-old porcelain dish with a single white paper inside, carrying a rectangle of fried chicken skin the size of a stamp, its surface bristled, like a scrubbing brush; two squares of fugu fish, the fish of deathly legend (the fish claims two lives a year), adorned with purple shiso flowers; two nuggets of wagyu beef, each the dimensions of an expensive chocolate, crowned with the soft, rust-pink roe of sea urchins.

Dessert? A crackle-glazed porcelain bowl the colour of thick honey, on a worn and obviously very old scarlet lacquer plate. A scoop of ice cream made from buckwheat tea. The tea they bring you in posh shops when you are paying your bill. The same tea they welcome you with at your ryokan. And then, a single scoop of sorbet the size of a bantam's egg, made from brown sugar syrup, stirred and frozen. A single bead of crystallised yuzu on top. A citrus pearl on a sweet, gritty oyster.

## Browned butter, rosemary and honey frozen yoghurt

I was inspired by the originality of those ices. Not to reproduce them, but to rethink the way I make them; the custard base, the crushed fruit, the slow churning. At home, I play (there is no other

word) with the notion of an ice of frozen yoghurt, sweetened with honey and infused with the resinous notes of rosemary. As so often, part my idea, part James's. The concept, which is either brilliance or bonkers, takes a while to get right; I want richness but not from eggs, and none of the often deadening effect of cream. The result is an ice that is herbal, refreshing, intriguing, thoughtful.

| | |
|---|---|
| butter – 250g | runny honey – 8 tablespoons, |
| rosemary – 6 single sprigs | plus a little to finish |
| flaked almonds – 50g | natural yoghurt – 700g |

In a small pan, warm together the butter and whole rosemary sprigs over a moderate heat until the butter melts. Remove from the heat and let the butter and rosemary infuse for about an hour.

Toast the almonds in a dry pan till golden brown and set aside. Remove the rosemary from the butter and discard. Return the butter to the heat, watching carefully as it cooks, removing it from the heat as soon as it starts to turn a warm, nutty, biscuity colour. Take care not to let it burn. (It will, in a heartbeat.)

Pour the brown butter into a mixing bowl, letting it cool for a few minutes, then add the honey and mix well. Stir in the yoghurt, then pour into the bowl of an ice cream machine and churn till almost frozen. Fold in half the toasted almonds, reserving the rest for decoration.

Remove from the ice cream machine, pack into a freezer box and freeze. To serve, throw over the reserved almonds and pour over a little honey, if you wish. For 6.

# Breakfast in Japan

## March 7

Kyoto wakes late, which at least gives me time to write. A perfect morning. Grey clouds. Mist hangs low over the hills like woodsmoke. Soft raindrops. An old woman rides her bike, wobbling, a transparent umbrella in her right hand. Breakfast is miso soup in a deep, black lacquer bowl, and grilled silver mackerel. A plate of pickles, vivid purple cabbage, white radishes, shredded daikon is salty, sour and crisp.

Japanese breakfasts are less sweet than ours. Smoke, salt, sour are here, but very little sweetness. There are similarities. The bowl of warm grain is rice here, not oats like at home. The smoked fish is salmon, not kippers. Tea is smoky buckwheat rather than Darjeeling. The bitterness of our beloved marmalade is replaced by pale green tea.

Breakfast is survival food for me. A slice of melon in summer. A wooden bowl of porridge in the snow. Coffee. Always coffee. Impoverished, newly arrived in London, I still ate breakfast. A world without breakfast is unthinkable. I would lose focus, stumble, probably faint.

In a ryokan, breakfast will be served to you in your own personal dining room. You will feel like an emperor. There will be a tiny bowl of bamboo shoots in spring, enoki mushrooms and stewed greens, a dish of sweet pickles, a grilled trout the size of a ballet shoe, melon, hot tea, the comfort of rice and miso soup. You may also have warm tofu in a bowl of sweet dashi.

Today I am in a large hotel, so the first food of the day comes in a vast buffet. A plate piled high with food is ugly, so instead I make several trips to the buffet. A bowl of shimmering miso with shredded omelette and cabbage floating amidst the broth. Grapefruit, brilliant pink, made for a grey sky. A tiny square plate with a piece of mackerel, grilled, all smoke and shimmer. Then that plate of pickles. I come back with greens too. Steamed and leafy with transparent stalks, a brilliant, life-enhancing emerald.

The Japanese woman next to me is tucking, as gracefully as anyone I have seen, into an English fry-up.

## Grilled fish with soy and sesame

mackerel, filleted – 2 (4 fillets)      sesame oil – 1 tablespoon
mirin – 3 tablespoons                sesame seeds – 2 teaspoons
light soy sauce – 2 tablespoons

Line a baking tray with kitchen foil, making sure there are no tears or holes. Place the mackerel fillets flat on the foil, skin side down, snugly next to one another.

Pour the mirin into a small mixing bowl, stir in the soy sauce and the sesame oil, then tip into a small frying pan. Bring to the boil, then, watching very carefully to make sure it doesn't burn, let it boil for approximately ten seconds and quickly remove from the heat. You should have a thick, glossy, dark caramel-coloured dressing.

Spoon the dressing over the fish, then sprinkle the fillets with sesame seeds. Place under a preheated oven grill and allow to cook for four to five minutes, basting halfway with any dressing that has escaped on to the foil. Serves 2.

## Espresso chocolate chip ice cream

We have long flavoured chocolate with spices, fruit and aromatics. Cinnamon, cherries, ginger, mint, the controversial orange and coffee are amongst the most famous. My own favourites are cardamom, cinnamon, ginger, yuzu and the aforementioned coffee. These are flavours I use above all others with chocolate.

We may of course disagree (chocolate and orange gets some people into a right old tizz), but some flavours do seem to me to work better than others. I am a fan of a plump, foil-wrapped chocolate orange, yet curiously I find that particular marriage works less successfully when we use dark chocolate. But generally I prefer the darker chocolates in the kitchen, with their deep and fruity notes.

As I am in Japan, I go with their habit of ice cream made with green tea. (The ground powder is also used for flavouring sponge cakes, custards and macaroons.) Today I take the train to Uji, a village where the smell of green tea hangs in the air, just to get a hit of their vibrant green ice cream, and where I eat it, Mr Whippy style, from a cornet.

There is also a tea ice flecked with chocolate chips, which doesn't quite work for me, but later, at home in London, I make one with coffee and little shards of chocolate that does. I include the recipe here, as it was in Japan the idea was hatched.

| | |
|---|---|
| milk – 500ml | egg yolks – 4 |
| double cream – 500ml | caster sugar – 150g |
| coffee beans – 50g, ground for espresso | dark chocolate – 150g |

Put the milk and cream into a saucepan, add the coffee and bring to the boil. As it comes up to boiling point, turn off the heat and leave the coffee to infuse into the milk and cream for twenty-five minutes.

Beat the egg yolks and sugar till they are light in colour. Pour the milk and coffee mixture through a fine sieve on to the egg yolk and sugar mixture, then stir thoroughly and transfer to a clean saucepan. Place over a low to moderate heat and stir until the custard starts to thicken slightly. If you take it too far it will curdle, so it is best to remove it from the heat the second it starts to coat the back of the spoon.

Pour into a jug and chill thoroughly. Transfer to an ice cream machine and churn till almost frozen. Chop the chocolate into small, rough pieces, then stir them into the ice cream and spoon into a freezer box. Freeze for a minimum of five hours. Serves 6.

# Street food in Fukuoka

So I'm sitting on a wobbly stool, cheek to cheek with gentle locals on their way home from work, a couple of American tourists and a camera-happy Korean food blogger, drinking pink plum wine from a thick glass tumbler. Puffs of smoke and the occasional crackles and sparks come from a small black grill at the back of the stall, the hands-on cooking hidden by a counter display of skewered meat, prawns and asparagus.

I have come for tarako, the lightly salted fish roe, mostly of pollock and cod, that appears all over Kyushu and much of the rest of Japan. Unapologetically salty, and deeply fishy, it is one of the reasons I come back year after year. It is so loved in this area, there are shops dedicated solely to it, selling packets of the opaque, orangey-pink roe both in its salted form and rolled in chilli seasoning.

Most often grilled whole or deep-fried in the thinnest tempura batter, these luminous sacs of eggs are also mashed into mayonnaise and stuffed into sushi. For breakfast I have eaten the unspiced roe sliced and stirred into warm rice and topped with crisp, dark green sheets of nori seaweed. As comforting a way to start the day as a bowl of warm oatmeal.

At the back of the stall, on a ledge behind the cook, lie skewers of chicken and pork-wrapped asparagus. They are grilled over charcoal and offered with chilli-flecked dip. I eat first the tarako, wrapped in shiso leaves and fried in tempura batter, then skewer after skewer of chicken and asparagus.

Later, at home in London, perhaps to remind myself of my trip, I raid the Japanese shelf and stir up a marinade for some pieces of chicken. It's an impromptu recipe, unauthentic yet delicious, with backnotes of citrus and chilli, sesame and soy.

# Chicken with yuzu and sesame

chicken meat, boned leg or
breast – 500g

shichimi togarishi –
half a teaspoon

*For the marinade:*
light soy sauce – 2 tablespoons
mirin – 2 tablespoons
sesame oil – 1 tablespoon
yuzu juice – 2 tablespoons

*To serve:*
a salad of crisp green lettuce
leaves, watercress, mustard
and cress and maybe a few
sprouted seeds

Put the soy sauce into a mixing bowl, together with the mirin, sesame oil, yuzu juice and shichimi togarishi, and stir to combine. Cut the chicken into finger-thick strips and push down into the marinade, then set aside for a good couple of hours. You can marinate the chicken overnight, but no longer as the texture may turn woolly.

Warm an overhead grill. Line a grill pan with kitchen foil. Thread the strips of chicken on to wooden skewers, packing them not too tightly, then place on the foil in a single layer and cook under the grill till sizzling. Baste them occasionally with the marinade. Some black edges here and there are more than a good thing, they are pretty much essential.

Serve with the crisp green leaves. For 2.

# The panko crumb

## March 16

Crumbs for thickening. Crumbs for coating or for giving a crisp crust to a pie. Crumbs for a fruit pudding or for toasting with sugar for a brown bread ice cream. Crumbs for fish and crumbs for fritters. Crumbs for the kitchen.

Breadcrumbs are a natural by-product of any home. A ciabatta left on the table overnight, a forgotten baguette, even stale sourdough and wholemeal loaves can be reduced to usable crumbs at the click of a switch.

I have the odd bag of them in the freezer, a squirrel store into which to dip when I decide to coat mashed potatoes or parsnips in a crust and fry them, or when I feel the need to thicken a soup on a chilly day. It has never occurred to me I might ever need, let alone want, to buy any.

And then I met panko. Ground from the lightest Japanese milk bread, these are the crumbs of the fairies, light and ethereally crisp, crumbs that provide a crisp coat whilst being so fine they are barely present. They are made from the bread with which the Japanese often make their sandwiches, a sweet, tight-crumbed loaf that smells like angel cake. Put a loaf into your shopping bag and it's so light you wouldn't even know it was there. I get my fill of it once a year, when I'm in Japan, but now panko crumbs are available at home, I use them in preference to any others for coating and crumbing. The perfect coating for, say, a fritter.

# Pea and bacon fritters

Use panko or make breadcrumbs from light, crustless bread and dry them out lightly in a very low oven till they are crisp.

| | |
|---|---|
| frozen peas – 500g | *To coat and fry:* |
| tarragon – 20g | eggs – 2, beaten |
| smoked streaky bacon – | crisp white breadcrumbs – |
| 4 rashers. | a couple of large handfuls |
| butter – 40g | butter – a thick slice |
| egg yolks – 2 | olive or vegetable oil – |
| crisp white breadcrumbs | a little |
| – 6 tablespoons | |

Boil the peas for about four minutes in lightly salted water, then drain them. Leave them in a colander under cold running water until they are thoroughly chilled. Tip the peas into the bowl of a food processor, add the tarragon leaves and process to a smooth paste.

Cut the bacon into small pieces and fry in the butter in a shallow, non-stick pan till crisp. Drain on kitchen paper, add to the peas and process briefly, then transfer to a bowl and chill thoroughly for a couple of hours.

Fold the egg yolks and 6 tablespoons of breadcrumbs into the pea mixture. Pour the beaten egg into a shallow dish, and spread the remaining breadcrumbs on a plate. Shape the pea mixture into six short, fat barrel-shaped croquettes. Roll each croquette in the beaten egg and then in the crumbs, then chill for twenty minutes.

In the same pan in which you cooked the bacon, warm the remaining butter and the oil, then fry the croquettes, over a moderate heat, gently rolling them over now and again to colour them evenly. Drain, briefly, on kitchen paper and serve. Makes 6, serves 3.

# Snow, sake and steak

## March 17

I am at a minimalist hotel in the wilds of Hokkaido, the sort where they bring you hot yuzu-scented tea on arrival and there are four different pairs of slippers at the entrance to your room. The vast square bath in my room is permanently full of hot spring water, lapping the edges and gently trickling over the sides and on to the floor.

Outside, there is snow on the ground. At night, the garden is lit by the stars and by low, stone lamps that send eerie shadows across the powdery snow. I take a short dash to the outdoor spring bath, jump in and stand in the steaming water for what seems like eternity. My body is toasty, but my hair feels crunchy with frost, so I clamber out and roll in the snow. After repeating this a few times, invigorated, shivering, I get dressed and return to the hotel with its long low bar and fine, beautiful and wafer-thin sake glasses that look like something from a science lab.

Sloe gin aside, sake is one of the few spirits I drink, and I warm myself up with several glasses. As regular drinkers know only too well, sake has a habit of creeping up on you. One minute you are stone cold sober. The next, pissed. It's the only way you can cope with the inevitable bill and its long row of noughts.

Expensive devil-may-care-drinking aside, you can use some of the more everyday sake in the kitchen. Made from rice, it has a similar use to the dry sherries and vermouths, but is more mellow and, I think, more interesting. Inspired by dinner, I scribble down the idea for a recipe that I will make when I return home.

# Braised steak, sake and shallots

After a bit of tinkering, the plan of adding a cheap brand of sake to a dish of braised beef works nicely, not overly sweet and deeply warming. You can use dry sherry if you prefer.

braising steak – 500g
groundnut oil – a little
young carrots – 200g
large banana shallots – 2

sake – 200ml
beef stock – 200ml
dark soy sauce – 2 teaspoons
pak choi – 2

Set the oven at 160°C/Gas 3. Cut the steak into two, then brown on both sides in a little groundnut oil in a heavy pan. Remove from the pan and set aside. Add the carrots, well scrubbed and halved lengthways, to the pan, then add the shallots, peeled and sliced in half. Let the vegetables brown a little, then add the sake, stock and steak. Cover with a lid and cook in the oven for an hour.

Check the flavour, adding soy sauce to taste – start with 2 teaspoons. Slice the pak choi in half and add to the pan, then return to the oven, uncovered, for ten minutes or until the greens have softened. Serves 2.

# Pork bone soup

It is just a hole in the wall really. A small door, with the usual crudely assembled menu and faded photographs in a frame outside. Nothing to distinguish it from any of the other places that seem to consist of ten seats, a counter, a single chef and a waitress.

What entices me in is the smell coming from under the door. Aniseed, something treacly and dark, but at its heart the deep, sweet smell of roasting meat.

As I walk towards the counter I am aware of my trainers half slipping on, half sticking to, the greasy concrete floor. I climb on to a stool, not quite sure where to put my bag, instantly aware that this is not the cleanest place I have ever eaten in. Untidy too. Unwashed pots and pans lie stacked in the sink; some less than spotless tea towels hang over the oven rail. Most would, in any other circumstances, turn and go. But for that smell.

The menu consists of eight or ten dishes, broths mostly, noodles, then a clutch of possible additions such as sheets of dark green nori to crumble into your soup or your rice, a soft-boiled egg sliced in half, its sticky golden yolk just visible through the murky liquor; greens by the handful. All of them, each and every dish, is based around three slices of pork and a bowl of broth.

Awash in its bowl of soup, the pork falls apart as soon as you touch it. Spoon soft. The fat quivers, the meat comes away with its dark edges, almost black and sweet with treacle, chilli, ground five-spice. Is there a hint of caramelised garlic too? There is a short row of bottles and pots to be explored. Stinging vinegar. Sticky soy. A tightly lidded pot of deep red spice paste. This last one brings a tear to your eye and a drip to your nose. At first, just the merest spot on the end of the tiny spoon, then a little more, the fearsome, slightly

addictive heat swirling through your lunch, leaving a rust-coloured rim around the dish as your soup goes down.

The liquor, opaque, the colour of thick honey, tastes not like a freshly made broth, but like the broth of time. A liquor that has been kept going for longer than anyone else cares to know. We are not talking of a newly made stock here, a shimmering liquid with an underlying note of bay or pepper, thyme or rosemary. This is just bones and water, simmered for who knows how long. Added to, boiled, simmered, ladled and then more bones added. A bit like the solera system in sherry, where one vintage is used to start the next. The flavour of ages.

And that is the magic here. The deep flavours that come, not via a shining kitchen and a crisp recipe, but flavours that are layered, day by day, week by week, possibly even longer. Flavours that mingle, mature and mellow. Where your bowl of broth and meat never tastes the same two days running.

If you dare to enter, to sit at the greasy kitchen counter, to order from the dog-eared, laminated menu, you will have a bowl of memorable food. You will watch as three slices are cut from a roll of roasted belly, black as sin, and put into a dish the size of a mixing bowl. A tangle of noodles. A ladle of steaming stock from a dented cauldron. As it is handed across the counter, you will take it gratefully, a little apprehensively. You will push the meat around in the liquor, crumbling it with a worn plastic spoon and watching it fall to shreds in the cloudy stock. You will haul out a chunk of flesh, an edge of trembling fat, a mahogany rim of sweet roasted spice, a floating piece of nori. You sip. You slurp. You dribble. You will rest your spoon and pick up your cheap, disposable chopsticks; your head will swoop down to the bowl, just like you were told never to do. You twizzle your noodles round the ends of your chopsticks as best you can. You suck. The dough, slithery and juicy with stock, slips into your mouth. It seems endless; you suck it up harder, determined not to let it go or, worse, to bite into it. Your noodles must not break.

As you pay and leave, your lips smarting, your tummy full, you have the faintest feeling of dread, that you might not have seen the last of your lunch, that you might live to regret the day you braved the greasy, but oh so delicious spoon in search of the smell of roasting meat and bubbling bones.

## Pork bone soup

water – 2 litres
dried shiitake mushrooms
– 25g
pork bones, thick ones, with
a little meat attached – 1kg

chicken wings – 750g
carrots – 2 large
onions – 2
thyme sprigs – 6
bay leaves – 2

Set the oven at 200°C/Gas 6. Pour the water into a very large pan, then add the dried mushrooms and bring to the boil. Lower the heat so that the water simmers gently and leave for 25 minutes, till you have a rich brown mushroomy stock.

Put the pork bones into a roasting tin in a single layer, then put them into the oven and roast for an hour, till deep gold.

Remove the shiitake from the water with a draining spoon – they have done their work. Lower the chicken wings into the water and leave to simmer for an hour, checking the liquid level from time to time and topping up to the original amount if necessary.

Lift out the chicken wings and lower in the roasted pork bones and their fat, pushing them under the surface of the liquid. Keeping the heat at a low simmer, making sure the liquid bubbles only now and again, let the broth cook for a good two hours.

Scrub the carrots, then tuck them in amongst the bones. Slice the onions in half, peeling them if you wish, then add to the stock together with the thyme leaves and bay leaves. Simmer gently, bubbles barely breaking the surface, for a further hour.

Drain the stock – I usually lift out the bones, vegetables and herbs with a pair of kitchen tongs – then set aside to cool. Season generously with salt. You should have a good litre to a litre and a half. It will keep, refrigerated at 3°C, for four to five days.

Note: The used shiitake I chuck, but the wings are something I feast on. Once they have simmered for about forty-five minutes, I lift them out of the broth with a draining spoon, tip them into the pork roasting tin, salt and pepper them, then trickle over olive oil and the juice from a squeezed lemon. I then roast them for half an hour or so, till golden and crisp-skinned. They serve as snacks, something to gnaw in lieu of a biscuit.

To use your bone broth: Reheat, adding cooked ramen, green vegetables such as bok choi or spinach, and/or slices of roast pork (my favourite and an excellent way of using up the Sunday roast), and serve in large, deep bowls. I like to season with a little dark soy, some lemon juice or ginger juice, made by squeezing grated ginger, and a dash of sesame oil as I serve.

# Well, hello, little dumpling

The problem with following the restaurant recommendations of the well-known guides is that you run the risk of being in a room full of tourists. And so we are. Australians, Americans, British, all taking photographs of every morsel. I wonder briefly whether I might have saved myself the air-fare and gone out to eat in Camden instead.

We eat gyoza tonight, the little dumplings known as potstickers. A cast-iron dish, worn from many years of stuck dumplings, full to the brim with neatly placed gyoza, a lacy web holding the plump little pouches together. There is vinegar and soy to dip them in. A splash of chilli. The first thing you notice is that the ratio of vinegar to soy is higher than at home. About ten to one in favour of vinegar, if you ask me.

The filling is minced pork seasoned with garlic, ginger and most definitely lemon grass. The dubious blessing of tourism has, somewhat regrettably, brought with it a Camembert version. The prawn and Chinese chive is very fine.

What separates these dumplings from so many others is that these stay true to the name. Their flat surface has indeed been allowed to stick to the pan, which is not always the case, resulting in a crisply crusted side and two softer sides, their surface like wet silk. They are worth the queue and the fact that you feel desperate to hear a Japanese voice. Partly due, I think, to their sharp dipping sauce and the inclusion of lemon grass. And perhaps the pressure of a million tourists, guided by the guides, hoping for, and indeed getting, the best gyoza ever.

# Gyoza with pork and lemon grass

dumpling wrappers – 20
oil – a little, for cooking
water – 100ml

*For the filling:*
spinach – 200g
spring onions – 6
sesame oil – 2 teaspoons

garlic – 3 cloves
lemon grass – 2 stalks
ginger – finely grated,
  2 teaspoons
minced pork – 250g
sugar – a pinch
white pepper, for grinding
soy sauce – 1 teaspoon

Wash the spinach leaves, remove the tough stems, then put them still wet into a non-stick pan, place over a moderate heat and cover tightly with a lid. Let the leaves steam for a minute or two, shaking the pan occasionally, till they have wilted and darkened, then remove them from the pan. Drain the spinach in a colander, then press in your fist till it is almost dry. Chop finely and put into a mixing bowl.

Finely chop the spring onions, then put them into a frying pan with the sesame oil and let them soften over a low to moderate heat. Peel and finely chop the garlic and add to the pan. Remove the outer leaves of the lemon grass and discard them. Finely shred the soft heart leaves of the lemon grass and stir them into the spring onions and garlic, then grate in the ginger, turn the heat up a little and add the minced pork to the mixture. Break up the mince with a wooden spoon to encourage it to brown evenly, stirring from time to time, but essentially leaving it to colour for about ten minutes. Stir in the pinch of sugar, a grinding of white pepper and the soy sauce. Turn off the heat and leave the filling to cool.

Place a gyoza wrapper on the work surface and put 2 generous teaspoons of the pork mixture in the centre. Dampen the edges of the wrapper with water, then fold in half to give a semicircle and press firmly to seal, crimping the dough as you go with your finger and thumb. Set aside and repeat with the remaining wrappers and filling.

Warm a thin layer of oil in a shallow pan and place over a low to moderate heat. Place the dumplings in the pan so their crimped edge stands uppermost. Let the base of each dumpling colour lightly to a golden brown, then pour the water in around the gyoza. Cover the pan with a lid and leave for five minutes.

Remove the lid and let the water in the pan boil for a minute or two, till it has almost totally evaporated. Serve the gyoza, which should by now have crisp, golden-brown bases, with the dip below. Makes about 20.

## Dip for gyoza with lemon grass

sesame oil – 1 teaspoon
rice wine vinegar – 1 tablespoon
sweet chilli sauce – 2 teaspoons
dark soy sauce – 1 tablespoon

caster sugar – 1 teaspoon
mirin – 1 tablespoon
lemon or yuzu juice –
  1 tablespoon

Put the ingredients into a small saucepan and bring to the boil. Simmer for two or three minutes, then leave to cool. The dip should be sweet, sharp and salty.

# A stir-fry of squid and peppers

## March 25

Serve immediately. The words have a needy, greedy quality that at the same time sounds unnecessary. And yet there are many recipes better for not being served the moment they come from the cooker: quiche or a fruit tart, for instance, which are best served at room temperature; a roast that needs time to relax so it doesn't spill its juices when we carve; stuffed peppers, whose Mediterranean origins demand a more laid-back approach. Anything involving béchamel or cheese sauce, such as lasagne or moussaka, needs to cool down if it is not to send us straight to A&E.

There are some dishes, however, that should wait for no one. They demand to go from pan to table and from plate to mouth as quickly as is humanly possible. These are meals where only the prospect of scorching our lips stops us from grabbing them right from the pan. Fritters of courgette flowers, aubergine or elderflower; pancakes; chips, or those heavenly little balls of deep-fried molten cheese known as croquetas; bacalau, crisp balls of deep-fried salt cod; bacon sandwiches and porridge. I would also add shepherd's pie to the list, but only because of some strange obsession I have about the need for the first forkful to be eaten so hot it makes my eyes water.

Stir-fries are another dish that sits nicely in hotter-the-better territory. Those prawns, chicken or beanshoots should still be sizzling when you tip them, spitting and popping, from the black pan. Earlier this week I made a little stir-fry of orange peppers and ghostly rings of squid that was actually smoking as I shook it on to our plates. The first mouthful eaten within seconds, the next, so quickly afterwards as to smack of bad table manners.

I will add sweetcorn to my hotlist too. I have given myself a nice 'trout-pout' before now by getting my mouth round those steaming kernels a minute or two too soon, but it was worth it. Sweet as sugar, still steaming from the water or smoking from the grill, corn needs instant attention, especially when the butter runs down its knobbly shaft. I made a chilli spread this week whose piercing heat, tempered by parsley, we melted over the corn within a minute or two of it leaving the water. Hot, sweet and spicy, it was eaten quicker than the time it had taken to rip the husks off.

I like a rice pudding off the heat scale too, baked apples (though only for the first mouthful) and treacle sponge. Puddings are the ones to be most careful with; with their sugar-based ingredients they can harm as well as heal, as anyone who has got to the tarte Tatin too quickly will know. But in terms of good eating, patience is not always a virtue.

## A little stir-fry of squid and pepper

Get the fishmonger to prepare the squid, thoroughly cleaning them and removing the ink sacs. (You will still have to do another quick clean at home.) If squid isn't your thing, this recipe is also good with prawns. Coriander is entirely optional here.

| | |
|---|---|
| squid – 300g (prepared weight) | Szechuan peppercorns – |
| a large red or orange pepper | 1 teaspoon |
| garlic – 2 cloves | black peppercorns – 8 |
| shallots – 2 medium-sized | sesame oil |
| ginger – 25g | a lime |
| groundnut or rapeseed oil – | coriander – a little (optional) |
| 2 tablespoons | |

Sort through the squid, cleaning and trimming anything the fishmonger may have missed. Cut the long body sacs into thinnish rings and trim the tentacles neatly.

Halve the pepper, remove and discard the seeds and core, then thinly slice each half. Peel and thinly slice the garlic and the shallots. Remove the skin from the ginger and cut the flesh into thin shreds about the size of a matchstick.

Heat the oil in a wok. Add the pepper, moving them round the pan from time to time till they start to relax and soften, then add the garlic, shallots and shredded ginger. Continue to fry and stir till the shallots are golden, then crush and add the Szechuan and black peppercorns, a good grinding of salt and the squid. Stir-fry for a minute or two only, till the squid is opaque, then shake over the sesame oil, the lime juice and, if you wish, a little chopped coriander.

Serve immediately. For 2 as a main dish.

# Home and a bowl of Japanese soup

## March 27

A single rat's hair. That is what I have been told. A willow, a crane, a stream, a leaf, in gold on a shining black lacquer bowl. Painted not with a brush, but with a single hair. Such a bowl and its lid demand contents as simple yet complex.

It was the lidded soup bowl, glossy black or deep burnished red, that attracted me at first. Set down on the right of the sushi or the tempura. A bowl whose contents were at first hidden by a tight lid, a lid that when removed revealed a story painted on its underside. The bowl, smooth, utterly faultless, its surface like a black mirror, home to a clear, shining broth. A broth that, once stirred, or lifted to the lips, produced a cloud of miso, swirling in the depths like a ghost under the surface of a dark pool.

I lift the bowl to my lips, inhale briefly, take a sip of the deeply savoury liquor and suddenly all is good with the world. A start to the day that is gentle yet not without substance. It's hardly porridge or a fry-up, yet miso soup sustains and sets you up for the day ahead. It's the hot broth, of course, hearty, fruity, virtually beefy in its intensity, perfectly clear when still, then intriguingly cloudy once stirred, but there's more to it than that. The feel of the smooth lacquer bowl in my hands, hearing the occasional whisper that emanates from the tight, steam-freckled lid, and the smell that is for me the essence of Japan, bringing with it a serene and slow-burning pleasure.

In Japan, whether I am eating grilled eel on sticky rice from a lacquer box, a piece of blistering aubergine tempura hauled out of bubbling oil, or chicken hearts cooked on skewers set over hot coals, you can almost guarantee there will also be a tiny bowl of miso soup offered alongside. Made from crushed soy beans and rice or wheat, left to ferment and mature, miso's variations in colour, from creamy white to a deepest mahogany, will generally signify how salty it is. The white (shiro) miso being the least salty and the place I first started.

Early this morning it came with some cubes of tofu and a sliver of seaweed. The broth has a milky quality, earthy yet tasting of the sea. In the last few days it has appeared with submerged scallops; a large, shelled clam; soft tofu in dainty dice and flakes; curls or sheets of kelp. With it comes a dose of umami, the fifth basic 'taste', along with bitter, salt, sour and sweet. Perhaps we should just call it 'savoury'. (Umami isn't solely a Japanese thing.) It's that deep, almost meaty note you get from hard cheeses, dried tuna and soy sauce.

Miso soup is often the first thing I make on returning from a trip abroad. There is almost always a tub of it in the fridge. Sealed and chilled it will keep for weeks. You just stir a couple of tablespoons of it into hot stock – I tend to use chicken or vegetable, rather than the traditional seaweed and bonito dashi. Introduce a handful of cooked noodles and you have lunch. Add shredded greens such as pak choi or spinach, and shavings of grilled chicken or tiny shreds of raw beef, and you have a light yet satisfying dinner.

The pastes are easy to deal with and readily available. Neither will I turn my nose up at the instant miso soups of which most wholefood stores have a dazzling range. It is just a case of boiling a kettle. But a homemade version gives you the option to alter the intensity by adding as much of the paste as you wish, and of course choosing whether it's a light miso day or a dark one. The paste makes a fine marinade for grilled chicken too, let down to a spreadable slush with equal amounts of sugar or honey, sake and mirin. Miso paste has become a staple ingredient in my fridge, just as Parmesan used to be. My umami fix. Today, though, it comes in a bowl, shining, calm, untroubled. A bowl of quiet perfection.

# A spring soup of young leeks and miso

A lovely, fresh-tasting soup for a winter-spring day.

leeks – 3 medium-sized
butter – 30g
a medium-sized carrot
a stick of celery
vegetable stock – 1 litre

light miso paste – 1 heaped
  tablespoon
spring greens – 4 handfuls
a small lemon

Trim and wash the leeks, and slice them into thin rings. Melt the butter in a large saucepan and add the sliced leeks, leaving them to soften over a low heat and covered by a lid. They should not colour.

Finely chop the carrot and celery and add to the pan. Pour in the vegetable stock and grind in a seasoning of salt and pepper, then leave to simmer for twenty minutes, until the vegetables are soft but the colour is still bright. Stir in the miso paste, adding more to taste if you wish.

Rinse the greens, then place them on top of one another and shred them into thin ribbons.

Finely grate the lemon zest and add to the soup with the greens. It is best to taste as you add, stopping when you feel it is sour enough. Simmer for two or three minutes, until the greens are just tender. Check the seasoning, squeeze over the juice from the lemon and serve. For 4.

# The day for a pie

## March 28

It's pie weather. A damp, misty morning followed by a dark evening. A sudden need for crisp pastry soaked on one side with sauce or gravy from a pie. It can be an open one with a creamy filling and a soft undercrust, or a pie with a pastry top, its face golden, its underside soaked in the filling. It could be one of the classics, of course, a Victorian steak and kidney or quaint cottage pie; a frugal shepherd's pie with deep fork-furrows of mashed potato or a pastry-topped fish pie made with white fish, prawns and dill-freckled cream.

But I don't want any of those. The pie I crave is something new yet familiar, a filling that I may have had in some other form – as a casserole perhaps or a sauté – but whatever, it must come with a pastry crust to soak up the sauce. I made two this week, the first with the familiarity of gammon and parsley and the second a spiced chicken pie with a tangled crust.

## Gammon, celeriac and parsley pie

*For the pastry:*
butter – 175g
plain flour – 225g
an egg yolk
cold water – 2–3 tablespoons

*For the filling:*
banana shallots – 5
groundnut or other oil –
  1 tablespoon

gammon, smoked or not,
  trimmed – 650g
plain flour – 2 level
  tablespoons
double cream – 250ml
parsley – 20g
celeriac – 150g
  (prepared weight)
melted butter – 30g

You will need a 24cm high-sided, fixed-base shallow cake tin or tart tin.

Make the pastry: rub the butter into the flour using your fingertips or a food processor, until it resembles coarse, fresh breadcrumbs. Mix in the egg yolk and enough water, probably about 2–3 tablespoons, to bring it to a firm but tender dough. Knead very gently for a minute or so.

Place the ball of pastry on a floured work surface or chopping board and roll into a disc large enough to line the base and sides of the cake tin or tart tin. Line the tin, pushing the pastry well into the corners and up the sides. Fill the pastry case with foil and baking beans and leave to rest in the fridge for at least twenty minutes.

Make the filling: peel the shallots and halve lengthways, then slice off the roots and separate the halves into layers. Warm the oil in a shallow pan over a moderate heat, then add the separated layers of shallot and leave them to soften in the oil, without letting them colour.

Cut the gammon into large cubes, roughly 2cm on each side, add them to the softened shallots and continue cooking for five minutes or so, then dust over the flour. Stir the shallots, ham and flour and let them cook for a minute or two, then pour in the cream and season with black pepper and a very little salt.

Lower the heat, so the gammon and shallots are simmering gently, and leave, with the occasional stir to make sure it isn't sticking, for about fifteen to twenty minutes. Remove the leaves from the parsley and roughly chop, then stir into the filling and remove from the heat. Set the oven at 200°C/Gas 6.

Peel the celeriac, then grate coarsely, as you would for a remoulade. This is done in seconds with the coarse grating disc of a food processor. (If you are not using the celeriac immediately, keep it from browning in a bowl of acidulated water.)

Bake the pastry case for twenty minutes, carefully remove the foil and beans, then return it to the oven for five minutes, until the pastry feels dry to the touch. Remove from the oven and fill with the gammon and onion mixture.

Drain the celeriac and toss it in the melted butter. Cover the top of the pie with buttered celeriac, brushing with any leftover melted butter. Season. Bake for thirty to forty minutes, brushing with a little more butter if the top appears dry. Serve when golden brown. For 6.

# Belly and beans

## March 30

I like the cold. Snow, frost, ice, and clear, pearl-grey skies appeal so much more to me than bright sun and fierce light. But then, with the cold comes a fearsome appetite and a need for velvet soups of artichoke or pumpkin; for casseroles of fat butter beans and parsnips; for pork belly and neck of lamb; baked potatoes and roast butternut; treacle sponge and baked jam roll. Food to warm the soul.

The smell of food as it slowly bakes and roasts, stews and braises, is half the reason I cook from scratch rather than heat up a microwave-ready meal. The sense of expectation brought about by the herb-scented fug that fills a kitchen as lamb slowly bakes with mint and lemon, or the lingering smell of caramelised meat juices and vegetables from a roast of pork loin and beans, is what brings me to the table.

The other attraction of slow cooking is that it allows us to use cheaper cuts – those pieces of a carcass that respond to long leisurely cooking in some sort of liquid. These are often pieces of meat with a good ratio of fat, and utilising that fat will only add to a dish's ability to warm as well as feed us. The fat that comes with a piece of pork belly is worth savouring, and this week I made a roasting tin of braised beans whose sauce was all the more effective by cooking pieces of pork belly in it so that the melting fat enriched the beans rather than burned on to the empty roasting tin.

## Pork belly and beans

While not being the bargain it once was, belly still represents value for money. It comes with or without skin and can be sold with or without its bones. For this recipe you need it with the skin scored by the butcher and the bones removed. There is a generous quantity here. Any that you don't eat at the time can be warmed the next day and served on toast.

dried cannellini beans – 500g
bay leaves – 3
onions – 2 medium-sized
olive oil
thyme – 6 little sprigs

vegetable stock – 1 litre
belly pork, bones out – 1.2kg
cavolo nero or other dark
  cabbage – 200g

Soak the beans in deep, cold water overnight. In the morning, drain them, tip them into a very large saucepan, add 3 bay leaves, cover with water and bring to the boil. Remove and discard any froth that floats to the surface with a draining spoon, then partially cover the pan with a lid and turn down to a lively simmer. Leave the beans to cook for a good forty-five to sixty minutes, until almost tender.

Peel and chop the onions, then soften them in a little oil in a large, solid roasting tin over a low to moderate heat, adding the whole thyme sprigs and a grinding of black pepper. Let them take their time, so the onions are truly soft.

Set the oven at 220°C/Gas 7. Drain the cooked beans as soon as they are almost tender, and tip them into the onions and thyme. You should include the bay leaves or, if they look tired, add a couple of new ones. Pour in the stock.

Using a heavy kitchen knife, slice the piece of pork belly into eight squares. Salt the skin generously, pushing the grains down into the slashes on the surface. Place the pieces snugly, but not quite touching each other, in the beans, making certain that the pork stands proud of the beans. Bake for twenty minutes, until the crackling is looking pale gold and lightly crisp.

Lower the heat to 160°C/Gas 3 and continue cooking for an hour and fifteen minutes. The pork should be crisp on top, soft but not meltingly so. Remove the pork to warm plates.

Place the roasting tin over a moderate heat, shred the cabbage and stir into the beans, then cook for a couple of minutes. Finish with salt, stirring it into the beans. Serve with the pork. For 6.

# Return to earth

## March 31

Baking grounds me. After three weeks away, amusing myself with cod's milt, baby eels, firefly squid, boiled fish heads, the meat of massaged bulls, cherry-blossom-scented rice and the roe of sea urchins, I need to get my hands into the flour. I need to mix and fold and roll and knead, to feel the warm, live bread dough in my palms, to watch it rise and bake to a golden loaf.

I make flatbread, a thick focaccia studded with marinated olives and freckled with thyme and crystals of sea salt.

## Green olive and thyme focaccia

I use lemon olives for this, the sort that have been marinated in lemon-scented olive oil. Get them at the deli. You could also use green olives and substitute lemon olive oil for the basic oil in the recipe. Failing that, just use green olives. Makes one round bread about 22cm in diameter.

strong white bread flour – 500g
easy bake dried yeast – 1 sachet (7g, 2 teaspoons)
sea salt – 1 teaspoon
olive oil – 3–4 tablespoons

warm water – 350ml
green or lemon-marinated olives, stoned – 85g
thyme – the leaves from 4 sprigs
sea salt flakes

Rub the bottom of a baking tin with a little of the oil. Set the oven at 220°C/Gas 7.

Put the flour and yeast into a large bowl and add the sea salt, finely crushed then 1 tablespoon of the oil and the warm water. Mix

thoroughly, then turn the dough out onto a well-floured board and knead lightly for five minutes or so.

As soon as the dough feels elastic, put it into a lightly floured bowl, cover with a cloth or clingfilm, then leave it in a warm place to rise. Once it has doubled in size – about an hour or so – gently press it down with your fist, knocking some of the air out. Remove the dough from its bowl (it will sink more, but no matter) on to a lightly floured work surface. Roughly chop the olives and thyme leaves and knead them into the dough. Place the dough in the baking tin and push it firmly to flatten it. Cover as much of the bottom as you can, but don't worry if it doesn't quite cover it. Set aside, covered with clingfilm, for a further thirty minutes or so, till well risen.

With a floured finger, push several holes deep into the dough, then spoon over half the olive oil. Scatter liberally with sea salt flakes. Bake for twenty-five to thirty minutes, till pale gold, then spoon over the remaining oil.

Whilst still warm, free the bread from the pan with a palette knife. Leave to cool a little, then tear into pieces. Serves 4–6.

# Spring
# eats

# Potatoes, anchovies and dill

floury potatoes, olive oil, rosemary, marinated anchovies,
dill, capers

Set the oven at 200°C/gas 6. Scrub **450g floury potatoes** thoroughly, then slice them thinly – the thickness of a pound coin would be about right. Put the slices into a mixing bowl and add **4 tablespoons olive oil**, salt, black pepper and the leaves from **2 large rosemary sprigs**. Toss the potatoes to coat them evenly with the oil and seasoning.

On a non-stick baking sheet, place the potato slices in a single layer, slightly overlapping. Make sure the surface of the potatoes is covered with a little oil, bake for about twenty-five to thirty minutes, until pale gold and lightly crisp here and there. Ideally the cooked potatoes will be crisp in parts and softer in others. Remove the baking sheet from the oven and place **6 marinated anchovy fillets** on top. Pull tufts of leaves from **a handful of dill** and scatter over the potatoes, then finally add **1 tablespoon capers** and serve, broken into pieces. For 3–4.

# Clams with picada

fish or vegetable stock, large prawns, parsley, bay leaves, shelled
almonds, garlic, lemon, tarragon, young leeks, cod fillet, small clams

Put **1 litre of fish or vegetable stock** into a saucepan over a moderate
heat. Shell **8 large prawns,** then add the prawn shells to the stock
together with **a small bunch of parsley stalks** and **a couple of bay
leaves** and bring to the boil. Lower the heat and leave to gently
simmer, partially covered, for 30 minutes. Reserve the shelled
prawns.

Put **50g of shelled almonds** into a shallow pan, add **a clove of
garlic,** peeled, and **a teaspoon of olive oil.** Toast until the almonds
start to brown, then transfer to a mortar and pound till coarsely
ground and crunchy. Stir in **3 tablespoons of chopped parsley
leaves,** the **finely grated zest of a lemon** and **3 tablespoons of
chopped tarragon.**

Cut **3 young, slim leeks** into short pieces approximately the
length of a wine cork. Skin **400g of cod fillet** and cut into 6 pieces.
Strain most of the stock through a sieve into a saucepan, add the
leeks and let them simmer over a moderate heat for 7 or 8 minutes
till soft, then lower in the cod, letting it cook for 4 or 5 minutes.

Put the remaining stock into a separate pan (you only need 50ml
or so), add **500g of washed and checked small clams,** and let them
cook for 3 or 4 minutes, till the shells open. Lift the clams out and
put them into the pan with the leeks and cod in, then pour in the
cooking liquor through a fine sieve. (This is a minor chore, but will
stop any fine grit from the clams getting into the soup.)

Add the reserved shelled prawns to the pan, continue cooking
for a minute or two, then carefully lift out the clams, cod, leeks and
prawns with a draining spoon and put them into deep bowls. Check
the cooking liquor for seasoning – it may need salt and pepper –
then pour into the bowls. Scatter the almond mixture over the
surface and serve. Serves 2–3.

# Chard with caramelised onions and sultanas

onions, sultanas or raisins, pumpkin seeds, lemon, chard

Peel and slice **a couple of small onions,** then soften them in a shallow pan with **2 tablespoons of olive oil** and **a thin slice of butter** over a low to moderate heat. When they are starting to brown a little around the edges, add **3 heaped tablespoons of sultanas or raisins** and the same of **pumpkin seeds** and let the fruit plump up a little. Add a little salt and the **finely grated zest of half a lemon.**

Wash **4 large handfuls (about 100g) of chard,** put it into a separate pan with a very shallow film of water, cover with a lid and steam over a high heat for a minute or so. As soon as the leaves have wilted, and while the colour is still bright, drain and transfer to a serving dish. Scatter over the sweet onion mixture and serve. Serves 2 as a light lunch or side dish.

# Bavette with avocado

### skirt steak, butter, small chillies, avocados, coriander

Season **a piece of skirt steak, about 450g** in weight and cut into two pieces, with salt and pepper. Warm **50g of butter** in a pan and, as it sizzles and starts to froth, add the steak and let it cook for about 3 minutes on each side, until it has coloured nicely and is lightly pink in the centre. Remove the steak from the pan, place it on a warm plate and cover with an upturned bowl or a piece of kitchen foil.

Halve, seed and finely chop **3 small chillies of assorted colours**, then add them to the juices left in the steak pan and cook over a moderate heat until they start to soften. Peel, stone and roughly chop **a couple of avocados**, then add them to the cooked chillies. Using a fork, roughly crush the avocados, letting them soak up some of the steak's cooking juices. Tear the leaves from **a few sprigs of coriander**, add them to the pan and mix gently.

Slice the two pieces of steak into thick slices and serve with the warm chilli guacamole. For 2.

### &

As the steak cooks, spoon the buttery pan juices over it almost continuously. Let it rest for a good 10 minutes before slicing. It will be all the juicier. Leave the seeds in the chillies for a hotter seasoning. Crush the avocado only lightly – it is more interesting texturally as a crush than as a much smoother purée.

### &

This works just as well with a thin pork steak. It will need a little longer than the skirt steak to cook, so keep the heat slightly lower. If you want a smooth and spicy cream for your steak or pork, blitz the avocado, chillies and cooking juices in a food processor.

# Lamb with tomato, ginger and basil

cherry tomatoes, yellow mustard seeds, olive oil, ginger, basil, lamb steaks, salad leaves

Put **75g of cherry tomatoes** into a blender or food processor. Tip **a tablespoon of yellow mustard seeds** into a shallow pan and fry them, covered with a lid, for a minute or two until they start to crackle and pop. Remove them and tip them into the tomatoes. Pour in **5 tablespoons of olive oil, 20g of peeled fresh ginger, 10g of basil** and a little salt and blitz to a rough, sloppy paste.

Season **2 thick lamb steaks** with sea salt and black pepper, then grill until nicely charred on each side using a ridged griddle pan or the oven grill. Keep the inside pink. Leave the lamb to rest for 5 minutes, then cut it into thick slices. Tip the dressing into a shallow dish or deep plate, add the slices of lamb and toss gently, coating the meat with the tomato and mustard seed dressing. Serve on a bed of **salad leaves**. Serves 2.

### &

You will probably want the lamb to be nicely browned on the outside and pink within, so oil the meat lightly, season it, place it on a well-heated griddle pan and cook for 4–6 minutes, then turn and cook the other side for slightly less. Alternatively, cook the steaks in a little olive oil and butter in a shallow pan, turning regularly and almost constantly spooning the butter over the meat as it cooks. Leaving the meat to rest (old advice, but so many people don't bother) will keep it more juicy inside.

### &

Use a pork or beef steak instead of lamb. Instead of ginger, or perhaps as well, add 2 cloves of mild, sweet garlic.

# Chinese sausage and rice

white basmati rice, spring onions, shiitake mushrooms,
wind-dried Chinese sausages, chicken stock, parsley

Wash **150g of white basmati rice** three times in a sieve under running warm water. Tip the rice into a medium-sized saucepan, tuck in **3 chopped spring onions, 80g of fresh shiitake mushrooms** and **200g of Chinese wind-dried sausages** and pour in **300ml of chicken stock.**

Bring the stock to the boil, then turn down the heat (you'll need little or no salt – the sausages often have enough already). Cover with a lid and cook for about 10 minutes, till the rice is tender and has absorbed most of the stock. You want it to be moist, but not sloppy.

Turn off the heat, then remove the sausages and slice into thick pieces. Fold them, together with **a little chopped parsley,** back into the rice and serve. Enough for 2.

&

Wind-dried Chinese sausages are available in Chinese grocery shops and supermarkets. The paler-coloured varieties are the mildest, and, I think, the nicest. In this recipe, they are placed in the rice, moistening the grains as they cook.

# Lamb fillet with lentils

lamb fillet, stock, Puy lentils, thyme, garlic, spinach, double cream


You will need **a neck fillet of lamb, roughly 300g** in weight. Warm **a little olive oil** in a roasting pan over a moderate heat, then add the lamb and brown lightly on both sides. Remove the meat from the pan and wrap lightly in foil. Pour **400ml of stock** into the pan and stir to dissolve any delicious stickiness from the lamb that might be present, then add **200g of Puy lentils, 6 small sprigs of thyme**, salt and pepper and **3 cloves of garlic**, smashed with the blade of a knife or a heavy weight.

Leave the lentils to cook at a fast simmer for about 10 minutes, then return the lamb to the pan and continue cooking for a further 15 minutes. Wash **200g of spinach leaves and their tender stems** and cook in their own steam for 2 or 3 minutes, until tender. Drain the spinach and squeeze out most of the moisture with your hands. Chop or tear into small pieces and fold into the lentils.

Stir **4 tablespoons of double cream** into the lentils, then check the seasoning and correct with salt and black pepper. Remove the lamb, slice into thick pieces and serve with the lentils. Serves 2.

### &
Let the liquid become almost entirely absorbed before adding the cream, so you have a rich, creamy lentil sauce. Drain and squeeze the spinach quite well before adding, so as not to introduce too much liquid.

### &
Rather than cooking the lamb with thyme, you could introduce a spice note. Add ground cumin and coriander seeds to the lentils and garlic, or even a little mild curry powder, but still use the cream and spinach.

# Rice, carrot and cashews

carrots, spring onions, cloves, ground coriander, brown basmati
rice, vegetable stock, cashews, nigella seeds, garam masala

Scrub and finely dice **2 medium carrots**. Warm **a slice of butter** and **a
little oil** in a frying pan, then add **a couple of roughly chopped spring
onions** and the diced carrots. Let the carrots and spring onions colour
lightly, then add **3 whole cloves** and **a teaspoon of ground coriander**.
Add **200g of brown basmati rice** and **500ml of vegetable stock**,
bring to the boil, season generously with salt, then cover tightly with a
lid and turn down the heat so the rice simmers gently.

Cook for 15–20 minutes, until the rice is almost tender. Leave
to settle, still covered with a lid, for 10 minutes. Toast **a couple of
handfuls of cashews** in a dry pan until they are lightly brown, then
set aside. Remove the lid from the rice, add **2 teaspoons of nigella
seeds, a teaspoon of garam masala, a thick slice of butter** and
the cashews. Fork the butter, nuts and spices through the mixture,
stirring well, then serve. Enough for 2.

## &

I always wash my rice three times in a bowl of warm water, swishing
it round with my fingers. This removes any surface starch and helps
to keep the rice separate. Partly necessity and partly ritual, it is
probably only truly necessary to do this once, but I have always
done it three times and my rice never sticks. It's best cooked with a
tight lid and is done when deep holes appear on the surface. Peep
occasionally to check.

## &

You could use parsnips instead of carrots, but cook them a little
longer before adding the rice, so the roots are caramelised. Use
white rice, cooking it for a shorter time. It will take about 12 minutes,
depending on the rice and how soft you like it. I have used soft spicing
here, but for a hotter mix use ground chilli, cumin and paprika.

# Spiced lamb patties

minced lamb, green peppercorns in brine, yellow mustard seeds,
mild curry powder, fennel, cucumber, yoghurt, mint


Put **500g of minced lamb** into a mixing bowl. Add **2 teaspoons of bottled green peppercorns**, rinsed of their brine, and **a teaspoon or two of yellow mustard seeds**. Stir in **2 level tablespoons of decent curry powder or home-made spice blend**, then season. Shape into four thick patties and set aside in a cool place for 15 minutes.

Thinly slice **a small fennel bulb**, then peel, halve lengthways and core **half a small cucumber**. Cut the cucumber into thin slices and add to the fennel. Lightly beat **350g of natural yoghurt** (not the strained variety) until it becomes soft and runny, then add the cucumber and fennel, **4 tablespoons of shredded mint leaves** and some salt and black pepper.

Fry the lamb patties in a shallow, non-stick pan in a small amount of oil. Turn them from time to time to encourage even cooking. When they are golden brown and sticky on the outside, lift, drain briefly on kitchen paper and serve with the fennel and yoghurt raita. Serves 2.

### &

A good meat patty should have an open texture, so it is best to avoid squeezing the meat too hard. However, this means the patties will be fragile in the pan, so put them into hot oil and leave them be, allowing a light crust to form before you carefully turn them over.

### &

Use chicken or beef mince if you prefer. Chicken can be a little dry when minced, so it may benefit from a couple of rashers of bacon per 400g of meat. Make up your own curry powder with cumin, cardamom and coriander seeds, finely crushed, then add chilli and black pepper to your taste to make the mix as mild or hot as you wish. I like to add a little ground turmeric, too.

# Duck with udon

duck legs, chicken or vegetable stock, udon or other thick
noodles, dulse or other seaweed, coriander, mint

Set the oven at 200°C/Gas 6. Put **2 duck legs** into a roasting tin (no
fat or oil needed), season lightly, and roast for 40 minutes, until the
skin is lightly crisp. Pour off any fat that appears in the roasting tin.
Place the duck on a chopping board, tear off the skin and set aside.
Remove the flesh from the legs and cut into pieces just large enough
to get on to your spoon.

Put the roasting tin over a moderate heat, pour in **1.5 litres of
chicken or vegetable stock**, then bring to the boil, stirring to
dissolve any tasty bits in the tin. Simmer the stock for 15 minutes to
reduce it slightly, then add **100g of udon noodles** and **2 handfuls
of dried dulse or other thin seaweed**. Continue cooking for 2 or
3 minutes, until the udon are tender and the dulse is soft. Add the
reserved duck meat and check the seasoning.

Lift the noodles out and divide them between two deep bowls.
Ladle over the soup, then drop **a small handful of coriander and
mint leaves** into each bowl. Tear up some of the crisp duck skin and
drop into the broth, then serve. Enough for 2.

&

If the duck skin isn't crisp, place it in a single layer on a baking sheet
and crisp it up under an overhead grill.

&

You can use chicken legs instead of duck. Roast them until the skin
is crisp, but add a little oil or butter to the pan before you put them
into the oven, and baste them once or twice during cooking. Use a
homemade chicken stock or a good-quality shop-bought product.
If seaweed isn't your thing, add very finely shredded ginger and let it
cook for 10 minutes.

# Salmon with macaroni

double cream, salmon, bay leaf, serpentelli, macaroni or similar
pasta, grain mustard, sourdough bread, fennel or dill

Pour **600ml of double cream** into a saucepan, add **a 400g piece of
salmon fillet**, a little black pepper and **a bay leaf** and bring almost
to the boil. Lower the heat and let the salmon cook gently for about
10 minutes, until the flesh comes apart in large flakes with ease, then
remove from the heat.

Boil **150g of serpentelli or macaroni** in generously salted water
for 9 minutes, then drain and tip into a baking dish. Remove the
salmon from the cream and break it into large pieces, discarding any
skin as you go, then tuck the fish into the pasta. Season the cream
with **2 tablespoons of grain mustard** and a little salt, then pour over
the salmon and pasta.

In a food processor, blitz **50g of sourdough bread** to coarse
crumbs with **a large handful of fennel fronds or dill**. Scatter the
herb crumbs over the pasta. Bake for 20–25 minutes at 200°C/Gas
6, until the crumbs are golden and lightly crisp. Serve with a crisp,
leafy salad and lots of watercress. Serves 3–4.

### &

The important thing here is to infuse the cream with the salmon and
bay, so leave the fish and bay leaf in the cream to cool a little once
the fish is cooked.

### &

Instead of salmon, use smoked mackerel. Peel the skin from the
mackerel, then break the fish into large pieces before tucking among
the pasta. Use dill or basil in the herb crust. Instead of mustard, try
green peppercorns rinsed of their brine.

# Spiced turnips and spinach

young turnips, small swedes, onion, cumin seeds, turmeric,
garam masala, spinach, yoghurt, coriander leaves

Peel 1kg of mixed young turnips and swedes and cut them into
halves or quarters depending on their size. Cook the turnips and
swedes either in boiling, lightly salted water, or in a steamer, for 15–
20 minutes, or until tender.

In a shallow pan, fry **a peeled and roughly chopped onion in a
little butter and oil** for 10–15 minutes, until soft and golden, then
add **a teaspoon each of cumin seeds, ground turmeric** and **garam
masala**. Continue cooking for a couple of minutes over a moderate
heat until all is fragrant.

Wash **200g of spinach** and remove any tough stalks. Place a
shallow non-stick pan over a moderate heat, add the wet spinach
and cover with a tight-fitting lid. Let the spinach cook in its own
steam for about 3 minutes, until wilted, then drain and gently press
the water from it.

Add the drained turnips and swedes to the onion and continue
cooking over a moderate to high heat until they are lightly golden
and have soaked up some of the flavour of the spices. A little
crispness here and there is a good thing. Season with a little salt.
Fold the spinach into the spiced turnips and swedes and serve, if you
wish, with a trickle of **yoghurt** and **a few coriander leaves**. Serves 4.

&

This gently fragrant dish works well with potatoes and parsnips too.
You could use another leaf, perhaps chard or kale. Steam these for
slightly longer than the spinach and use a little more water, to give
them time to soften.

# Pancetta and leek tortilla

pancetta, button mushrooms, leeks, butter, eggs

Chop **150g of smoked or unsmoked pancetta** into small dice and fry for 4 or 5 minutes in a shallow 22cm non-stick pan. If it crisps a little, all to the good. Remove and set aside on kitchen paper, leaving any fat behind in the pan.

Halve **150g of button mushrooms** and fry them in the pancetta fat, adding **a little oil or fat** if necessary, until they are golden. While the mushrooms cook, wash and shred **300g of leeks**. Lift the mushrooms out and set aside, then add the leeks to the pan with **30g of butter** and cook over a low heat until soft and sweet. Try not to let them colour.

Break **6 eggs** into a bowl, whisk thoroughly, then season with salt and black pepper. Return the pancetta and mushrooms to the pan with the leeks, then pour over the beaten egg and leave to cook, over a lowish heat, until the bottom is golden and the edges are starting to set.

Warm an overhead grill, place the pan under the heat and leave for a few minutes, until the egg has set lightly. The omelette should still wobble when gently shaken. Serves 3–4.

### &

It's all about temperature. Perfection involves getting the heat right – high enough to cook the eggs but low enough to let them cook through before the tortilla browns too much on the bottom. Practice helps. I start off with a moderately high flame, then turn it almost as low as it will go for the remaining time. Finishing the cooking under an overhead grill is a bit of a cheat but diminishes the chances of an overcooked base.

# Hot-smoked salmon with oatmeal

shallots, butter, oatmeal, hot-smoked salmon, parsley,
double cream, nutmeg

Peel and finely chop **2 medium-sized shallots**. Melt **60g of butter** in a heavy-based pan over a moderate heat, then add the chopped shallots and cook for 7–10 minutes, until soft and pale gold. Pour in **150g of coarse or medium oatmeal or fine porridge oats** and turn in the butter until coated and glossy. Sprinkle with a little water and continue to cook for 10 minutes, until the oats smell nutty and toasted.

Break **200g of hot-smoked salmon fillet** into large flakes and fold gently into the warm, soft grain. Add salt, black pepper and **3 tablespoons of chopped parsley**. Pour **100ml of double cream** into a small pan, season with more salt and pepper, and add **a little grated nutmeg**. Warm gently. Serve the salmon and oatmeal warm, spooning over the cream as you go. Serves 2.

### &

The oatmeal needs only a small amount of cooking – just until it smells warm and toasted. The coarser your oats, the longer they will need. Probably not a good idea to use large rolled oats for this. Stir the oatmeal and shallots regularly. Once the salmon has been added, try not to stir too much, as you will crush the fish. Hot-smoked salmon does not need cooking, just warming through.

### &

Cook a few large handfuls of spinach or chard in a very small amount of water. Drain and press the water out, then chop roughly. Fold through the warm grain. Instead of butter, use bacon fat or dripping. Instead of cream, finish with a poached egg.

# Carrot and cardamom soup, ricotta dumplings

carrots, celery, onion, bay leaves, peppercorns, cardamom pods, vegetable stock, plain flour, oatmeal, baking powder, butter, ricotta, parsley, watercress, thyme

Scrub and roughly chop **400g of carrots**. Cut **2 ribs of celery** into short lengths. Peel and roughly chop **an onion**. Put the carrots, celery and onion into a deep pan with **a couple of tablespoons of olive oil** and cook over a moderate heat for 10 minutes. Add **a couple of bay leaves** and **6 black peppercorns** to the pan. Crack open **6 cardamom pods**, extract the seeds and grind them to a coarse powder, then add to the vegetables with a little salt and **1 litre of vegetable stock or water**. Bring to the boil, then lower the heat and simmer for 25 minutes, or until the carrots are soft. Blitz the soup in a blender or food processor till quite smooth.

Make the dumplings: put **70g of plain flour** and **70g of fine oatmeal** into a mixing bowl with **a teaspoon of baking powder** and a couple of good pinches of salt. Using your fingertips, rub in **75g of butter** until the mixture resembles fine breadcrumbs. Stir in **200g of ricotta**. Blend **3 teaspoons of water** with **30g of herbs** to a rough paste. I suggest equal amounts of **parsley leaves** and **watercress** and a generous palmful of **thyme leaves**. Stir the herb paste through the dumpling mix. Check the seasoning, adding black pepper and more salt as you think fit. Roll the mixture into 12 balls.

Bring the soup to the boil, checking it is not too thick and adding a little more stock or water if it is. Drop the dumplings into the simmering soup, then cover with a lid and let them steam for 15–20 minutes, till cooked. Serve in shallow bowls. Enough for 4.

&

The dumplings need to be cooked as soon as they are made, so get them into the soup just after you have rolled them. For the deepest flavour, use large maincrop carrots for the soup rather than the small spring carrots.

&

You could change the herbs in the dumplings to suit what you have around. Basil works well, as does tarragon. Avoid rosemary in this instance. For a more pronounced cheese note, add Parmesan – a couple of tablespoons, finely grated and added with the ricotta, should be enough.

# APRIL

## Hiding bunny

### April 2

If you are thinking of cooking rabbit and haven't made the rabbit with tarragon in *Kitchen Diaries II*, then may I suggest you do? It's a recipe with spring written all over it.

Today I make a rabbit salad, deploying grain mustard, honey and cider vinegar as seasoning for the pan juices. It is really quite delicious. And most people think it's chicken until you happen to mention it.

### Warm rabbit and watercress salad

rabbit – a saddle and 2 legs
butter – 40g
olive oil
garlic – a whole, large head
apple juice, unfiltered – 500ml
cider vinegar – 1 tablespoon

mild honey – 1 tablespoon
wholegrain mustard –
   1 tablespoon
young spinach – 100g
watercress – 100g

Salt the rabbit lightly. Warm the butter and a little oil in a large, heavy sauté pan, then brown the rabbit in it. A relatively even, golden brown is what you are looking for. Break the head of garlic into individual cloves, peel them, then add to the rabbit, letting them colour lightly.

Pour over the apple juice and leave the rabbit to cook for fifteen minutes, or until you can slice the meat easily from one of the legs. Remove the rabbit from the pan, leave to rest for ten minutes, then pull the meat from the bones in as large pieces as possible.

Let the rabbity, appley pan juices bubble down to half their volume over a moderate heat, stirring in the cider vinegar, honey, mustard, salt and pepper. Squash the garlic cloves into the dressing with a fork.

Wash the spinach and watercress, discarding any tough stalks as you go. Return the rabbit momentarily to the pan, add the washed leaves, toss tenderly, and immediately divide rabbit, leaves and dressing between two plates. Serves 2 as a light main dish.

# A piquant sauce for chicken

## April 3

Of all the ingredients that introduce a snap of acidity to a recipe – lemon, lime, passion fruit, verjuice, vinegar, yoghurt – it is only soured cream that brings with it a touch of richness too. Even a spoonful stirred into the hot pan juices will turn a straightforward sauté into something memorable.

Soured cream is not a pot of cream that has gone sour. You know that. It is single cream whose clean, sharp flavour has been deliberately created by the addition of lactic cultures. (Called sour cream by most of us, it is generally sold as 'soured' cream.) As an ingredient in the kitchen it brings more to the party than a pot of double cream. Where cream takes the edge off the flavours in the pan, softening their bright notes, soured cream does the opposite, sharpening, lifting, lightening the existing flavours.

The bum note is that soured cream tends to curdle slightly, or at the very least turn the sauce grainy. You could faff around with cornflour or arrowroot to prevent this, but I don't see the point. There will be a little graininess, so let's just go with it. The trick to minimising the effect is not to boil the sauce once the cream has been added.

Soured cream dresses a salad of crisp ingredients with little need for anything else. The acid notes of lemon or vinegar are already there, as is the emollient that makes the dressing coat the salad, but I do occasionally stir in a splash of olive oil to make it less clumpy to toss and provide a more easily incorporated dressing. You can flavour it with herbs, particularly dill, fennel, caraway and celery seed. Spices incorporate well enough, especially cumin, coriander seeds and cardamom. Toast the spices in a dry pan before adding.

If I have a pan full of roasting juices I generally leave them as they are or may perhaps add a little wine or Marsala to them, but if I feel in the mood for something more substantial (richer and smoother), then soured cream is a possibility. Added to a sauté pan that has been used to cook some chicken pieces, a few spoonfuls of soured cream give an instant sauce without the need to reduce or thicken.

A small pot of soured cream made its way into a chicken sauté at home this week, and was further sharpened with a few sliced gherkins. The recipe, made with a glass or two of Riesling and some tiddly little mushrooms, was only just short of being a stroganoff, and with all the glorious piquancy you would expect. Floury potatoes would be my own choice, though others may prefer rice.

Shopping for soured cream is easy enough in a major supermarket but it is not always the easiest ingredient to find. You can make a near substitute by stirring a few drops of lemon juice into a pot of cream, but it must be done with care and the flavour isn't quite the same. It's an emergency tactic. In many ways crème fraîche has taken its place. It is certainly easier to track down, but, good though it is, it doesn't have the same clean, bright tang to it. And that, surely, is the whole point.

## Chicken with soured cream and gherkins

I used large free-range chicken legs for this. You could also use breasts or drumsticks.

| | |
|---|---|
| small shallots – 12 | Riesling – 500ml |
| chicken legs – 2 | soured cream – 150ml |
| butter – a thick slice | |
| button mushrooms – 250g | *To serve:* |
| gherkins – 6 | steamed potatoes or rice |

Pour boiling water from the kettle over the shallots and set aside for ten minutes to soften the skins and make them easier to peel. Season the chicken legs, then brown them lightly on both sides in a little butter. Peel the shallots, leaving them whole, then add them to the chicken pan, letting them colour nicely on all sides.

Halve the mushrooms, then add them to the chicken and shallots, letting them colour lightly. Slice the gherkins into thick pieces and add to the pan together with the wine. Leave the wine to come to the boil, continue cooking at an enthusiastic bubble for three or four minutes, then lower the heat to a gentle simmer.

Let the chicken simmer for about twenty minutes, then stir in the soured cream, keeping the heat quite low. Allow to warm through, check the seasoning, and serve with potatoes or rice. Serves 2.

# A letter to an old friend

## April 4

Dear Mashed Potato, I don't see you much any more, but I still think of you. I imagine you sitting in fat clouds on a white plate, a pool of shining gravy lapping at your edges. Heavy with butter, maybe hot milk, or cream or olive oil, you always were my go-to food, the recipe that sorted me out, put my world to rights, tucked me in at night.

I still see you, of course, as an occasional smear on the plate at a posh restaurant dinner, like seeing a picture of your first love in a photo album. Or when I am making the crust of a shepherd's pie, to be browned in the oven in deep furrows like a freshly ploughed field. I see glimpses of you in fishcakes too, or in ham croquettes on the counter of tapas bars.

You were loved in all your guises: as an almost liquid pool under a fillet of red mullet or thick slices of lamb; beaten with cheese to an unctuous and buttery mess; hidden inside the brittle, salty skin of a baked potato; or piled, lumpy and cold, into a pan with shredded cabbage only to emerge as a sweetly singing bubble and squeak. But most of all, I remember you as you were when I first fell in love with you, whipped to a waxy cloud with masses of butter, pure and simple.

Today, we shall once again meet up, as you are folded with roasted caramelised onions and the sort of matured Cheddar that makes your lips tingle. Better still, you will be made not from boiled or steamed potatoes but from roast. The mash will be soft and fluffy, but with pieces of crisp roast potato crust in there too. An old friend loved all the more for being an occasional visitor.

# Cumberland sausage, shallot
## and Cheddar roast potato mash

floury potatoes – 900g
large banana shallots – 2
olive or groundnut oil – 50ml
Cumberland sausage ring –
    500g, held together by skewers

Cheddar, such as Montgomery's
    or Keen's – 75g
chopped parsley – a small
    handful

Peel the potatoes and boil them for fifteen minutes in deep, salted water.

Set the oven at 200°C/Gas 6. Peel the shallots and halve them lengthways. Pour the oil into a roasting tin and add the shallots, cut side down. Drain the potatoes and put them in amongst the shallots. Place the Cumberland ring amongst the potatoes and shallots and bake for about an hour, till the shallots are golden and soft and the potatoes are lightly crisp.

Grate the Cheddar. Remove the shallots and sausage to a warm place, then add the grated Cheddar to the potatoes in the tin, with a little salt and pepper, and roughly crush with a potato masher to give a coarsely textured, crusty mash. Fold the shallots and parsley through the roast potato mash, and serve with the sausage. For 3.

# A new cure

## April 7

I have been using herb-scented salt for some time, most often by chopping dill into the dry salt marinade for making gravlax, which I usually do at Christmas and Easter. The salt preserves, the dill flavours. But seasonings like this are too good for special occasion cooking alone.

Earlier in the week I flavoured a packet of sea salt flakes with lemon and orange zest, both finely grated and stirred through the white flakes with a little chopped dill leaf. Mixed with black peppercorns, mint leaves and gin, I used it as a marinade for salmon. Sliced thinly, the fish looked clean and smart against a white plate, and needed just a triangle or two of treacle-coloured rye bread at its side. The second day we served it with a frost-crisp salad of paper-thin slices of fennel, blood orange and black pepper.

Flavoured salts are good with grilled meats too, and making them is easy. You chop the herb leaves, mix them one third to two with salt, let the mixture dry a little, then keep it in a stoppered jar. Where the process becomes even more interesting is when you marry a couple of herbs together, or introduce a little spice, or even a clove or two of garlic. Right now my favourite is a salt that has thyme leaves and crushed juniper folded through it. In the last couple of weeks its cold Nordic notes have seasoned lamb cutlets from the grill and a sea bream baked whole. The salt also had an outing with sautéd potatoes, scattered over as they finished cooking.

Rosemary needles, dill fronds, fennel, thyme, savory and celery seeds can be used to add a herbal note to salt. But less popular herbs are interesting too. Lavender works nicely with grilled chicken. I grew myrtle last year, a herb that has seen less of the inside of my kitchen than it could. Its slight bitterness needs to be tamed – I pick the leaves out as one might do bay. It worked well enough in a pork casserole (with apples and cider) but I like the leaves best when they are pounded with salt (use a pestle and mortar), then used to bring life to a beef casserole.

We can crank the herb salt up with other flavourings too. The idea of serving grilled chicken skin, salty and crisp, with a dish of mayo is one of the better ideas I have come across lately, but we can take it on a bit. By grilling the skin till it crunches, then crushing it to a coarse powder and tossing the result with sea salt and a few herbs, we have an original and extraordinary seasoning that can be used with both green and root vegetables, potatoes and popcorn.

Of course you can do the work in a food processor, but I prefer to chop the herbs by hand or to mash them with a pestle and mortar. Herb-flavoured salts will keep, in a sealed jar, for several weeks. The crucial detail is to let them dry for twenty-four hours first. The most successful way to do this is to scatter the pounded herbs and salt on a tray, in a shallow layer, and leave in a warm but airy place. Bottle tightly, then keep near the cooker, using the salt as the mood or whim takes you.

## Salmon with mint and citrus salt

Get your fishmonger to fillet a salmon tail for you, leaving the skin on.

| | |
|---|---|
| a medium to large salmon tail, filleted – 450g | gin – 4 tablespoons |
| golden caster sugar – 25g | the zest of a lemon |
| sea salt – 8 tablespoons | the zest of an orange |
| black peppercorns – 1 tablespoon | mint leaves – 10g |
| | dill – 10g |

Carefully check the fish for any stray bones or scales. Wipe it with a piece of kitchen paper. Put the sugar and salt into a mixing bowl, then coarsely grind the peppercorns and stir in. Add the gin and the lemon and orange zest.

Roughly chop the mint and dill, then stir into the salt and sugar mixture. Place the fish on a large flat dish or platter and spread the salt mixture over with your hands. Lay a piece of clingfilm over the fish, then place a flat weight such as a chopping board on top.

Place the fish in the fridge and leave for a minimum of twenty-four hours, but no longer than forty-eight. Wipe the fish thoroughly with kitchen paper, removing every morsel of salt – it has done its work. Slice the fish thinly like smoked salmon or into thicker pencil-thin strips. It will keep for two or three days, wrapped in clingfilm, in the fridge. Serves 4–6.

# A sticky pudding for a chilly day

There is an unspoken challenge to smother a hot cross bun with as much butter as humanly possible. It is something I am always up for. But there is more to the fruited Easter bun than tea and toast. The hot cross bun is more interesting than a round of 'white sliced' when used in a bread and butter pudding; it provides a more substantial alternative to panettone as a cushion on which to sit baked fruits and makes a sweet breadcrumb crust when crumbled, fried in hot butter and scattered over stewed apples.

Today I tear the little buns to pieces and tuck them into a loaf tin with sliced bananas and butterscotch sauce. There is a touch of both banoffee pie and sticky toffee pudding to its layers of sweet fruit and caramel sauce.

## Hot cross bun, toffee and banana pudding

bananas – 3, slightly underripe    vanilla extract – half a teaspoon
hot cross buns – 3
light muscovado sugar – 150g    *To serve:*
double cream – 375ml    double cream

You will need a loaf tin measuring approximately 18cm × 9cm × 7cm deep.

Set the oven at 180°C/Gas 4. Peel the bananas and slice into thick rounds. Slice the hot cross buns in half and tear each half into small pieces.

Put the sugar and cream into a small saucepan and bring to the boil. As soon as the sugar has melted, add the vanilla extract and set aside.

Line the loaf tin with baking parchment, leaving a little overhanging the edges. Pour some of the butterscotch sauce into the tin, then pile in the torn pieces of hot cross bun and the banana. Pour over the rest of the butterscotch sauce and press the bun pieces down so that they become saturated with the sauce.

Bake for thirty minutes, until lightly firm. Leave for ten to twenty minutes before turning out and cutting into thick slices. Serve with double cream. For 6.

# A roast with a spring in its step

## April 10

The Sunday roast, joyous, generous, the pinnacle of shared meals. A gathering of family, in some cases the only one of the week, or a long and leisurely meal for friends. For all its generosity and pass-the-peas bonhomie, the dish itself splits into two halves, the hot roast and the glorious leftovers.

Cold beef, cooked pink and carved thin, sharing a plate with pickled walnuts and baked potatoes. Cold roast chicken tugged from its bones, dipped into a bowl of garlicky, tarragon-freckled mayonnaise. Or as it is today, the remnants of a roasted shoulder of lamb, seasoned with rosemary and anchovy, sliced thick and piled on to hot toast. No garlic mayonnaise, but instead crushed peas seasoned with wasabi and softened with butter, layered with cool, roasted lamb and salad leaves.

The lamb was a roast from which I used the juices to cook a handful of summer greens. Pink-stemmed beetroot leaves, young red chard whose stems were barely pencil thick, and peas from the pod. I also tossed in a few late shoots of purple sprouting, as tender and precious as asparagus spears. I could have boiled the vegetables, but instead decided to steam them in the roasting juices and stock, still in the roasting tin, over a moderate heat. They took less time than it took the lamb to rest.

## Roast shoulder of lamb with young greens

I use shoulder for its flavour and the crispness of its fat. It is often cheaper than the leg. I am the first to admit a shoulder is less straightforward to carve than the other cuts of lamb, and usually resort to hacking off large juicy pieces of meat rather than neat slices.

shoulder of lamb – 2kg
olive oil
anchovy fillets – 8
rosemary – 3 bushy sprigs
thyme – 8–10 sprigs

*For the vegetables:*
mixed greens – 250g (purple
sprouting broccoli, young
beetroot leaves, red chard, etc.)
vegetable stock or water – 200ml
shelled peas – 250g

Set the oven at 180°C/Gas 4. Place the lamb in a roasting tin, rub all over with olive oil and season lightly with sea salt. Pierce the fat in fifteen or so places with the point of a knife, cutting 3 or 4cm down into the flesh.

Stuff the slits in the meat alternately with anchovy fillets and tufts of rosemary. Scatter with the thyme sprigs, tucking a few underneath the meat.

Roast the lamb for one and a half hours, until the fat has turned translucent and pale honey-coloured and the meat is light rose-pink. Remove the roasting tin from the oven, lift out the meat and place somewhere warm, covering lightly with foil. Leave to rest for fifteen minutes or so.

Trim the broccoli and the beetroot and chard stems, removing the leaves and setting them aside. Place the roasting tin over a low to moderate heat, then pour in the stock or water and bring to the boil. When the liquid starts to bubble, stir with a wooden spoon or spatula to dislodge the roasted meat juices and herbs, then add the peas, broccoli and the chard and beetroot stems and cover with foil. Leave the vegetables to steam in the roasting juices for three or four minutes, turning them from time to time.

Add the leaves of the chard and beetroot, turn them once or twice in the hot liquid till they have wilted, then lift all the vegetables out into a warm serving dish. Turn the heat up under the roasting tin and reduce the liquid to a thin, deeply flavoured dressing. Carve the lamb on to a warm serving dish or directly on to plates, and serve with the roasting juices and vegetables. For 4–5.

# Roast lamb sandwiches with crushed peas and wasabi

Lamb is good when eaten as a cold cut, but I think it benefits from being used at room temperature or even still slightly warm, rather than from the fridge. That'll be a Sunday evening sandwich rather than Monday night then.

peas – 250g
wasabi paste – 1 tablespoon
butter – 40g
sourdough bread – 4 thickish
  slices
olive oil

salad leaves (mustard,
  watercress, little gem lettuce,
  micro-leaves)
leftover roast lamb – 4 handfuls
roasting juices (optional, but
  good if you have some left)

Put a pan of water on to boil, salt it lightly, then add the peas. Cook until tender (three or four minutes only if you are using frozen, four to ten minutes if using fresh, depending on their age).

Drain the peas, add the wasabi paste and butter, then crush with a vegetable masher. I like the peas to retain quite a bit of texture, others may prefer to mash them to a smoother consistency. Taste and season.

Toast the pieces of sourdough lightly on both sides. I say lightly, but I must admit to a personal preference for a few charred edges to mine. Sprinkle the surface of the toast with a little olive oil, then lay a few of the salad leaves on each slice. Place a couple of spoonfuls of the crushed peas on top of the leaves, then some slices of the cold roast lamb. Salt the lamb generously, then trickle over a few spoonfuls of either olive oil or hot roasting juices. Enough for 4 open sandwiches.

# A coffee mousse

## April 11

There is no cheque you could write that would tempt me to eat an egg. It is to my eternal regret that I will never know the pleasures of one softly cooked with its blanket of hollandaise sauce and doughy raft of English muffin; the childish joy of dipping a buttered soldier into the dripping yolk of a morning boiled egg in its little striped cup; the quivering delight of a perfectly poached egg on a square of toast or the cheerful face of a pert yolk and wibbly white, fried and tucked amongst its friends in a full English. (Note to new parents, do not force your child to eat anything they don't like. They may end up hating it for the next fifty years.)

And yet, hidden in a soufflé, a cake, a pâté or a frittata, I am up for an oeuf or two. I get much pleasure from seeing them, in the style of a Cedric Morris painting, in a bowl on the kitchen table. Or of running my fingers over their blue, cream, brown or ivory shells in a peaceful Zen moment. I am happy to cradle one from henhouse to kitchen as I did the summer we filmed on the farm. I am often enchanted by the sight of a stray feather found in an egg box. But put one in an egg cup and I will run faster than a flock of Welsummers from the jaws of a hungry fox.

Which brings me to the mousse. Twenty years ago there was barely a menu in the land without a salmon, ham, avocado, lemon, orange or chocolate mousse. And when I say chocolate I mean one of those wobbly gelatine-based numbers they used to teach at Cordon Bleu rather than the wannabe truffle version thick enough to stand a spoon in. But they have all but disappeared, which is a shame because I rather like the cloud-like fluff of a sweet or savoury mousse with its hidden cargo of eggs. Just don't even say the word coddled.

164

# Coffee mousse

Light, creamy, delicate. Tastes like a cappuccino. Use the strongest espresso you can make.

eggs – 5
golden caster sugar – 120g
gelatine – 6 small sheets

double cream – 250ml
strong espresso – 100ml
a little cocoa powder

Separate the eggs, and put the yolks into the bowl of a food mixer and the whites into a large mixing bowl. Add the sugar to the yolks and whisk till light, thick and creamy, occasionally scraping down the sides of the bowl with a rubber spatula.

Soften the gelatine sheets for five minutes or so in a bowl of cold water, until they are soft and jelly-like. Whip the cream until it will sit in soft folds. It should not be stiff. Make the espresso – it needs to be very strong – then add the softened gelatine to it, stirring until it has dissolved.

Gently, but thoroughly, fold the whipped cream into the egg yolks and sugar mixture, followed by the coffee and gelatine. Beat the egg whites till stiff, then, using a large metal spoon, tenderly fold them into the mousse, making sure they are fully mixed in. Spoon or ladle the mixture into cups or small bowls and refrigerate for a couple of hours till set. Don't leave overnight.

Dust the top of each mousse with a little cocoa powder before serving. Enough for 8.

# Lamb chops and apricots on focaccia

## April 17

I am asked, a little too often, 'What should I serve with that?'

Such questions remind me how difficult it is to shake off our meat and two veg heritage. Most times, I will make a single dish for dinner. I don't see the need for 'with'.

A salad or some green vegetables, maybe some roast potatoes, will appear on the table at some point, though almost never on the same plate. Or should I say on the same plate at the same time. I guess I just hate an overcrowded plate.

Today, some chops. Thick cut, cooked with juniper and apricots. I sit them on a slice of toasted focaccia, for the sole reason of soaking up the glossy juices. Toast soaked with lamb gravy? Oh yes please.

## Lamb chops with cider and apricots

A jacket potato would be another sound accompaniment for these sweet and juicy chops. Failing that, some plain mashed potatoes, into which you can fork the cooking juices as you eat.

olive oil – 2 tablespoons
large, thick lamb chops
(or boneless steaks) – 4
(about 1kg)

sparkling cider – 700ml
juniper berries – 15
dried apricots – 200g
focaccia – 4 slices

Preheat the oven to 180°C/Gas 4. In a large, wide casserole, heat the oil and lightly brown the chops on both sides, seasoning them with salt and black pepper as you go. Pour in the cider, scraping at any sticky residue left behind by the chops. Roughly crush the juniper

berries, flattening them with a heavy weight, then add them, with the apricots, to the lamb. Cover with a lid, then transfer to the oven and bake for approximately half an hour, till the meat is tender.

Toast the slices of bread, place a chop on each, then spoon over the pan juices. Serves 4.

# Sweetness and light

## April 19

There is a bowl of egg whites in the fridge to use up. At least, that's my excuse for making light, marshmallow-hearted clouds of crisp egg white and sugar. Clouds that I will fill not with cream, but with a sharp lime curd, made at home. Shop-bought lemon curd, at its best, is a fine substitute for those disinclined to grate, squeeze and beat.

My meringue-making has improved tenfold since I learned to warm the sugar in the oven before adding it to the egg whites, and, once added, to beat the mixture at high speed till it turns stiff and glossy.

## Meringues with lime curd and pistachios

*For the meringues:*
caster sugar – 250g
egg whites – 6
cornflour – 1 tablespoon
white wine vinegar –
  2 teaspoons

*For the filling:*
limes – 2
lemons – 2
butter – 100g
egg yolks – 4
salted pistachios – 100g
  (50g shelled weight)

Set the oven at 200°C/Gas 6. Scatter the sugar in a fine layer over a baking sheet and place in the oven for five minutes or so to warm.

Put the egg whites into a deep mixing bowl, preferably the bowl of a food mixer, and beat fairly slowly, till white and fluffy. I find the process works best with a food mixer and a whisk attachment, but a hand whisk will do the trick too.

Tip the warm sugar, a few tablespoons at a time, into the egg whites, beating all the time at a moderate to high speed. The sugar added, continue beating for a good five minutes, till the egg whites

and sugar are stiff and glossy. They should be able to stand in stiff, shiny peaks. Mix in the cornflour and the vinegar.

Line a baking sheet with non-stick baking parchment, or use a very lightly oiled baking sheet dusted with a very fine layer of flour.

Using a large serving spoon, place eight generous piles of the mixture, each about the size of a goose egg, on the baking sheet. Place in the preheated oven and immediately lower the heat, door closed, to 140°C/Gas 1.

Bake the meringues for thirty-five to forty minutes, till crisp outside. They should be soft and marshmallow-like within. Allow the meringues to cool on the tray before moving, with the help of a palette knife, to a cooling rack.

To make the filling: finely grate the zest of the limes and lemons into a heatproof bowl that will sit comfortably in the top of a small saucepan. Squeeze the lemon and lime juice into the bowl, then place the bowl over a pan of simmering water.

Cut the butter into small pieces, then drop them into the juice and zest and leave to melt, stirring occasionally. Beat the egg yolks lightly to mix, then pour into the juice and zest, a little at a time, stirring regularly.

Warm the butter, egg and juice mixture and leave to thicken, over the hot water, for roughly twenty minutes, beating regularly with a wooden spoon. The curd won't actually set till it has cooled. Remove the curd from the heat and let it cool, then refrigerate.

To serve, place the meringues on individual plates or a serving dish, lightly crush the top of each with a spoon, then place a spoonful of curd in each hollow. Roughly chop the pistachios and scatter over the top. Makes 8.

# A roasting tin dressing

## April 23

As meat or vegetables roast, chicken, say, or ripe peppers, their juices and sugars stick to the roasting tin. This is good. This is more than good. This is the heart and soul, the essence, of the meat or vegetable. It will concentrate and in doing so darken, stubbornly sticking to the tin in the form of a glossy, umami-rich gel. I think of it as the spirit of the roast.

This essence is the backbone of a good gravy or, god forbid, jus. It can also be the spine of a dressing. Think of pieces of crisp-skinned chicken, the scorching meat wrenched from its bones, the skin torn into shards, tossed with ice-cold, thick-stemmed salad leaves. A little bitterness perhaps, or just sweet iceberg or buttercrunch. Now think of it with a dressing made from its essence, that shining goo stuck to the pan.

We can dissolve the essence by pouring in a little red wine or tarragon vinegar. Some lime or lemon juice (blood orange with pork) and a very little oil. Heat it, gently, scraping and dissolving as you go. Taste for salt, for pepper and for sweetness. It is no crime to add the merest pinch of sugar.

Now return the meat to the pan, toss it in the juices, then place on top of the cold – they must be crisp – leaves. The leaves will wilt briefly, the juices will form a puddle in the plate. You will have hot meat, cold leaves, savour, sweetness, crunch and spirit. Stuff vinaigrette.

# Roast chicken, lime and mint

For a midweek salad I use thighs or drumsticks, so the chicken cooks quickly. It will of course work with a whole bird too.

large chicken drumsticks – 4
groundnut oil – a little
butter – a thick slice
a small cucumber
mint leaves – 8
watercress – 2 handfuls

radish sprouts – 4 small handfuls

*For the dressing:*
limes – 2
fish sauce – 1 tablespoon

Set the oven at 200°C/Gas 6.

Put the chicken drumsticks into a small roasting tin, pour over the oil, season with salt and pepper and add the butter. Roast for thirty minutes or so, till the drumsticks are golden and the skin is lightly crisp. Remove the flesh from the bones, leaving it in large, juicy but manageable pieces.

Squeeze the lime juice into the roasting tin and place over a medium heat. Add the fish sauce and warm gently, scraping at any sticky bits on the pan and stirring them into the dressing. Check for seasoning – it may need a little ground black pepper. Slice the cucumber with a vegetable peeler, to give long, wide shavings. I do this by shaving on all four sides, then discarding the central core of seeds.

Return the chicken pieces to the pan and toss gently in the dressing. Tear the mint leaves into large pieces, then toss them with the cucumber and the watercress. Assemble the salad by putting the watercress, cucumber and radish sprouts on to plates, then spooning over the warm chicken and its dressing. Finish with a few more radish sprouts and mint if you wish. Serves 2.

# A gutsy toast

## April 25

I need something to quell my avocado-toast habit. That moment when I take an avocado, skin, stone and smash it, stir in a little olive oil, coriander and salt, then slather it on toasted sourdough. Nothing wrong with that, other than the regularity with which it replaces lunch or even dinner.

I need something less soft and green, something with a heart, soul and balls. So today, I toast a thin slice of sourdough over which I pour olive oil, then add 'nduja, the spreadable, spiced Italian sausage available from supermarkets and Italian grocery shops. Put it back under the grill, I then calm its chilli heat down with a thick slice of soft, chalky white goat's curd.

## 'Nduja bruschetta

a thick slice of sourdough
  or ciabatta
olive oil
'nduja – 85g

soft goat's curd or cheese
  – 50g
thyme – 3 sprigs
black olives – 4–6

Toast the bread lightly on both sides. Trickle enough olive oil over one side of the toast to thoroughly moisten it. Place the slice of 'nduja on the bread, add the goat's curd and thyme leaves, a little trickle of oil, then slide under the grill for a few minutes till the 'nduja is warm. Add the olives, trickle over a little more olive oil, and eat immediately. Per sandwich, serves 1.

# Bread and honey

## April 29

The clear sky tempted me back into the garden to rake and dig, prune and, perhaps, sow. I come inside for tea, scratched and aching, to be restored by tea and toast. My reward is pouring honey over the surface of the hot, crisp bread.

A pot of honey is often my souvenir from a trip to a farm shop or a day in the countryside, but I have been enjoying a batch of urban honeys of late, from hives in unexpected locations, such as back gardens of shops and on the roofs of tower blocks. A world away from the buttercup fields and heather-clad hills of country honey. This week alone I tasted a very floral version from bees in Kensington; a more resinous one from hives in Hyde Park; a light and lemony pot from Devon bees now living six floors up in Chelsea; and a honey from Spitalfields and another from Notting Hill. I like the idea of hives in the hood as much as in a clover-dappled field.

In this kitchen, honey is not just found in a glass pot on the table, and is as likely to end up in a recipe as it is on a piece of bread. Not only is it a golden prize on top of your crumpets or spooned on to your porridge (incidentally the best way yet to get the subtle notes of a fine pot of gold to show its hand), honey is a useful addition when making bread dough too, just as it is to the tighter dough of a batch of crispbread. Its presence gives not only a mild sweetness, but depth too, and a pleasing, mellow quality to the finished bread. I also feel it helps the keeping quality, but that may be my imagination.

For cooking I use a lightly flavoured honey, avoiding the chestnut and strongly scented types that can dominate. (I have a pot of French honey in the cupboard that smells not dissimilar to chest rub.) When you cook with a delicate honey, most of its more interesting qualities are lost, so it is best used on toast, English muffins or crumpets.

A better idea is to trickle a little lightly flavoured honey over a slice of goat's or sheep's cheese. The more strongly flavoured cheeses work best, but a spoon of floral 'bee jam' on a soft, fresh goat's cheese has a certain elusive charm. Reward indeed.

## Rosemary and honey bread for cheese

Moist, sweet and salty, these spongy loaves will keep for two or three days if wrapped in clingfilm. With its sweet fruits and herbal notes, this is a perfect bread for cheese.

| | |
|---|---|
| strong wholemeal flour – 250g | rosemary leaves – |
| strong white plain flour – 250g | 2 tablespoons, chopped, |
| salt – 1 teaspoon | plus a few for the top |
| warm water – 350ml | dried cherries – 50g |
| honey – 1 tablespoon | dried apricots – 50g |
| fresh yeast – 40g | golden sultanas – 50g |

Put the flours into a large mixing bowl, add the salt and mix thoroughly. Pour the warm water into a small bowl, then stir in the honey and yeast. When they have dissolved, add the chopped rosemary.

Tip the yeast and honey mixture into the flours and stir in the cherries, apricots and sultanas. If you are using a food mixer armed with a dough hook (a flat paddle will work just as well), mix for four or five minutes. You should have a dough that is really quite sticky. Cover it with a cloth and leave in a warm, but far from hot, place for about an hour, till risen and lightly spongy.

Flour a large chopping board or work surface, then tip the dough on to it and slice in half. Roll each piece of dough into a ball and place on a lightly floured baking sheet. Scatter the surface of each loaf with a few rosemary leaves and a few pinches of sea salt flakes. Cover with a cloth and leave for about twenty minutes, till the dough has flattened and spread slightly. Set the oven at 230°C/Gas 8.

Bake for 25 minutes, till dark brown, then remove from the oven and transfer to a cooling rack. When cool, slice and serve with goat's cheese and mild honey. Makes 2 small loaves.

# MAY

## Crab and asparagus

### May 4

I like to use every bit of an animal, a vegetable or a fish. The bones for soup, the pan juices for a sauce, the vegetable peelings in a stock. Even pastry trimmings, brushed with butter and scattered with Parmesan or sugar, then baked to nibble with a cup of coffee as soon as they come from the oven.

There is much flavour to be had from a crab shell too, or even those of a bag of prawns or crayfish. To resign them to the bin unused is as wasteful as throwing out the bones of the Sunday roast before you have used them for an impromptu stock or gravy. (A quick stock from cooked bones will never have the body and soul of a carefully made bone broth, but it is a shame not to use what we have.)

As you crack the claws of a crab and pull out the coral-flushed white meat, keep the empty claws and the body shell safe. You can smash them with a heavy weight, cover them with water, tuck in a bay leaf or two and a few parsley stalks and simmer for twenty minutes, till you have a rose-pink stock. Use it as the base for a noodle soup or a sauce.

The shells and heads of a bag of prawns seem thin and light beside that of the lobster and the crab and are more likely to be tossed aside as useless. Yet bring them to the boil with a few aromatics and in twenty minutes or less you will have produced a delicate bouillon, mild and sweet, a good start for a broth of prawn, lemon grass and ginger. You can add greens such as pak choi or spinach and some long thin rice noodles too. (A suggestion: cook the noodles separately to keep the fish broth clear and fresh-tasting, then add them to the broth with shredded Chinese greens, grated ginger and chopped fresh mint leaves.)

The bisque of the classic French kitchen, made with crushed lobster or crab shells, the flesh, and then thickened with stale breadcrumbs, is generally too rich for me, but it has its fans. Traditionally made by pounding the shells, claws and heads to a paste, this is the stuff of hard kitchen labour. But we can still make a sound stock for the home kitchen by smashing up the carapace and simmering it with water, thyme and a few aromatic bits and bobs.

This week I made a surprisingly deeply flavoured crab sauce by leaving the broken shells to infuse with warm cream and a couple of bay leaves. I bolstered the flavour with a few spoons of brown crabmeat and used it to dress a salad of white crab and asparagus. An occasional and rather special early summer treat.

## Asparagus with crab sauce

I like my asparagus to be cooked longer than most, until it bends a little. The flavour is better that way. That said, I cook the spears lightly for this, keeping them quite crisp. Works nicely with the soft, sweet crabmeat.

| | |
|---|---|
| the shell and cracked claws of a crab | ginger – a large thumb |
| | double cream – 250ml |
| lemon grass – a long, plump stalk | asparagus spears – 10 |
| | brown crabmeat – 175g |
| garlic – 2 cloves | white crabmeat – 150g |

Smash the crab shells and claws into manageable pieces and put them into a medium-sized saucepan. Crush the lemon grass with a heavy weight so it splinters, then tuck it amongst the crab shells. Squash the garlic cloves and drop into the crab shells, then peel the ginger, slice into thick coins and add to the pan. Pour in the cream and bring to the boil, then turn off the heat and leave, covered, to infuse for about half an hour.

Warm the grill or griddle pan, lightly oil the asparagus spears, trimming the ends if necessary, and cook till they are lightly coloured and still (just) crisp. Sieve the crab sauce to remove the lemon grass, ginger, garlic and shells, then stir in the brown crabmeat and warm gently.

Divide the hot asparagus between two plates, add the white crabmeat, fresh and unseasoned, then spoon over the sieved crab sauce. Serves 2.

# Sweet and earthy

Generally, the backbone of a dish, the 'flavour base', is set early on in the recipe, long before the final seasonings – the 'top-notes' – are added. This flavour base can be set by cooking onions slowly till they are sweet, or toasting meat with spices such as cumin and coriander, or sweating finely chopped carrots, celery and onion with bay and garlic. We are setting down a foundation on which to build.

Today, I start an aubergine stew by frying chorizo, torn into chunks and left to cook over a moderate heat, so it sizzles mostly in its own paprika-spiced fat. The sweetness from the sugars in the sausage and the deep savour of the fat form the base-layer of flavour on which I might add onions, dried fruit and stock. (Pancetta or bacon is another good way to produce that backbone, fried in a film of olive oil, as is garlic, ginger and spring onion.)

The reason for choosing chorizo is the sausage's intense smoky flavour, something to balance the sweetness of the prunes and apricots with which I want to bulk up my aubergine stew. A deep earthy base that will take the sugary notes of the dried fruits.

## Prune, apricot and chorizo stew

| | |
|---|---|
| olive oil – 3 tablespoons | a medium aubergine |
| cooking chorizo – 250g | cumin seeds – 1 teaspoon |
| a large red onion | coriander seeds – 1 teaspoon |
| soft dried apricots – 75g | chicken stock – 300ml |
| soft dried prunes – 75g | coriander leaves – a handful |
| skinned whole almonds – 50g | |

Warm the olive oil in a deep saucepan, then break the chorizo into large pieces and add to the oil. Let the chorizo cook over a moderate heat for two or three minutes. Peel and roughly chop the onion, add to the pan and continue cooking till it starts to soften. Stir in the apricots and prunes and the skinned whole almonds.

Set the oven at 180°C/Gas 4. Halve the aubergine lengthways, cut into thick slices and then into small cubes, add to the pan and continue cooking until soft and tender. Grind the cumin and coriander seeds to a fine powder in a pestle and mortar and stir into the onion and sausage mixture.

Stir in the chicken stock, season with salt and pepper, bring to the boil, then cover with a lid, transfer to the oven and bake for about 45 minutes. Stir in the coriander leaves and serve. For 3–4.

# A bit of a pickle

One of those pure, early summer days, when the light is pale and clear, and pours in through every window in the house. The freshness is heightened by the acid greens of the young hornbeam and robinia leaves, the young, effervescent greens of a garden full of rising sap. Eating-wise, it is a day for mild flavours, a light lunch outdoors.

I like the modern approach to pickling, where fish or vegetables have their flavours brightened by a short rest in a mild vinegar or lemon juice mix, more like a ceviche than a pickle or a souse. When used for fish, there are subtle textural changes; the outside firms up a little, but the centre stays rare and soft.

The fishmonger has some salmon, and I buy a couple of tails, which he lets me have a bit cheaper. Doing so much work, they tend to be a little firmer in texture, which appeals to me. You could use a piece of salmon fillet if that is what you have.

# Pickled salmon and cucumber salad

The time you marinate your fish for will depend on how you like it. I like mine to be soft and raw in the middle, so four hours is usually enough. Leaving it overnight will produce a firmer texture. There is no need for salt in this, by the way.

| | |
|---|---|
| a large cucumber (400g) | granulated sugar – 100g |
| salmon – 600g, made up | mustard seeds – 1 tablespoon |
| of 2 tails | coriander seeds – 1 tablespoon |
| | white peppercorns – |
| *For the marinade:* | 1 teaspoon |
| white wine vinegar – 500ml | cloves – 3 |
| 1 small red onion, finely sliced | a whole star anise |

Lightly peel the cucumber, halve it lengthways, then scrape the core of seeds out with a teaspoon. Cut the cucumber flesh into thin pieces, no thicker than half a centimetre. Cut the salmon into four pieces.

Pour the vinegar into a wide saucepan, then add the onion, sugar, mustard seeds, coriander seeds, white peppercorns, cloves and star anise. Bring the vinegar to the boil, stir to dissolve the sugar, then let it cool down. You can speed this up by pouring the hot vinegar and spices into a bowl standing in a sink of cold water.

When the marinade is cool, slide in the salmon pieces, add the cucumber, cover with clingfilm and refrigerate for a minimum of four hours.

Serve in whole pieces with some of the marinade, or gently break the fish up and pile it loosely in the centre of the plate. Serves 4.

# A bejewelled ice

## May 8

I have long suspected that I enjoy shelling pistachios, prising their teasing, salty shells apart and extracting the tiny purple and green kernels within, far more than I do eating them. The almond has a better flavour, the brazil is more meaty, the hazelnut is sweeter and the cashew altogether more salty and plump. (The shelling of cashews, by the way, is an extraordinary task to watch – the danger and hard work involved makes you appreciate them even more.)

It was whilst making Christmas mendiants, the thin slabs of chocolate studded with nuts and pieces of crystallised fruits (see page 465), that I discovered the marriage of pistachio and white chocolate. The sight of white chocolate the colour of clotted cream, pebbled with pale green and mauve nuts, has a quiet charm and the flavours a serenity and calm.

From crisp slabs of chocolate to soft, nut-studded ice cream is a small but worthwhile jump.

## White chocolate and pistachio ice cream

full-fat milk – 500ml
double cream – 500ml
vanilla extract – a few drops
egg yolks – 4

caster sugar – 4 tablespoons
white chocolate – 200g
shelled pistachios – 100g,
chopped

Pour the milk and cream into a non-stick saucepan, add a few drops of vanilla extract and bring to the boil. Turn off the heat. Put the egg yolks and sugar into a bowl and whisk till thick and creamy, then pour the hot vanilla cream over the egg yolks and sugar, stirring with a wooden spoon.

Rinse the pan, then pour in the custard mixture and place over a moderate heat. Stir almost constantly, without allowing the custard to come to the boil. When the mixture will coat the back of your wooden spoon, remove from the heat. If it shows any sign of curdling, plunge the saucepan into cold water and whisk furiously till all the steam has gone and the graininess has disappeared.

In a pan over hot water, melt the white chocolate, then pour the custard into the chocolate and stir.

Leave the custard to chill, then pour into an ice cream machine and churn till almost set. Add the chopped pistachios just as the ice cream is approaching readiness, then scoop the mixture into a cold freezer box and leave to freeze. Serves 6.

# Goat's cheese and thyme

## May 11

Most of Britain's goat's cheeses have names that evoke Domesday Book villages and stone-walled, oak-beamed farmhouses: Innes and Ticklemore; Dorstone and St Tola; Chidwickbury, Wellesley and Ragstone. Peaceful names, calm and timid, like the white-walled creameries in which we assume they are made. The names are mostly modern inventions, but not whimsical, named with good reason after a local hill, ridge or patron saint. Mary Holbrook's Cardo, for instance, is named after the cardoon stamens she uses in place of rennet.

It is rare I don't have a goat's or sheep's cheese in the house. Their floral, lemony, lactic flavours often appeal to me more than the cow's milk cheeses. Invariably, these cheeses end up on a plate with a fig or a piece of toasted sourdough. Some are eaten straight from the cheesemonger's waxed paper, but rarely, perhaps too rarely, do they end their days being cooked with. But I have cooked with them twice this week, first whipped up into a herb cream to accompany some grilled lamb cutlets (there's a recipe in *Eat*), and then today, in some little tartlets of thyme and cream.

Thyme, medicinal, resinous, redolent of rock-strewn Greek or French hillsides, is the first herb I think of as a seasoning for goat's cheese. The romantic in me likes to imagine white-bearded nanny goats scrabbling up rocky mountain passes, nibbling at wild thyme and oregano as they go. The truth is that the marriage is as old as the hills. My local cheese shop sells a Corsican Fleur de Maquis, a firmish goat's cheese rolled in a crust of dried herbs that includes thyme. It smells like a parched mountainside and tastes aromatic, sweet and faintly of cedar. I sometimes make shallow, square pastries filled with goat's cheese cut from a log and thyme, or mash cheese, cream and the herb together to make a filling for baked potatoes.

The low fat content of many goat's cheeses means they are good for adding to a tart or a quiche. The flavours are clean and fresh, unlike the fattier cheeses that add luxury but also a certain blandness. Using a cheese like this, especially one with a bit of lactic bite, is a way of keeping the weight of cheese down and the flavour up. More piquant than most of the cow's milk cheeses, a little goes a long way.

Today I make a dozen wee tarts (you need two per person) with just 150g of cheese. Sounds on the wrong side of frugal, but it is enough.

The goat's cheese tarts are not served on the plate alone. They come with a salad. I can never resist those first white-tipped bunches of summer radishes. I usually buy two at a time in the hope they will keep me from reaching for the biscuit jar, but a loud crunch is about the only thing they have in common and the salad bowl is probably a better place. An early summer salad of crisp, cold cucumber, lightly peeled so its green colour shines through, then tossed with pea shoots, the salad leaf du jour, with watercress for spice and a simple dressing of fairly bland olive oil and salt. (In my house, a radish never goes unsalted.)

## Goat's cheese and lemon thyme tartlets

goat's cheese – 150g
an egg yolk
double cream – 225ml
lemon thyme – a few sprigs

*For the pastry:*
plain flour – 200g
butter – 100g
an egg yolk
a little milk or water

You will need a twelve-hole tartlet tin.

Put the flour and butter, cut into small pieces, into the bowl of a food processor. Add a pinch of salt and blitz to fine breadcrumbs. If you prefer, rub the butter into the flour with your fingertips. Add the egg yolk and enough milk or water to bring the dough to a firm ball. The less liquid you add the better, as too much will cause your pastry cases to shrink in the oven.

Pat the pastry into a flat round on a floured surface, then roll out fairly thinly. Cut twelve discs from the pastry using a large pastry cutter or saucer as a template, then push the pastry into the tartlet tins. Chill thoroughly for at least thirty minutes.

Bake the tartlet cases at 200°C/Gas 6 for about fifteen minutes, till they are pale biscuit-coloured. Remove from the oven and turn the heat down to 180°C/Gas 4.

Crumble the goat's cheese into small pieces and drop into the pastry cases, leaving room for a little of the custard. Mix the egg yolk and cream in a measuring jug and season with salt and black pepper. Tear the thyme leaves from the stems and add to the custard mixture.

Pour the mixture into the tartlet cases, then bake for about twenty minutes, till the filling is lightly set, and serve with a frisée salad. Makes 12.

# Salt and the radish

## May 15

Bright red is probably my least favourite colour. Brash, loud, hot. A colour that screams. Of course some reds are good, even sought after. The black red of a dinner-plate Monarch dahlia; the deep maroon of a fat-marbled rib-eye or the burnished rust of a Japanese lacquered soup bowl, perhaps. Red tartan can be a joy, as can a Negroni. But as a rule, the screaming red of London buses and tomatoes is not the hue for me. Curiously, I have a piercing orange umbrella. It raises a smile on a grey, rainy day.

This may explain why I never buy the 'clown's nose' round red radishes yet happily pounce on a bunch of the long, elegant white-tipped French Breakfast variety. Vermilion and white, their tuft of green leaves still perky, looking like they were picked yesterday. I simply cannot resist. Those that aren't eaten on the way home are dunked into a bowl of ice cubes and water and left to crisp further still. They are usually brought to the table with very cold, unsalted butter and a tiny saucer of sea salt. After three or four I give up on the butter and just dunk the wet radishes in the salt flakes, just as I did with rhubarb and sugar when I was six.

A radish sandwich, made with thick-cut, soft-crumbed, flour-dusted bread, sweet butter from a new packet and a few sprigs of watercress, is as good as any sandwich can be. One for a shady corner of the garden. I like them in a salad of course, especially with soft-fleshed, buttery lettuce to balance their heat and crunch. And yet I rarely use them in any other way, forgetting how useful they are as bringers of mild, sweet heat to summer soups (particularly one of yoghurt, chopped cucumber, spring onion, capers and dill) and chopped up in grain salads such as tabbouleh and couscous.

I see no reason not to cook a radish, just as we cook with mouli and turnips, its larger cousins. Its texture softens like any other vegetable, its heat mellows a little, and it loses its cheery colour, but it is pleasant enough with white fish or salmon. Radishes are rather cool when sautéd too. I toss them in a pan with butter and dill, continuously basting them with the herb butter as they cook. Be gentle, they don't need to brown; by that time the life will have gone from them. You need to leave a bit of bite in them, so no more than seven or eight minutes in the pan. And, of course, salt. Radishes love salt.

## Baked sea bass with tarragon and radishes

It need not be sea bass. This method will work with most fish. The cut should be quite thin – fillets are probably most suitable – and the cooking time needs to be short and sweet, so the radish is crisp.

| | |
|---|---|
| a medium-sized sea bass | radishes – 6 |
| butter – 75g, melted | a small red onion, very |
| tarragon – 5g | thinly sliced |

Set the oven at 180°C/Gas 4. Ask the fishmonger to clean and fillet the fish for you, but leave the skin on. Melt the butter in a small pan, then tip it into the bowl of a food processor. Remove the leaves from the tarragon stems and drop them into the butter with a light seasoning of salt and black pepper, then process to a smooth, green dressing.

Cut two pieces of baking parchment large enough to loosely wrap the fillets of fish, one per parcel. Place a fillet on each and fold into a parcel, open at the top.

Slice the radishes in half lengthways, then place them inside the parcels on top of the fish. Peel the onion and slice it very finely, then add to the fish. Divide the tarragon butter dressing between the two parcels, then seal the edges by folding and securing with a skewer.

Bake the paper parcels for about twenty to twenty-five minutes. Each parcel should be opened at the table, allowing the tarragon-scented steam to waft up. Serves 2.

# Snap, crackle and heat

## May 16

## A salad of spiced chickpeas and puffed rice

A particularly aromatic and crunchy salad.

| | |
|---|---|
| seeds of a small pomegranate | whole, skinned almonds |
| a large cucumber (400g) | – 50g |
| coriander seeds – 1 teaspoon | chickpeas – a 400g tin |
| cumin seeds – 1 teaspoon | hemp seeds – 30g |
| groundnut oil – 2 tablespoons | sunflower seeds – 30g |
| garam masala – 1 teaspoon | puffed rice, unsweetened |
| curry powder – 1 teaspoon | – 30g |
| | olive oil |

Peel the cucumber, lightly, then cut in half lengthways. Scrape the seeds out, then cut the flesh into small dice. Toss the cucumber and pomegranate together.

Put the coriander and cumin seeds into a shallow pan and warm them over a gentle heat. Let them cook, moving them around the pan, until they are crisp and fragrant. Remove the pan from the heat and tip the toasted seeds into a mortar. Crush them to a fine powder.

Warm the oil in the shallow pan, then, keeping the heat low, add the ground cumin and coriander, the garam masala and the curry powder, then the skinned almonds. Warm the nuts and spices, moving everything round the pan so it doesn't burn. Drain the chickpeas and stir them into the spices and almonds, together with the hemp seeds, sunflower seeds and puffed rice.

Tip the warm chickpea mixture into the pomegranate and cucumber, add a trickle of olive oil, then toss gently together and serve. For 4.

# Radish and cucumber

## May 17

## A radish gazpacho

For a more substantial, light lunch, I like to make open-textured toast, from a ciabatta-style loaf, and place it in the bottom of the dishes before ladling over the soup. If it appears a bit thick, you can let it down with a dash of vegetable stock or more cucumber juice.

a large red pepper
garlic cloves – 3 large
olive oil – a little
a cucumber, medium-sized
radishes – 100g

sherry vinegar – 2 tablespoons

*To finish:*
radishes – 3

Set the oven at 200°C/Gas 6. Put the three radishes to finish in a bowl of iced water and set aside for them to crisp up.

Slice the red pepper in half and remove and discard any seeds or tough cores. Peel the garlic. Place the halves of pepper in a roasting tin, tuck in the garlic cloves, trickle with oil and bake for thirty to forty minutes, till the skin of the pepper is dark brown in colour. Peel off the skin, saving any juices from the roasting tin, then put the skinned pepper flesh and the garlic into the bowl of a food processor.

Peel the cucumber, cut into large chunks and add to the pepper. Clean the radishes and add them to the pepper with the sherry vinegar, then process the ingredients for several seconds, until you have a rough, thick soup. I would avoid the temptation to process to a smooth purée. Taste, adding more salt or vinegar as you wish.

Slice the chilled radishes in half lengthways. Ladle the soup into bowls, add the halved radishes and serve. For 3.

# Pork and the gooseberry

## May 23

A walk round the garden this morning under a piercing blue sky. I stop under the golden robinia, its canopy as acid bright as lime cordial, vivid azure peeping through the wisteria-like leaves. Outside in the street, instead of the slow, head-down trudge to the bus, people are laughing even before 8 a.m. It is as if the air is full of happy gas. There are gooseberries at the greengrocer's today, which would probably take the smile off a few faces.

My love of the gooseberry – as a barely set jam, in an undulating, soft-crusted pie or as a vital, smartingly sharp breakfast compote – is no secret and I have previously given a recipe (in *Tender II*) for a cordial-soaked gooseberry cake. But their possibilities with savoury recipes need considering too if we aren't to lose this less than popular fruit. (They get more difficult to find with each passing year.) I use the fruit regularly with grilled, crisp-skinned mackerel and as a seasonal alternative to apple sauce with roast pork, but I want to experiment with this a little more.

A relish – pink onions, purple-black juniper berries and tart green gooseberries, simmered till the onions are soft and the hairy berries have burst – comes up trumps today. Its acidity slices through the sweet meat. Each mouthful is a nice little balancing act between sharp and sour. Hit.

# Pork chops, gooseberry, mint and juniper relish

red onions – 2
olive oil – 3 tablespoons
juniper berries – 8
gooseberries – 500g

honey – 2 tablespoons
mint leaves – 10 medium-
  sized
pork chops – 4

Peel and roughly chop the red onions, then put them into a deep pan with the olive oil and leave to cook slowly, without any browning, till soft and tender.

Coarsely crush the juniper berries, using a pestle and mortar. Wash the gooseberries, top and tail them, and tip them into a saucepan with the crushed juniper berries, honey and a couple of tablespoons of water. Put the pan over a medium heat and bring to the boil, then lower the heat and let the fruit stew for ten to twelve minutes, till the berries start to burst. It would be good to catch them before they start to collapse into jam.

Shred the mint leaves and stir them into the gooseberries, then turn off the heat. Leave the fruit to settle and cool for ten minutes or more before serving. If you plan to serve the relish cold, chill thoroughly before serving. If you are serving it warm, keep it in a warm place, covered, till the chops are ready.

Using a very sharp knife, score the chops through the fat to the flesh. This will help the fat crisp nicely on the grill. Rub the chops lightly with olive oil, then season with salt and black pepper. Set the chops over the barbecue or on a preheated griddle pan and cook, depending on their thickness, for five to six minutes, then turn and cook the other side for a further five. The fat should be golden and lightly crisp, the pork slightly pink and very juicy within.

Serve the relish, warm or chilled, alongside the chops. For 4.

# Podding peas, shelling beans

## May 27

I must tell you about the chicken minestrone. This meal in a bowl, a 'soup-stew', came about because of the need for a thick, warming dinner for a cool May evening, but one with a fresher, brighter feel to it than the usual bean soups. Bean soup being, by its history and nature, a thing of deepest winter.

By this time of year I have had my fill of the faux Tuscan peasant bean broths. Sustaining and cheap though they are, with their bags of soaked borlotti and cannellini, their ham hocks and carrots and garlicky croutes, they can, once the weather lightens and spring sun shines, start to feel out of place.

Enter the new season's beans, the early peas and first broad beans. Fresh green replacements for the dried brown and cream pulses of winter. Swap chicken for the ham, broad beans for dried fava and garden peas for cannellini and you have an old friend in a new coat. A plate of food warming enough for a cool May day, yet one that feels light and more in tune with the calendar. Add to that the child-like joy of shelling peas and beans, collecting the green pulses in a colander, and crunching on the occasional pea pod, and you have a celebration. Albeit a small, rather personal one.

This dish, incidentally, is a great one for large parties. You can double or quadruple it without it coming to grief. But unlike the cold weather versions, it is not a soup for keeping overnight. Eat it the day it is made and revel in the freshness of spring.

# A green chicken minestrone

chicken thighs – 4
oil
small leeks – 2
chicken stock – 1 litre
broad beans – 450g
  (in pod weight)

linguine – 50g
peas – 200g (podded
  weight)
parsley – a handful

Season the chicken thighs, then brown them on both sides in a little oil in a casserole or heavy, deep-sided pan. Roughly chop and thoroughly wash the leeks. Lift out the browned thighs and set aside, then tip the chopped leeks into the pan and let them soften over a low heat, stirring regularly so they do not brown. Return the chicken thighs to the pan, pour over the chicken stock, and leave to simmer for about twenty minutes.

Remove the broad beans from their pods. Break the linguine into short lengths (about 2cm) and add to the pan, turning the heat up so the liquid boils, then cook for eight or nine minutes, till the pasta is cooked. Three or four minutes before the pasta is ready, add the podded beans and the peas to the soup. Finish with a good handful of freshly chopped parsley, check the seasoning and serve. For 2.

# Green spears. Glossy mash.

A pile of mash, so loose and silky it is on the verge of becoming a purée. The season's asparagus, grilled and glistening with olive oil. The bright notes of lemon zest. A treat today, but something I could happily eat all summer long. By the way, I use Maris Pipers for this very soft mash, but a waxy-fleshed potato such as Charlotte would be good too; unorthodox, but capable of giving an even smoother, more velvety mash.

## Griddled asparagus, lemon mash

| | |
|---|---|
| asparagus – 250g | one and a half lemons |
| olive oil | full-fat milk – 300ml |
| | olive oil – 5 tablespoons |
| *For the mash:* | |
| potatoes – 850g | |

Peel the potatoes, cut them into large pieces, then bring to the boil in a pan of lightly salted water. Turn the heat down to an enthusiastic simmer and leave to cook for about twenty minutes, till they are tender to the point of a knife. Finely grate the zest of the whole lemon and put to one side.

Warm the milk in a small saucepan and set aside. Squeeze the lemons. Drain the potatoes thoroughly, then put them into the bowl of a food mixer fitted with a flat paddle beater attachment.

Beat the potatoes at slow speed, slowly introducing the warm milk and lemon juice as you go, beating until you have quite a loose mash. Now beat in the olive oil. The mash should be very soft and creamy, with no lumps.

Brush the asparagus with olive oil, then cook for three or four minutes on a heated griddle, turning the spears occasionally so they colour evenly.

Divide the mash between two plates, and place the asparagus alongside. Generously trickle olive oil over both the asparagus and the mash, then finish with the lemon zest. Serves 2.

# Thin, tender biscuits for a summer's day

## May 29

A slim biscuit that is crumbly on the outside and lightly chewy within is a thoroughly good thing. These biscuits, very simple to make, are the result of two mixtures, one baked inside the other. It is essential not to over-bake them, and if possible they should be served slightly warm. They are fragile, with a soft scent of almond and rose. They would be heavenly with a bowl of vanilla ice cream or pannacotta.

## Rose and almond shortbread

*For the almond filling:*
ground almonds – 100g
icing sugar – 50g
caster sugar – 50g
an egg

*For the shortbread:*
butter – 200g
icing sugar – 90g

vanilla extract – a few drops
ground almonds – 140g
plain flour – 140g
the zest of a lemon

*To decorate:*
large crystallised rose
  petals – 3
caster sugar – 2 tablespoons

For the almond filling: put the ground almonds in a mixing bowl and add the icing and caster sugars. Beat the egg lightly with a fork to mix the white and yolk, then stir or beat into the almonds and sugar. When the mixture is soft and thick, set aside and make the shortbread.

Put the butter, cut into small pieces, into the bowl of a food mixer. Add the icing sugar, then cream with a flat beater attachment to a soft, pale fluff. Mix in a few drops of vanilla extract, then add the

ground almonds and plain flour. Grate the lemon zest finely into the mixture and gently stir in.

Set the oven at 160°C/Gas 3 and line a baking sheet with baking parchment. Break the almond filling into sixteen pieces and roll them into balls. Divide the shortbread mixture into sixteen, flatten a piece in the palm of your hand, then place a ball of almond paste in the centre. Pull the shortbread around the almond paste and squeeze to seal. Roll into a ball. Repeat with the remaining mixture.

Place the balls, generously spaced to allow them to spread, on the lined baking sheet. Press the top of each ball down with a fork and bake for twenty to twenty-five minutes, till the biscuits are pale and still soft. Remove to a cooling rack with a palette knife. Leave for ten to fifteen minutes to set.

Put the rose petals and sugar into a food processor and blitz to a coarse powder. Scatter over the warm biscuits. The biscuits are best eaten soft and warm, and on the day of baking. Makes 16.

# JUNE

## Asparagus and blue cheese

### June 2

Asparagus needs fat. Shining butter sauces; runny saffron-hued egg yolks; crisp bacon with stripes of glossy fat; cheeses that melt languidly over the stalks; even the quaint accompaniment of buttered bread will make the spears of asparagus on our plates more interesting to eat.

There's more. Crisp grains of toasted, grated Parmesan; the liquid ooze of a melting Tunworth or Brie; a white-collared slice of Parma, serrano or speck; the rustle of a dusting of freshly toasted white breadcrumbs translucent with butter or bacon fat. They all work.

Tonight, I get two plates of asparagus, with a scattering of shattered crisp bacon and a spoonful or two of hollandaise sauce, on the table for barely a fiver. I introduce sustenance with a toasted English muffin, lending a sort of 'eggs Benedict' feel to the whole affair. It goes down well, despite the butter sauce being left for fifteen minutes before serving. (A bloody good whisking every few minutes soon put a stop to the sauce's threatened curdling.)

It is the butter, pork and bacon fat that makes the asparagus so good to eat, but the flavour depends much on the cooking time. I can't go along with the idea that the spears should always be cooked al dente. Crisp, bright green asparagus just tastes exactly that, crisp and green. The real flavour of this particular vegetable is evident only when it is cooked longer than has become usual. That is why canned asparagus tastes so much of itself. If only it weren't so flaccid. I retrieve the spears from the water or steam once they have passed the vibrant green stage, when they have started to soften a little in colour. Frog rather than pea green. Timing depends on the thickness of the stalks, but it is generally a good five or six minutes at a rolling boil. If the spears will stand erect they are not quite ready. Wait a minute or two longer and they'll taste more richly of what they are supposed to.

The best asparagus dish I have encountered recently was at a food stall in Fukuoka, in Kyushu, Japan, where the spears came wrapped in very thin belly pork and grilled. (I thought it was streaky bacon until I tucked in.) The meat was sliced barely thicker than a sheet of paper and coiled around the meat like a ribbon round a maypole. It then sat on the grill, the fat from the pork basting the spears as they cooked and sending clouds of smoke heavenwards. I ate six at one sitting which, if you have seen the size of the asparagus in Japan, you will know was a little excessive.

If you can't make a pot of egg and butter sauce, then a spoon or two of crème fraîche will do. I let it melt in a small pan, then stir in a little tarragon vinegar and a palmful of the chopped herb. Another possibility is to thin mayonnaise with a little milk or olive oil, or to dress the spears with (so friends tell me) a poached egg, placed on top of the spears, then broken, a few drops of very good red wine vinegar trickled over the running yolk.

After years of letting Camembert or the gentle British equivalent Tunworth melt over piles of plated asparagus, it is today that I realise how well blue cheese works too.

## Asparagus and Roquefort tart

You can use Roquefort of course, but some of the British blues such as Stichelton, Stilton and Beenleigh or Crozier from Ireland will work nicely too. Use whatever looks good. Because of the deep flavour, you need very little.

*For the pastry:*
butter, fridge cold – 90g
plain flour – 150g
an egg yolk
very coarsely ground black
  pepper – 1 teaspoon

*For the filling:*
asparagus spears – 12
eggs – 2
double cream – 300ml
Roquefort or other blue
  cheese – 200g

You will need a 22cm tart tin with a removable base.

Make the pastry: cut the butter into small dice and rub into the flour with your fingertips, or reduce to fine crumbs in a food processor. Add the egg yolk, the pepper and a tablespoon or two of water and bring the mixture to a firm, even-textured dough. Wrap in clingfilm and refrigerate for twenty minutes. Set the oven at 200°C/Gas 6.

Bring a pot of water to the boil. Cut the asparagus into short lengths and cook in the furiously boiling water for five minutes or so, till almost tender, then remove with a draining spoon (they will get a further cooking in the oven). Make the custard by beating the eggs very lightly into the cream, then seasoning with black pepper, and, depending on how salty your blue cheese is, a little salt.

Place the tart tin on a baking sheet and line it with the pastry, making certain you have pushed it deep into the edges and that there are absolutely no tears or cracks. Line with greaseproof paper and baking beans and bake for fifteen to twenty minutes, then carefully remove the beans and return the pastry case to the oven for a further five minutes, or until the pastry feels dry to the touch.

Turn the oven down to 180°C/Gas 4. Place the asparagus spears in the pastry case and crumble the blue cheese over the top. Pour in the custard, then carefully transfer to the oven and bake for about forty minutes. Leave to cool, then transfer to a board or plate and serve. For 8.

# Serves you right

## June 8

Pigeons are not regular visitors to this garden. Magpies, nesting blackbirds, robins and jenny wrens, yes, but pigeons tend to flock further down the terrace, where they are fed by a neighbour. Occasionally they perch, fat as ducks, on the branches of my fig tree.

For a long time I confused these urban birds with the wood pigeons on sale at the butcher's. The feral city pigeon, scavenger, mess-maker, allotment thief, is probably what puts people off buying the pink-breasted wood pigeon, or culver as it is known in the south-west. Away from a diet of pizza, and other city detritus, the country cousin lives on young shoots, crops and garden scrumpings.

Shoot a city pigeon and you risk a large fine. Take your 12-bore to the countryside and you will make a farmer happy. In the kitchen, their downfall is their lean flesh. There is almost no fat to baste the meat naturally as it cooks. I get round this by soaking the birds in olive oil and aromatics (bay, juniper berries, peppercorns and thyme) or by swaddling them in pork fat or streaky bacon to prevent them drying as they roast.

The pigeon's lack of fat is the reason they are often cooked long and slow with red wine or cider, where the liquid keeps their meat soft as they cook. Even then, they will never fall apart the way a long-cooked chicken will. When I cook pigeons I apply the same rule I do for squid, cooking them either fast and furious or long and slow, never in between.

I am no butcher. Nevertheless, this evening I spatchcock a couple of pigeons for the grill. The birds, chubby and with no dark red bruises or split skin, come from the butcher ready for the oven. I run my fingers over the skin, tugging out a couple of stubborn feathers and a lump of dark, bloody gore the pluckers have left behind (evidently plucking isn't what it used to be), then put the birds on a chopping board, plump side down.

Using the kitchen scissors, I cut each of the carcasses on the upper, flat side, right through the backbone, then open them out like a couple of miniature books. The job takes about two minutes. I was taught to keep spatchcock birds flat during cooking by impaling them on crossed skewers like a heraldic shield, but I have honestly never found this necessary and instead I place them plump side up on a baking sheet. A trickle of olive oil to moisten the skin, then I grind together some black peppercorns, flakes of sea salt and a palmful of juniper berries and scatter the black and white freckled seasoning over the skin.

The barbecue aside, I find the oven grill is the best way to cook birds such as these, placing the tray a good 20cm from the heat. Fifteen minutes or so later they emerge toasted, crisp-skinned, rare-fleshed and smelling of salt, smoke and juniper.

You can faff around with a knife and fork for a while, splicing off the juicy little breasts and winkling the meat from the frail legs, but the most satisfying way to eat them is to tear the meat from the bones like a caveman, gnawing and tugging and chewing the salt-crusted skin and meat. Today, I make a purée of green peas, slushy, like a professional chef's olive oil potato mash, in which to dip the meat and bones as we go.

## Pigeon and peas

pigeons, oven-ready – 2
juniper berries – 12
olive oil – 4 tablespoons
peas, frozen or podded
  weight – 300g

butter – 40g
tarragon leaves –
  4 tablespoons

Place the pigeons on a chopping board plump breast side down. Using kitchen scissors or a heavy cook's knife, split the birds down

the backbone (there will be a loud crack), then open them out flat. Put them into a roasting tin or a grill pan.

Lightly crush the juniper berries with a heavy weight – I use a pestle – to release their fragrance, then add them to the olive oil together with a generous pinch of sea salt and a grinding of black pepper. Trickle the oil over the birds and leave them for an hour or so, turning them once or twice. I find this softens and lubricates the flesh, making for a juicier eat.

Heat a barbecue or oven grill. The time they will need depends very much on the heat of your grill and how rare you like your meat. You will see their skin darken and crisp, but reckon on about fifteen to twenty minutes, a good 20cm from the elements of the oven grill. Turn them occasionally during cooking.

Cook the peas in deep boiling water till tender (about five minutes for frozen, eight for freshly podded), then drain in a colander and tip them into the bowl of a food processor. Melt the butter in a small pan. Add the tarragon leaves to the peas, followed by the melted butter, and process to a soft creamy purée.

Divide the tarragon pea mash between two plates and add a pigeon to each one. Serves 2.

# A salmon tale

## June 10

I tend to reject extravagance. But that doesn't mean I don't push the boat out occasionally. The wild salmon season has been going for long enough now. The price has come down far enough to entertain the idea of its firm, pink flesh served with sliced cucumber, a pile of thin-skinned new potatoes and a bowl of homemade mayonnaise. Gentle and timeless flavours for the still, warm days of June.

The fishmonger had a wild salmon tail today, a cut that does a lot of work in an active swimming fish, and tends to be slightly cheaper than the front end. At Christmas I often marinate a side of fish with beetroot and slice it thinly. A jewel-coloured gravlax (*Kitchen Diaries II*). I wonder if the flavours might also work with a fish served hot, and I set about marinating the tail in the pulp and juice of some young beetroots. I add fresh ginger root, lemony and bright-tasting, set the fish aside for a few hours, then bake it wrapped in foil.

Pretty as a picture, sweetly earthy and yet soft enough for the flavour of the fish to shine, it is a success. We eat it with new potatoes, their gossamer-thin skins intact, shining not with butter, but with the pink juices from the fish. There's lettuce too, a young crinkly-leaved Webb's Wonder, for those who want it.

# Baked salmon, beetroot and ginger

fresh ginger – 50g

groundnut oil – 8 tablespoons

a large raw beetroot

salmon tail – 500g

Peel the ginger and the raw beetroot, cut each into large pieces, then put them into the bowl of a food processor. Process the ginger and beetroot until finely crushed, pouring in the groundnut oil as you go.

Pour the beetroot mixture into a sealable plastic bag, then slide in the salmon tail fillet and close the bag so that none of the marinade can escape. Place in the fridge and leave for a minimum of four hours.

Set the oven at 180°C/Gas 4. Place the fish in a roasting tin with a little of its marinade. The rest has done its job and can be discarded. Season the fish with salt and black pepper, cover loosely with kitchen foil and place in the preheated oven for twelve minutes.

Take off the foil and continue roasting the fish for a further eight minutes, then remove from the oven, place the foil over the top to keep the fish warm, and leave to rest for five minutes. Serves 2.

# Sirloin and sweet garlic

## June 12

I leave for the market in Bermondsey. A Saturday ritual that fills the fridge and revives the spirits. I dislike the ubiquitous and wasteful supermarket plastic bag for the way everything arrives home squashed and sweating. I rely on two old faithfuls, a charcoal horsehair bag made for me by Marianna Kennedy in Spitalfields and a soft, indigo canvas bag I bought in Japan. Initially expensive purchases, they have, like many quietly well-made objects, paid for themselves a hundred-fold with their resilience and sustainability. The first is deep, square-sided and capacious and appreciated for its firm, flat base that prevents fragile purchases such as punnets of fruit from tipping over. Practical for plants too. The latter is so soft I can fold it up and stuff it into my satchel or I can swing it over my shoulder like a backpack. They will probably be with me till the day I die.

This morning, there is a faint whiff of garlic in the vegetable stall, soft and subtle, like the ghost of a French farmer. This first garlic of the season, plump, waxy, its pliable skin flushed with mauve, has a gentle quality that I prefer to the dried, flaky-skinned bulbs that keep us going through the winter. These young bulbs are juicy and mild, though their scent will permeate the fridge, ruining the milk and leaving their fingerprint on anything unsealed. They will kill a melon at twenty paces.

A head of spring garlic feels alive and full of juice, its character softer and less rasping. When we are told to rub a cut clove of garlic around a salad bowl, this is the stuff the writer means, not one with the heat and bitterness of the dry winter bulbs. At home, I unpack the shopping: a bunch of radishes, a lettuce the size of my head, a couple of small cucumbers, a pair of avocados, unwaxed lemons that smell like a winter's day in Amalfi and a bunch of flowers for the kitchen table. There are also six heads of spring garlic. (And no melon.)

Two of the heads of garlic I roast. Another I use to scent a steak for Saturday dinner.

## Sirloin steak with aubergines

Aubergines have the ability to soak up olive oil and butter, changing the texture of their flesh from spongy and bland to soft and silky. Tonight I cook steaks and aubergines, the pan juices scented with new, mild garlic.

| | |
|---|---|
| butter – 60g and a little extra | sirloin steaks – 2 large, about |
| olive oil – a little | 250–300g each |
| a whole head of new garlic | an aubergine |
| rosemary – 3 sprigs | half a lemon |

Melt the butter in a shallow non-stick (or well-used cast-iron) pan. Add a little oil to stop the butter from burning. Slice the whole head of garlic in half across the middle and place it cut side down in the butter, together with the whole sprigs of rosemary. Let the garlic cook, gently, for about 10 minutes, adjusting the heat so it colours only lightly. When the garlic is soft and pale gold in colour, season the sirloins and add them to the butter, removing the garlic if necessary to stop it over-browning. Cook the steaks on both sides, then remove and leave to rest for six to eight minutes, covered lightly with foil.

Add the aubergine, diced into very small cubes, to the pan and let it cook, constantly spooning over the butter and steak juices, adding a little more oil if the aubergines are particularly thirsty. Let them brown lightly and make sure they are thoroughly tender. Squeeze the half lemon into the aubergine and serve with the nicely rested steak. Serves 2.

# New garlic and mushrooms

## June 13

There is a head of roasted garlic left from yesterday, its fat cloves sweet and caramelised, still inside their papery skins.

The mellow, barely-there quality of baked garlic has little in common with the hot, piercing bite of chopped garlic that spits and fizzes in a wok over a fierce flame. Squeeze the butterscotch-coloured cloves from their skins, then mash the flesh with a trickle of olive oil to make a scented paste the hue of old ivory. That paste can be spread on thick toast that you cover with slices of chalk-white goat's cheese; used to season cream in which to toss pasta ribbons; or, as I did today, used as a filling for a thin, flaky tart of mushrooms.

## New garlic and mushroom tarts

puff pastry – 325g
an egg

olive oil – 3 tablespoons
dill, chopped – 4 tablespoons

*For the mushrooms:*
large button mushrooms – 300g
butter – a thick slice

*For the paste:*
a whole head of roasted garlic*
double cream – 6 tablespoons

Roll the pastry into a rectangle 30cm x 40cm, place on a floured work surface with the longest side towards you, then cut into four equal rectangles. Place them on a baking sheet lined with baking parchment and set the oven at 200°C/Gas 6.

Score an inner rectangle on each of the pieces of pastry, about 2cm in from the edges. Try not to cut through to the baking sheet. Brush the rim of each rectangle with a little of the beaten egg, then bake for about twenty to twenty-five minutes, or until crisp and golden.

Halve or thickly slice the mushrooms, then cook them in the butter and olive oil in a shallow pan till golden and slightly sticky. Season with salt, pepper and the chopped dill.

Peel the roasted garlic, then put it into a small bowl and crush to a paste with the back of a spoon. Pour in the cream, a couple of spoonfuls at time, letting it thicken slightly as you go. Season with salt and pepper.

Remove the tarts from the oven and push the inner rectangle of each one down with a spoon or palette knife to give a shallow hollow in each. Spread the garlic cream over each hollow, then add the sautéd mushrooms and dill. Serve immediately. Makes 4.

*Starting from scratch, wrap a whole head of garlic in kitchen foil and bake at 180°C/Gas 4 for thirty-five to forty-five minutes, till soft.

# Earthy potatoes, sweet sharp mayonnaise

## June 17

Overnight rain. The potato plants that stood tall in the shade of the medlar tree are now bowed, their heads hanging from last night's downpour. I did not plant these, they just appeared on the site of last year's crop from the potatoes I failed to harvest. This was supposed to be the year I gave their bed over to gymnocarpium, the oak and beech ferns that will thrive under the slowly expanding green canopy of the medlar. Next year.

The sodden soil means this is not the day to dig potatoes, but I have made up my mind that we are to have potato salad. When it is really good, a potato salad can be worth elevating to main dish status. By 'really good' I mean that the potatoes are creamy-fleshed and earthy and have been cooked by someone who is fearless with the salt pot. Potatoes that are cooked well past al dente, even a little crumbly, and have been dressed thoughtfully, imaginatively, and – this is crucial – while they are still warm.

I honestly don't care whether the potato peeler is involved or not. I like both the silky texture of a young, naked spud and the sort of skin-on salad that could be politely referred to as rustic. We shouldn't be bullied into peeling our King Edwards if what we fancy is a rough-hewn, gutsy accompaniment to a fat, char-crusted rib-eye. Just make sure the other ingredients are in a similar vein, herbs torn instead of finely chopped, and plenty of lip-smarting vinegar in the dressing.

The dressing is just as important as getting the right potato. There is a style of salad that involves diminutive, waxy-fleshed tubers, barely as big as a blackbird's egg, fine parsley and tarragon (use only the youngest leaves), and a dressing of mayonnaise that has been given a lactic sharpness with crème fraîche. Charlotte, Jersey Royals and Belle de Fontenay if we are talking varieties. Or an even simpler recipe where, fresh from the pot, they are sliced and tossed with nothing but olive oil and soft, fruity red wine vinegar.

Large, floury-textured potatoes can be wonderful in a salad despite what purists say. The whole 'salad potato' dictum is a bit of a red herring. At this age, though, they are best peeled, cooked to the point of crumbling before being drained thoroughly, then stirred carefully with a mustard-spiked dressing and the generous amount of parsley you would use if you were making a tabbouleh. But always, the dressing should be applied when the main ingredient is still warm and has just been sliced. That way it will be soaked up more effectively. The dressing needs to get to the heart of the matter.

I like to roast new potatoes for salad too, and toss them in the dressing so you get a nutty, caramelised quality and a fudgy texture. Even heartier with some meat involved, slices of sirloin if you are feeling flush, or bits of bacon, fried crisp as splintered glass, if not. We eat our potato salad not with cold cuts but with big fat sausage rolls from the deli, the sort that need a knife and fork.

## A piquant salad of potato and chicory

The amount of mayonnaise here is the smallest amount you can effectively make in a food mixer. Save half for later.

| | |
|---|---|
| new potatoes – 400g | groundnut oil – 100ml |
| watercress – a handful | olive oil – 200ml |
| chicory, radicchio or other | lemon juice – a good squeeze |
| bitter leaves – a handful | honey – 1 tablespoon |
| | grain mustard – 1 tablespoon |
| *For the dressing:* | cornichons – 15 |
| egg yolks – 2 | capers – 3 teaspoons, rinsed |

Wipe or rinse the potatoes, then boil them in deep, generously salted water till they are as tender as you wish. They will take about fifteen to twenty minutes, maybe less, depending on their size. For this recipe I cook them a little more than I would usually, a good twenty to twenty-five minutes.

Make the dressing: put the egg yolks into a large bowl, add a pinch of salt, then slowly add the oils, the briefest trickle at first, beating all the time, then a little faster, until you have a thick, wobbly mayonnaise. Add the lemon juice and a little finely ground black pepper.

Stir the honey and mustard into half the mayonnaise, putting the other half away for another time. Slice the cornichons in half lengthways, then stir, together with the rinsed capers, into the mayonnaise and season to your taste with salt and pepper.

Remove and discard the toughest of the watercress stems, then pick over the leaves, keeping only the very freshest. Wash the chicory and tear into large pieces. Drain the potatoes, then, using the back of a spoon or a potato masher, press down lightly on each potato to crack it open.

Drop the potatoes into the dressing, mixing gently so the warm potatoes soak up as much of the dressing as possible, then add the torn chicory leaves and the watercress. Serves 2–3.

# Rabbit and cucumber

## June 18

The farm dogs got my rabbit. I still remember, over forty years on, hearing furious growling and squealing up in the orchard, running up through the long grass to see the terriers from the next door farm playing tug-o'-war with my vast white pet. A scene of horror on a school morning, blood and fur and bared teeth and tearful screams of 'Daddy, Daddy, the dogs have got the rabbit.' I left him to deal with the remains, just as now I leave the butcher to joint the meat for my stew.

Rabbit is good summer meat, light, lean and mild. It works well with cucumber, tarragon and new potatoes in a salad. But we had a mayonnaise-dressed salad yesterday. Instead, I make a thin but intensely flavoured dressing from the roasting juices and a sweet vinegar.

## Rabbit with new potatoes and sherry vinegar

One of those dressings made using the cooking juices, this time from roasting a rabbit and potatoes with olive oil. The rabbit, incidentally, will never be falling-off-the-bone tender cooked this way – you want it to have a bit of bite as a contrast to the soft, sweet roast potatoes. I daresay you could use chicken, thighs and drumsticks, if the thought of a fluffy white tail bobbing through the fields still haunts you.

new potatoes – 600g
a whole wild rabbit, jointed into 6

olive oil – 3 tablespoons
a cucumber, medium-sized
sherry vinegar – 1 tablespoon

Set the oven at 180°C/Gas 4. Rinse or wipe the potatoes, then halve or quarter them depending on their size and put them into a roasting tin. Place the rabbit pieces with them, tucking them amongst the potatoes, then trickle over the oil, season generously with salt and black pepper and roast for approximately thirty minutes, till golden, giving the rabbit and potatoes the occasional turn.

Peel the cucumber lightly, slice it in half down its length, then scrape out and discard the seeds. Cut into thick slices.

Remove the rabbit from the tin and take the flesh off the bones, tearing or cutting it into large, bite-sized pieces. Transfer the potatoes and the rabbit pieces to a mixing bowl. Put the roasting tin over a moderate heat and pour in the sherry vinegar. Add the cucumber. Scrape at any crusted-on pan juices and stir into the vinegar, then pour over the rabbit and potatoes, toss gently and serve warm. For 3.

# Crisp duck. Ripe apricots.

## June 21

When an apricot disappoints me, as it so often does, I warm its cold heart with sugar, honey or spice. Ground cinnamon and a lightly flavoured honey will do the job, and can be added to the fruit destined for a tart or to be baked in a slow oven. Cardamom and anise work too, but ginger swings both ways, and can be added to the halved fruits in a mild, creamy curry (see *Kitchen Diaries II*) or used, in its syrupy form, as a glaze for a sweet tart. The quickest rescue remedy I know for lacklustre apricots is to halve, stone and brush their cut side with syrup from the ginger jar, then cook them under a low grill. That way, the fruit gets to wallow in both its favourite luxuries, sweetness and heat.

The apricots I buy from the greengrocer's today are the richest and sweetest I've had for years. I usually pick the deepest-coloured fruits from the box, leaving the pale, hard fruits be, then settle them in a single layer on a plate near the kitchen window for a day or two. Warmed by the summer sun, they become softer, sweeter and more interesting within forty-eight hours. But unless you are on the side of the angels, cooking your fruit is probably a better idea than trying to eat them as they are, the way you might a peach.

Another trick is to make a spiced sugar by crushing cardamom seeds and sugar using a pestle and mortar, rolling the fruit in it and baking till soft, then pouring over a generous amount of double cream or crème fraîche and returning it to the oven till the cream is warmed through.

There are other possibilities too. Apricots slipped on to brioche or panettone, spooned with honey and a little lemon juice, and baked till their syrup caramelises in the heat; the fruit chopped and stirred into warm sticky rice with sesame seeds and coconut milk; baked with a white-bloomed creamy cheese or, if you can find a reasonably priced supply, made into jam.

In possession of the apricots from heaven, I eat a few of them straight from the brown paper bag, while the rest go into a salad with the meat from a couple of crisp-skinned, roasted duck legs. Served as a main course with a bowl of perfect buttercrunch and iceberg lettuce at its side, we eat it shortly after the bird has been roasted, its skin still crunchy. The meat needs to be pulled from the bones with two forks in the style of pulled pork, so you get long strands of roasted meat and shattered, salt-flecked skin to toss with the sweet fruit and the sharp lime and black pepper dressing.

## Roast duck and apricot salad

I use legs for this recipe rather than the breast. The meat on the roasted duck legs pulls into shreds much more successfully than the breast meat and the skin roasts more crisply.

duck legs – 2
lime juice – 100ml (2 limes)
olive oil – 4 tablespoons
chilli – 1 medium-sized
small ripe apricots – 6–8
coriander – a handful

Set the oven at 200°C/Gas 6. Place the duck legs in a roasting tin, rub with a little salt and pepper, then roast for forty-five minutes, till the skin is crisp and golden. Remove the duck from the tin, place on a chopping board and pull the meat and skin away from the bones into thick juicy shreds, using two forks.

Mix the lime juice with a good pinch of sea salt flakes and stir in the oil. Shred the chilli, finely, removing the seeds if you prefer a cooler dressing, then add to the lime and oil. Halve and stone the apricots, slice into segments, then add them to the dressing. Toss with the warm, shredded duck.

Remove the coriander leaves from their stems, leaving them whole, then add them to the duck and apricots. Serve whilst the duck is still slightly warm. Serves 2.

# Loving the unfashionable herb

## June 27

Despite the general advice that mint is a herb to be used with discretion, I sometimes like to go in the opposite direction, using it boldly, like tucking whole leaves into a hot, chilli-scorched roast pork sandwich or chopping it and tossing with fried breadcrumbs and lemon zest to scatter over scallops or chicken livers.

You can soften mint's punch by mixing it with another suitable herb. Classic garden mint probably works best in conjunction with coriander and basil. The presence of another strong herb stops the mint dominating the dish, and the blend can be quite intoxicating. Mint is so part of our culture, from mint sauce with lamb (which I continue to love no matter how much it is frowned upon) to sweets and chocolate. The herb's use comes as a breath of fresh air to marry with the flavours of the Mediterranean or the Middle East, when it suddenly becomes exotic and tantalising.

For mint recipes it is always worth looking east. The herb, strangely cool and hot at the same time, goes well with aubergines, especially when they are chargrilled; with meatballs and grills; and chopped and folded into grain salads such as tabbouleh. Of all the suitable partners for this clean-tasting herb, lemon is perhaps the most neglected. I use them together in dressings for carrot salads, sometimes with a little cream. Lemon and mint is also a sparkling dressing, mixed with olive oil, for courgettes.

The simple salad of crisp, pale lettuce, beanshoots, thinly sliced peppers, mangetout and shredded roast chicken with a dressing containing nam pla and soy that I made yesterday became worth making again once a mixture of chopped mint, coriander and sesame oil became involved. A clear broth made from the chicken bones, with mushrooms, dark soy, a little miso paste and some beanshoots, took on a vitality once a handful of mint leaves was stirred in. Mint freshens, invigorates, stimulates.

And that is the point. There is no herb that brings with it such freshness and spark. Of course this will vary according to which mint you use. The variety is virtually endless, from those with hairy leaves or a slightly smoky note to them to the sweet mints more suited to dessert. Try a pesto made, not with the usual basil, but with mint. As a sauce it has far fewer possibilities, but is excellent on grilled lamb.

Out of step I know, but I do like to put a bunch of mint in with the new potatoes from time to time. It tastes of childhood, though probably only if your mother was, like mine, the sort to put mint in her potatoes.

There is a place for mint at the end of a meal too, often in partnership with chocolate (in a mousse or cake, a tart, or as a sauce for a pile of little choux buns). A favourite way to finish dinner when oranges are at their best is to slice them, steep them in a light sugar syrup with fresh mint, and chill them very thoroughly.

Of all the uses for mint this summer, the most successful by far has been in a frozen yoghurt freckled with dark chocolate chips. Although I have used an ice cream machine, I wanted a recipe that anyone with a freezer could do. Rather than churning the mint syrup and dairy produce (I used yoghurt, but it could have been custard), I simply beat the ice particles from the outer edges of the freezing sorbet into the liquid middle with a small whisk. Do this two or three times and you will have a much more light and airy ice than if you just freeze it into a block. Together, the yoghurt and mint made the most refreshing dessert of the year.

# Mint frozen yoghurt

A mint and chocolate sorbet, without the need for an ice cream maker.

caster sugar – 250g
mint sprigs – 15g
water – 250ml

yoghurt – 650g
dark chocolate – 60g

Blitz the sugar with 10g of the mint sprigs, leaves and stalks, in a food processor. You should end up with moist, green sugar. Put the sugar and water into a saucepan and bring to the boil, then, as soon as the sugar has dissolved, remove from the heat and cool the mixture. I find the quickest way to do this is to put the pan into a sink of cold water, or pour the hot syrup into a bowl set in a larger basin of ice cubes.

Blitz the remaining mint leaves briefly with the yoghurt, then stir into the cooled syrup and mix gently. Transfer the mixture to a plastic freezer box. Keep in the freezer for a couple of hours, or until ice crystals start to form on the outside edges, then stir or whisk them into the liquid centre and return to the freezer. Repeat a couple of times until almost frozen, then roughly chop the chocolate into small pieces and gently fold in.

Return the mixture to the freezer and leave till frozen. Scoop into bowls and serve. For 8–10.

# A summer lunch. Wasabi and salmon.

## June 28

Salmon and wasabi does it for me. The pale green horseradish paste, so fiery and vibrant, is my condiment of choice, and I will admit to using it somewhat adventurously, just as others might use mustard. It is particularly flattering to the oily, firm-fleshed salmon in all its forms, smoked, fresh, cured and raw. I never seem to tire of salmon sashimi, crunchy Japanese pickles and wasabi.

In this kitchen, wasabi turns up in anything from mashed potato (sloppy verging on the soupy, flecked with palest jade green) to a thin film spread on smoked eel. It introduces a subtle warmth to a bowl of pure white rice; can be stirred into mashed pea purée or spread on cold roast beef or pork destined for a sandwich.

The pastes and powders made from ground wasabi root are fine. Fresh wasabi is a rare and special visitor to my kitchen, and is treated with reverential respect. It is milder, less rasping, more subtle, yet unmistakably horseradish. If it was more widely available I would be a happy man. Then my wasabi grater, with its beautiful iridescent scaly surface, would get more of an outing.

I use the paste today, ready mixed and squeezed from a short green tube, giving a slow tingling warmth, the sort that creeps up on you as you eat, to a tub of mayonnaise. The condiment is for a dish of raw salmon that is to be eaten as a tiny salad before we start the main meal. To balance the softness of the salmon I grill the skin until thin enough to shatter, catching it just as it turns from silver to amber. We pile the fish on to tiny rye crackers and eat them before we sit down.

# Salmon in wasabi mayonnaise

It is not really practical to make a very small quantity of mayonnaise. Inevitably, there will be some left over from making this recipe. A thoroughly good thing to have in your fridge if, like me, you are a midnight fridge raider.

| | |
|---|---|
| salmon – 500g | groundnut oil – 150ml |
| purple radish sprouts | extra virgin olive oil – 50ml |
| | lemon juice |
| *For the wasabi mayonnaise:* | wasabi paste – 1 tablespoon |
| egg yolks – 2 | (to taste) |

Place the salmon on a chopping board and remove the skin in one piece. Cut the skin into three strips and set aside.

Make the mayonnaise. Put the egg yolks into a mixing bowl and very slowly beat in the oils, a few drops at a time at first, then add salt to taste and a squeeze of lemon juice. Beat in the wasabi, starting with a teaspoon, then adding more until you have a mayonnaise that is mildly spicy.

Cut the salmon into tiny dice. Add 3 heaped tablespoons of the mayonnaise and mix briefly.

Salt the salmon skin generously, then cook under an overhead grill till very crisp. Place briefly on kitchen paper, then chop or crumble into small pieces. Scatter over the salmon mayonnaise with some radish sprouts, and serve. Serves 4.

# Mango and blueberry lassi

The blueberries have a pinch of acidity which lifts the rather mild and soothing puréed mango.

*For the blueberry syrup:*
blueberries – 150g
caster sugar – 2 tablespoons
water – 100ml

*For the lassi:*
large mangoes – 3
juice of half a lemon
ice cubes – 2 large handfuls
yoghurt – 250g

Tip the blueberries into a saucepan, add the sugar and water and bring to the boil. Lower the heat and simmer for five minutes, or until the berries have popped and the juice is rich purple. Blitz till smooth. (If you don't mind lumps in your lassi you could simply crush the berries with a fork.)

Peel the mangoes and slice the flesh from the large flat stones. Put the flesh into a blender together with the lemon juice and the ice cubes and process to a thick smooth purée.

Add the yoghurt and combine. Pour into glasses, and add a couple of spoons of blueberry syrup to each. Serves 4.

# Currant buns

## June 29

Blackcurrants, pastry and cream.

*For the cream cheese pastry:*
plain flour – 250g
baking powder – half a
 teaspoon
butter – 75g
full-fat cream cheese – 75g
an egg
beaten egg for brushing

*For the filling:*
blackcurrants – 225g
caster sugar – 3 tablespoons

*To serve:*
double cream

Put the flour and baking powder and a good pinch of salt into a large mixing bowl, then add the butter, cut into small dice, and the cream cheese and rub the ingredients together with your fingertips until they resemble coarse, fresh breadcrumbs. Beat the egg, then fold into the mixture, bringing the dough together and then into a ball with your hands. Wrap in greaseproof paper or clingfilm and refrigerate for twenty minutes. Set the oven at 200°C/Gas 6. Toss together the blackcurrants and sugar.

Divide the mixture into six and roll each one out into a thin 16cm disc. Put one piece of pastry on a baking sheet and place a sixth of the blackcurrant and sugar filling in the centre. Brush the rim of the pastry with beaten egg, then pull the edges into the middle and press tightly to seal. Turn the bun upside down, push it into a neat round and brush with beaten egg. Make three small slashes in the top. Dust with caster sugar. Continue with the rest of the pastry and filling.

Bake for twenty-five minutes, or until golden. Serve warm, not cold, with double cream. Makes 6.

# Agnello rapido

June 30

A fillet of lamb, the long, fatless strip of meat from the loin, has no bones to pick at, no wrapping of fat to keep it succulent, and none of the crisp-skinned majesty of a glistening shoulder of meat in its roasting tin. Yet it remains a useful little cut for a midweek dinner. Lean as a whippet, with no sinew to remove, this elegant piece can be on the plate in the time it takes to lay the table, make the accompanying salad and open the wine. Unfussy, quick to cook, neat and fairly cheap. Not to be confused with neck fillet, a much more hard-working joint altogether, and one for the pot. Slow cooking in liquid is probably the best way to go with that one.

Unlike most meat, which will roast to perfection with no more than a cursory seasoning, fillet needs our help if it is to be truly delicious. Olive oil – lots of it – some black olives, a spice paste, maybe a thin sauce made from the roasting juices and a glug or two from the Marsala bottle. I have roasted fillet of lamb successfully with a paste made from rosemary, garlic and olive oil, and with another from sun-dried tomatoes in oil and fresh basil leaves. You can smear it with mild mustard or pesto before roasting, introducing an intriguing crust around the rare meat. Once or twice I have spread it with mustard and coated it in breadcrumbs too.

This is not for those who take their meat well done. Rose pink is preferable for something as lean as this. One fillet will serve two, cut into strips as thick as a finger. To bulk it out, I toss it with lightly steamed spinach leaves, a tomato salsa or a mixture of salad leaves, using the olive oil and juices in which it roasted, spiked with a dash of red wine or sherry vinegar, as a dressing.

I find it useful to sizzle a loin fillet of lamb in olive oil for a couple of minutes before putting it into a very hot oven. It encourages a

238

delicious outer crust. Rosemary or thyme sprigs go into the pan, maybe a crushed clove of garlic too. What you bring to the table is a mini Sunday roast, easy to carve and sweet as a nut. The lack of bones, of fat and its size means this is not the cut for a feast. Its usefulness and speed is what gives it weekday space in my kitchen.

## Roast lamb with olives and ciabatta

As the lamb cooks, the slices of ciabatta soak up the olive oil and juices from the meat.

lamb loin fillets – 2 large
rosemary – 4 bushy sprigs
olive oil – 100ml
ciabatta – 4 thick slices

black olives – 60g
mixed salad leaves – 2 large
handfuls

Set the oven at 200°C/Gas 6. Season the lamb fillets with salt and pepper. Bash the whole rosemary sprigs lightly with a pestle or rolling pin to release their oil. Warm the olive oil in a roasting tin, add the lamb and brown evenly for no more than a couple of minutes, on all sides.

Put the slices of ciabatta into the roasting tin, turning them in the oil to moisten them, then place the lamb fillets on the bread. Tuck a couple of the rosemary sprigs under the lamb, and the remainder on top. Tip the olives into the pan, then roast for fifteen minutes. Wash the salad leaves.

Remove the meat from the oven and leave to rest, covering the tin with foil, for about eight minutes, then remove the fillets from the bread and slice into thick pieces. Divide the bread, which will by now have soaked up the rosemary-infused oil, between four warm plates.

Toss the slices of lamb with the washed and dried salad leaves and pile on top of the ciabatta. Trickle over any remaining juices from the roasting tin, scatter over the olives and a pinch or two of sea salt flakes, and serve. For 4.

# Summer
# eats

# Grilled lamb cutlets with crushed avocado

avocados, lime, coriander leaves, cucumber, spring onions, lamb cutlets, celery salt

Halve, peel and stone **2 small avocados**, then crush the flesh roughly in a small bowl. Trickle in **a couple of tablespoons of olive oil**, the **juice of a lime** and a grinding of black pepper. Roughly chop **a handful of coriander leaves** and add them to the bowl.

Halve **half a cucumber** lengthways, scoop out its watery core and discard, then chop the flesh into small dice and add to the bowl. Finely chop **2 spring onions**, then fold into the avocado with the coriander and cucumber to give a rough, vivid green mash.

Season **6 lamb cutlets**, then grill on both sides until they are done to your liking. Dust the cutlets with a pinch of **celery salt or sea salt flakes** and serve with the crushed avocado. Enough for 2.

# Grilled halloumi, carrot and chilli

green chilli, red chilli, halloumi, carrot, mint, yoghurt,
white wine vinegar, iceberg lettuce

Halve, seed and very finely shred **a medium-hot green chilli
and a red one**. Put the shredded chillies into a shallow dish with
**2 tablespoons of olive oil**. Slice a **250g block of halloumi** into two
or three pieces horizontally, then place in the chilli and oil. Leave for
15 minutes or longer, turning from time to time.

Coarsely grate **a large carrot** and finely shred **8 mint leaves**. Stir
the carrot and mint into **4 tablespoons of yoghurt** and season with
black pepper and **a teaspoon or two of white wine vinegar**.

Cook the halloumi on a preheated griddle for 4 or 5 minutes on
each side. It will soften and turn golden brown in patches, but not
melt. Tuck into **a large, crisp leaf of lettuce** (iceberg is good for
this), then add the mint and carrot yoghurt. Fold the leaf over the
warm halloumi and eat. Enough for 2 as a light snack.

&

Halloumi softens rather than melts. In order for it to colour nicely,
but not to become dry and overcooked, you need to keep the heat
quite high, so it colours quickly. Turn the cheese once or twice during
cooking to colour both sides. Watch it carefully, as it can burn quite
suddenly.

&

Feta is a slightly more piquant alternative, but it's softer and more
fragile to handle. Bake it after marinating rather than cooking it on the
grill. The contrast between the heat of the chillies and the coolness
of the lettuce is almost the point of the recipe, but you could serve
the warm cheese crumbled among watercress or rocket instead.

# Aubergine and mozzarella

aubergines, basil, olive oil, mozzarella

Wipe **a large aubergine, or 2 small ones**, remove and discard the stalks, then slice into rounds, roughly ıcm thick. Heat an oven grill, and place the aubergine slices in a single layer on a baking sheet. Blitz **ı5g of basil leaves and stalks** with **8 tablespoons of olive oil** to a vivid green dressing in a blender or food processor. Trickle two-thirds of the basil oil over the aubergines, sprinkle with a little sea salt and place under the grill. Leave the aubergines to cook for ıo minutes or so, watching them carefully and turning them once so they cook evenly. They should be soft and lightly toasted.

Thinly slice **a ball of mozzarella** and place the slices on top of the aubergines. Season with salt and black pepper and the reserved basil dressing. Return to the grill and leave to cook until the mozzarella starts to melt into pools. Finish with a few basil leaves if you wish, and serve with toasted ciabatta. Serves 2.

&

Mozzarella should melt rather than cook. It needs just a minute or two under the grill in order to soften. Once it has started to change colour to gold, it will toughen. Keep the cooking quick and watch the cheese carefully. There is no need to salt the aubergines first.

&

Try spreading a thin layer of pesto on the grilled aubergines before adding the mozzarella. Use a little tomato or chilli sauce on the aubergines, under the cheese. Add garlic to the basil dressing.

&

Goat's cheese is an alternative to the mozzarella – use it in thick slices cut from a log. Rosemary, thyme sprigs and pine kernels could be scattered over the cheese before grilling.

# Sausages with summer vegetables

Romano peppers, red and yellow peppers, courgettes, tomatoes, olive oil, thyme, herby sausages, bread

Slice **2 Romano peppers** in half lengthways. Halve **a red and a yellow pepper**, remove the seeds and core, then cut each lengthways into four pieces and put them into a large roasting tin. Halve **2 courgettes** lengthways, then cut each half into thick chunks and add to the tin. Halve **6 medium tomatoes** and add them to the courgettes and peppers. Pour over **6 tablespoons of olive oil**, season with salt and pepper (be generous), then add **2 tablespoons of chopped thyme** and toss the vegetables in the oil.

Tuck **6 plump and herby sausages** among the veg. Bake for about 35–45 minutes at 180°C/Gas 4, turning occasionally, until you have tender vegetables, golden sausages and lots of cooking liquid. Serve with **chunks of bread** to soak up the gloriously fruity juices. Serves 3.

&

It's all about the juices. Get hold of some great bread to accompany this. Sourdough, possibly, or a light and airy ciabatta will do fine. The point here is not only the sizzling sausages and tender vegetables, but the sweet, thyme-scented cooking juices. Chunks of decent bread ensure that you won't waste a single drop.

&

I avoided putting garlic in this, but you could if the mood takes you. You could also cook it more slowly, on the hob instead of in the oven, letting the mixture sweeten and concentrate. Cool, chill and serve as a salad the following day. An aubergine or two wouldn't go amiss either.

# Duck with apple

duck breasts, cucumber, apples, white vermouth, honey

Season **a couple of duck breasts** with salt and black pepper. Warm a shallow non-stick pan over a moderate heat, place the duck breasts, skin down, in the pan and let them cook for 5 minutes, until the skin is golden and lightly crisp, then turn and cook the other side for 5 minutes or so. Remove from the pan and leave to rest for 10 minutes. Leave the fat from the duck in the pan.

Peel **2 small cucumbers, or half a medium-sized one**, then cut into thick slices. Halve, core and segment **a couple of apples**. Add the apples and cucumber, together with **a little oil or butter** if there is not enough duck fat, to the pan, and leave them to cook for about 5 minutes.

When the apple is lightly golden and tender, add **3 tablespoons of white vermouth**, such as Noilly Prat, and let it bubble briefly. Stir in **a tablespoon of honey (or 2 if you wish)**. Season carefully with salt and black pepper, then serve with the duck. Serves 2.

&

If you leave the duck in place to brown nicely, without moving it too much, a rich dark film of caramelised meat juices and sugars will appear in the pan. When you add the cucumber and apples and pour in the liquid, the film will dissolve and flavour the pan juices splendidly. If the apples are of the sweet dessert variety rather than 'cookers', such as Bramley, they won't break up as they cook.

&

You could use chicken breasts. Keep the skin on. You are unlikely to need the honey. Try a few cubes of smoked pancetta, added to the pan just prior to the apple, in which case you are unlikely to need any extra fat.

# Lamb, chickpea and feta

cubed lamb shoulder, ras el hanout, tinned chickpeas, lemon,
mint, feta, salad leaves

Dice **300g of lamb shoulder** into very small cubes, no bigger than
1cm in diameter. Warm a thin film of oil in a non-stick frying pan and
add the lamb. Brown nicely on all sides. Add **2–3 level tablespoons
of ras el hanout** and fry briefly.

Drain a **400g tin of chickpeas** and tip them into the lamb. Let
the lamb and chickpeas cook for 5 minutes, until the chickpeas are
thoroughly hot, then add **a generous squeeze of lemon, a handful
of shredded mint leaves** and a little black pepper. No salt. Crumble
**200g of feta** into the lamb and stir briefly, then tip on to plates or
into bowls and serve with **a little crisp salad**. Serves 2.

### &

If you buy ready-cubed lamb, cut the pieces into smaller dice. The
cooking time here is short. Leg or shoulder cuts are best for this. If you
want something even leaner, use a lamb loin fillet. Like garam masala,
ras el hanout spices are already roasted, so there is no need to cook
them for long after adding them to the lamb.

### &

Sweet and mild ras el hanout spice mix is available from large
supermarkets and Middle Eastern grocers, but you could use garam
masala for a change. You could make this recipe with beef, too, though
a lean cut would be best. A few rocket leaves, added to the pan when
the chickpeas go in, is a sound idea, but not spinach, which will produce
too much liquid.

# Trout with pink onions and samphire

trout, lemons, red onion, samphire, cucumber, cornichons, capers

Place **2 whole, medium-sized trout**, cleaned and gutted, in a roasting tin or baking dish. Cut **a lemon** into six slices, then stuff three into each trout. Peel **a red onion** and slice into fine rings, stuff half into the belly of the fish, then scatter the remainder around the roasting tin. Squeeze the juice of **a large lemon** around the fish, tuck **a large knob of butter** inside each one, then season with salt and pepper. Bake for half an hour at 200°C/Gas 6.

Trim any tough roots from **150g of samphire**. Cut **150g of cucumber** into quarters lengthways, then into thick pieces. Halve **50g of cornichons**. Mix the three ingredients together, then remove the fish from its roasting tin and toss the samphire mixture in the warm fish juices. Stir in **a tablespoon of capers**, a little black pepper, but no salt, and serve with the trout. Serves 2.

### &

Ask the fishmonger to gut and clean the trout but to leave the heads on. If you prefer to cook with fillets instead of whole fish, place them skin side up in the tin and tuck the onion and lemon underneath.

### &

Any small round fish is suitable here, such as mackerel or small sea bass. If using mackerel, try stuffing it with orange and fennel, or perhaps slices of tomato and shredded basil. Instead of adding samphire and cucumber to the dressing, add shredded iceberg lettuce or cooked green beans.

# Roast courgettes

black olives, Parmesan, rosemary, breadcrumbs, courgettes

Stone and chop **4 tablespoons of black olives** and put them into a mixing bowl. Add **6 tablespoons of grated Parmesan, 2 tablespoons of chopped rosemary** and **4 tablespoons of breadcrumbs**. Season with salt and black pepper.

Set the oven at 180°C/Gas 4. Cut **2 large or 4 medium-sized courgettes** in half lengthways. Score the cut sides, taking care not to cut too deep. Place the courgettes, snugly and cut side up, in a small roasting tin, then rub **a little olive oil** over the cut sides.

Spoon the olive and herb stuffing over the courgettes, pressing down lightly without compacting the stuffing. Trickle a little olive oil over the surface and bake for 45 minutes to an hour, until sizzling. Serves 2.

&

To get the courgettes to cook right through, score deeply into the cut sides with the point of a small knife. Try not to cut too far, otherwise the oil will leak out.

&

You could add a few anchovies to the stuffing. Chop them finely and mix with the olives. A little thyme, finely chopped, would be good, as would lemon thyme. As an alternative to the courgettes, slice large, ripe tomatoes in half round their middles, then stuff and bake as above, adding shredded basil to the stuffing.

# Baked tomatoes with tarragon oil

large tomatoes, anchovy fillets, cucumber, olive oil, tarragon,
parsley, sourdough or ciabatta bread

Slice **4 large tomatoes** in half and put them on a baking sheet.
Trickle over **a little olive oil**, season with black pepper, then add **an
anchovy fillet** to each one. Cook under an overhead grill until hot
and lightly toasted. Peel **a cucumber**, slice down its length, then
scrape out the seeds with a teaspoon and discard. Make a dressing for
the cucumber by pouring **5 tablespoons of olive oil** into a blender
or food processor, adding the leaves from **3 or 4 large sprigs of
tarragon** and **a few leaves of parsley**, and blitzing until you have a
bright green dressing.

Grill 2 slices of the **bread**. Spoon the dressing over the tomatoes,
cucumber and the toasted bread. Serves 2.

&

Ripe sweet tomatoes are best for this, to balance the salty qualities
of the anchovy. You don't need to put salt on the tomatoes, the
anchovy is salty enough. Use good sourdough and flavoursome
olive oil.

&

Use basil or chervil in place of the tarragon. Serve the whole lot as
a filling for a warm pitta, tipping the cooked tomatoes and crunchy
cucumber into the toasted pitta pockets. Add a crumbling of feta
cheese and a few torn basil leaves.

# Spiced chicken and noodle soup

red chillies, lemon grass, garlic, lime, coriander, mint, turmeric,
chicken breast, coconut milk, fish sauce, noodles

Into a food processor put **2 small hot red chillies, 2 roughly chopped inner stalks of lemon grass, 2 cloves of garlic, the juice of a lime, a handful each of coriander leaves and mint, 3 teaspoons of turmeric and 3 tablespoons of groundnut oil**. Process to a rough paste.

Warm a griddle pan and cook **500g of boned chicken breast** for 5–7 minutes on each side, until cooked. Remove from the pan and slice into thick strips. Warm a deep-sided sauté pan or wok over a moderate heat and fry the paste for a minute, moving it round the pan so it doesn't burn. Add the pieces of griddled chicken, then pour in the contents of a **400ml tin of coconut milk** and bring to the boil. Shake in **a few drops of Thai or Vietnamese fish sauce**.

Drop **100g of fine noodles** into boiling water, then drain and divide among four deep bowls. Ladle in the chicken and its sauce and serve. Enough for 4.

### &

Organisation is the key here. There are more ingredients than I would usually want to put into a quick, everyday dish, but they require little prep other than roughly chopping and blitzing in a food processor. So have all the ingredients ready before you start. Then the whole thing will only take minutes. You could cook the chicken using an overhead grill if you prefer.

### &

Add a thumb of ginger or a teaspoon of dried shrimp to the spice paste, or a handful of Thai basil. The flavour of the grilled chicken is part of the dish, but if you prefer something more soothing, poach it in the coconut milk instead. Use thick fresh noodles if you prefer, or leave them out altogether.

# Freekeh with peppers and artichokes

freekeh, yellow peppers, preserved artichokes, dill,
coriander, lemon

Put **150g of freekeh** into a bowl, cover it with warm water and set aside for 10 minutes.

Slice **2 yellow peppers** in half, tear out the core and any seeds, then slice each half into four strips. Warm **3 tablespoons of olive oil** in a heavy-based shallow pan, then add the peppers and let them cook over a moderate heat, covered with a lid, for 10–15 minutes or so, until tender and silky. Pour in **4 tablespoons of water** and shake the pan, letting any sweet residue from the peppers dissolve. Season lightly.

While the peppers are cooking, boil the freekeh in deep, lightly salted water for 25 minutes till nutty and giving (I like it a little al dente and chewy, but you should cook it to your own liking).

Slice **250g of cooked, preserved artichokes** in half and add to the pan of peppers. Finely chop **20g of dill** and add, together with **3 tablespoons of chopped coriander, the juice of half a lemon** and **4 tablespoons of olive oil**. Warm briefly, then drain the freekeh and toss with the peppers and the sweet, lemony juices in the pan. Serves 4.

### &

I have been using a lot of freekeh lately, liking its mild roasted flavour and chewy texture. Most of the major stores have it, but it can also be found easily in Middle Eastern food shops.

# Pearl barley kedgeree

pearl barley, vegetable stock, eggs, butter, curry powder, peas,
smoked mackerel

Put **200g of pearl barley** into a saucepan with **500ml of vegetable stock** and bring to the boil. Lower the heat to an enthusiastic simmer and leave to cook for about 20 minutes, until almost all the stock has been absorbed.

Put **2 eggs** on to boil. Warm **50g of butter** in a shallow pan and add **3 teaspoons of your favourite curry powder**. Sizzle the spices for a minute or two, then add **150g of cooked peas**. (Frozen peas, cooked for 2 minutes then drained, are perfect for this.)

As soon as the peas are hot and coated in the spiced butter, stir them through the cooked pearl barley. Tear **250g of smoked mackerel** into large shards and fold gently through the barley. Shell the eggs and cut into quarters, then tuck them into the barley and serve. Enough for 2.

&

Take care cooking the barley. It is worth keeping an eye on the liquid levels, topping up with a little more hot stock if needed. Ideally there should be a thin film left in the bottom of the pan at the end. Note that 'pot' barley still has its husk and will take a lot longer to cook than 'pearl'.

&

You could happily swap the mackerel for poached smoked haddock and use rice instead of pearl barley. My own temptation would be to include some wild rice, for the textural contrast.

# Baked eggs and tomatoes

banana shallots, courgettes, garlic, cherry tomatoes, thyme, dried oregano, duck eggs

Peel **4 banana shallots**, then slice them in half from root to tip. Warm **3 tablespoons of olive oil** in a shallow heavy-based ovenproof pan and lightly brown the shallots on both sides. Keep the heat moderate. Halve then quarter **2 medium to large courgettes** lengthways and cut into large dice. Peel and finely slice **2 cloves of garlic**. Set the oven at 200°C/Gas 6.

When the shallots are soft, push them to one side of the pan and add the courgettes and sliced garlic to the other, letting them lightly colour. Cut **800g of cherry or other small tomatoes** in half. When the courgettes are pale gold, add the tomatoes, **6 whole sprigs of thyme** and **a teaspoon of dried oregano** and let them cook for a minute or two, then transfer the whole pan to the oven.

Bake the vegetables for 25 minutes, until the tomatoes are soft and the vegetables are truly tender. Remove the pan from the oven and make two small, shallow hollows among the vegetables, then crack **a duck egg** into each of them. Return the vegetables and eggs to the oven for 4–5 minutes, until the eggs are just set. Serves 2.

# Red mullet and couscous

vegetable stock, couscous, red onion, pumpkin seeds,
ras el hanout, red mullet

Bring **400ml of vegetable stock** to the boil in a saucepan. Put **200g of instant couscous** into a heatproof mixing bowl, then pour over the hot vegetable stock, cover with a plate and set aside for the couscous to swell.

Peel and finely chop **a red onion**, then let it sweat and soften in **a little olive oil** in a small pan over a low heat. Roughly chop **4 tablespoons of pumpkin seeds** and add them to the softening onion. Stir in **2 teaspoons of ras el hanout** – a mild, sweet North African spice mixture – and a little salt.

Brush **4 small red mullets** with olive oil, then season inside and out with salt and pepper and cook them on a preheated grill or griddle pan until just cooked. They shouldn't need more than 6–8 minutes per side, depending on their size.

Fluff the couscous with a fork, then fold in the onion and seeds. Season generously and serve with the grilled fish. Serves 2.

&

The couscous can be cooked in water if you prefer, but the best flavour comes from plumping it up in vegetable or chicken stock. The couscous should soak up all the stock – if it doesn't, drain it in a sieve before mixing in the onion.

&

If you don't want to use the mild and fragrant spice mix ras el hanout, you could add a fiery element and stir in a little chilli sauce. Dried fruits are good here, particularly golden sultanas and chopped apricots. Stir them in with the onions, perhaps with a little chopped mint too.

# Noodles with prawns and egg

rice noodles, carrots, spring onions, red chilli, garlic,
cashews, raw prawns, light soy sauce, sesame oil, egg,
dried shallots, coriander

Bring a pan of deep, salted water to the boil, then add **100g of flat
rice noodles** and turn off the heat. Cover tightly with a lid and leave
for 5 minutes, then drain.

Peel **2 small carrots** into ribbons with a vegetable peeler, then
roughly chop the slices. Roughly chop **2 spring onions**, then finely
chop **a small hot red chilli** and set aside. Peel and thinly slice **2 large
cloves of garlic**. Toast **50g of cashews** in a shallow pan in **a little oil**,
then remove. Set aside. Heat **2 tablespoons of oil** in a wok or frying
pan, then add the carrots, garlic, chopped spring onions and chilli
and cook over a high heat for a few seconds until golden. Add **240g
of shelled raw prawns** and continue cooking over a high heat for a
couple of minutes, until they are pale pink.

Drain the noodles, add them to the pan and continue cooking for
a minute. Pour in **3 tablespoons of light soy sauce** and **3 teaspoons
of sesame oil**, add **a beaten egg**, and stir. Add **2 tablespoons of
dried shallots** (optional), **a handful of coriander** and the toasted
cashews. Serves 2.

**&**

Success is all in the timing. This is one of the rare occasions I like to get all the chopped ingredients prepared first. The cooking happens quickly and at high temperature. A thin-based pan, ideally a wok, is essential so the ingredients can cook quickly.

**&**

Other good things to add: shredded ginger or lemon grass. Fat pork such as belly. Squid, cut thinly into rings. Button mushrooms, halved. Omit the egg if you wish. Finish with fresh mint and a squeeze of lime.

# JULY

## Loganberries, cream and oats

### July 5

The loganberry is the happiest of all accidents, created in 1883 by James Logan; a meeting of the plump American blackberry with an old variety of raspberry. The mulberry aside, the logan is the most fragile of the berries, soft and translucent, each cluster of tiny drupelets appearing almost dusty, the faintest bloom covering their surface. Once crushed, their juice is the deepest ruby, like a bottle of cassis caught in sunlight.

There were little cardboard punnets of loganberries at the vegetable stall in Bermondsey this morning, much earlier than those on the prickly canes in my garden, which are still hard and green. I buy two and bring them home, my precious cargo balanced on top of the shopping as if it were a box of bird's eggs.

Once in the kitchen I debate (with myself of course, so I get the answer I want) as to the fruit's fate. Simplicity wins, as it so often does. No tart, no cake, no cobbler or pie. Just a persuasive, juice-releasing crush with a fork and a folding in of thick, sweet cream. A fool of the purest sort.

But as with any soft, 'custard cup' dessert, some textural contrast is needed. Crisp, almondy biscuits the length of a cat's tongue; a scattering of softly crushed meringue, like glistening snow; smashed butterscotch to add a warm golden crunch. All valid candidates, but I opt for a sweet oat mixture, soft and flapjack-like, crumbled amongst the cream and scarlet fruit.

# Loganberry oat cream

*For the oat mixture:*
butter – 140g
demerara sugar – 60g
golden syrup – 125g
jumbo oats – 115g
medium rolled oats – 115g

*For the berry cream:*
double cream – 500ml
loganberries – 250g

You will need a 32cm × 24cm square non-stick cake tin, lined with baking parchment if you wish.

Set the oven at 200°C/Gas 6. Melt the butter in a deep, heavy-bottomed saucepan. Weigh the sugar on to the scale pan, then measure the golden syrup on top of it. (That will save you getting the scales sticky with syrup.) Tip the sugar and syrup into the melted butter, add a generous pinch of salt and the oats and stir well. Scoop the mixture into the cake tin and smooth level, but try not to compact the mixture. Bake for fifteen to twenty minutes, till deep gold and lightly set, then leave to cool.

Lightly whip the cream. It should sit in soft folds rather than be stiff enough to stand in peaks. Using a fork, lightly crush the berries, till their juices run, but stop well before they turn into a purée.

Tenderly, fold the crushed berries into the whipped cream and divide between the dishes, breaking up and scattering the oat crumble as you go. There will be some of the oat mixture left over. No bad thing. Serves 4.

# Something stuck to the pan

## July 6

James, without whom everything would have collapsed long ago, was telling me how his mother makes fideuà, the Valencian pasta dish that is cooked in the style of a paella. The one that uses tiny macaroni-style pasta instead of rice, similar to what is sold here as stortini bucati. And, best of all, how it is left to form a delicious crust on the bottom of the pan.

Fideuà is one of those dishes best made in quantity, so is perfect for the big sharing lunch we are having this weekend. We made it here the other day, first browning sliced squid and prawns in a wide shallow *paellera* (I could have used a thin frying pan), then setting them aside to make a soft sweet backbone to the dish with garlic, tomatoes, paprika and saffron, cooked to a brilliant scarlet slush.

The pasta cooks for about nine minutes, but then, and this is the crucial bit, you must stop stirring, so the pasta and sauce form a crust on the base of the dish. Now James's mother apparently gets very insistent about this. No stirring or fiddling, prodding, poking or peeping. The crust, known by various terms including *soccarat* – from the verb *socarrar*, to singe – will only form if you have the ability to leave the dish alone to get on with things itself. It should stick to the pan, as it does in a correctly made paella, firm enough to be scraped off with a spoon, but caught before it burns. It is the sort of utterly delicious, crusty, flavoursome, almost accidental treat that you either understand or you don't. I can think of a few people who would regard it not as something special, a morsel of culinary treasure, but as a nuisance, something that will stick to the pan and make washing up a pain. It probably says something about our cooking that we have no word in our language for such a delicacy.

So how do you know when the crust is ready? It's a mixture of experience, faith and luck. But also of having faith in your own intuition. If I'm honest I like this dish much more than paella and I'm sorry that it is not better known here. The way the pasta soaks up the juices from the seafood and tomato, the crisp yet luscious crust that forms on the base, not to mention the no-stir rule, though that comes at a price. Despite the stern warnings I was given about resisting the temptation to stir, fideuà is not a dish to leave unattended. This is not something to cook by the clock or by the book. It is something you have to get to know, by making it over and over again, by which time you will have learned to trust your pan, your ingredients and your skill.

# Fideuà

If you can't find the pasta above, use very fine spaghetti, broken into short lengths, or the ready-cut spaghetti tagliati. Better still, perhaps, would be to try and track down fideo, the traditional pasta for the dish.

a medium onion
squid – 2, cleaned
olive oil – 3 tablespoons
garlic – 4 cloves
tomatoes – 600g
sweet smoked paprika –
  2 level tablespoons
saffron – a generous pinch
  (optional)

pasta, such as stortini bucati
  – 500g
chicken or fish stock – 1 litre
large prawns, uncooked – 12
clams – 250g
mussels – 12

Peel the onion and cut it into small dice. Remove the tentacles from one of the squid. Cut the body sac into small dice and set aside. Cut the second squid into wide strips, removing the tentacles as you go.

Place a shallow pan over a moderate heat and pour in 2 tablespoons of the olive oil. When the oil is hot, add the diced squid and cook quickly, letting it sizzle and colour lightly on both sides.

Peel the garlic and slice each clove very finely, then add to the pan, still set over a medium heat, together with a little more oil if needed. Chop the tomatoes, fairly finely, add them and all their juice to the pan, and cook for two minutes. Stir in the paprika, saffron and pasta.

Let the pasta toast for a minute, then pour on the stock, season with salt, bring to the boil and leave to cook for eight minutes, or until two-thirds of the liquid has evaporated. At this point do not stir again until a fine crust has formed on the base.

While the pasta cooks, warm the remaining tablespoon of oil in a shallow pan, add the reserved raw squid and the prawns and cook for two minutes, till lightly browned. Remove immediately.

Place the clams and mussels, and the squid and prawns, over the surface of the pasta, then make a loose dome of kitchen foil over the pan and leave everything to steam for two or three minutes, till the mussels and clams have opened. Serve immediately. For 6.

# Lean and clean

## July 10

Fillet is a rare visitor to this kitchen. Too lean, too clean, too damned expensive. I like my beef to come with blackened, crusted edges and bloody inside, with a casing of wobbling, creamy fat.

The only other beef fillet recipe I can find is one in the first *Diaries*, rolled in peppercorns and served with a dressing of egg yolks, mint and mustard. It's good. Despite the not inconsiderable cost, it has been a popular recipe. I placed a second fillet recipe in my *Observer* column, expecting howls of anger at using such a wantonly extravagant cut. Wrong. It went down so well that I include it here, all rose-pink flesh and peppercorn crust, and with a juicy, fragrant accompaniment of matchstick courgettes tossed with lemons and basil.

## Fillet of beef with basil and lemon courgettes

If you want something to go with this, I would sauté some potatoes.

| | |
|---|---|
| white peppercorns – 2 tablespoons | courgettes – 2 large or 4 small |
| black peppercorns – 2 tablespoons | garlic – 2 plump cloves |
| olive oil | thyme – 8–10 bushy sprigs |
| fillet of beef – 700g | basil leaves – a good handful |
| | half a large lemon |

Lightly crush the peppercorns (I use a pestle and mortar). They should resemble fine gravel rather than powder. Tip the ground peppercorns on to a plate and mix in 2 teaspoons of sea salt flakes. Lightly oil the fillet of beef, then roll it in the salt and pepper, pressing down firmly so the meat is encrusted.

Wipe the courgettes, then cut them into thick matchstick-shaped strips. Toss them in a little salt and set them aside in a colander to drain for twenty minutes. This will prevent them becoming 'wet' during roasting. Drain them, pat them dry with kitchen paper, then add a tablespoon of olive oil. Peel and crush the garlic and add to the courgettes with some ground black pepper and the leaves from the thyme sprigs, then toss gently so the courgettes are evenly oiled and seasoned. Set the oven at 230°C/Gas 8.

Tip the courgettes into a roasting tin and place the peppered beef on top. Roast for ten minutes, then lower the heat to 180°C/Gas 4 and continue to cook for a further twenty-five minutes. Remove the meat from the tin, place on a warm plate, cover with foil and leave to rest for ten minutes. Return the courgettes to the oven; you want them to be tender and golden.

When the courgettes are ready, add the basil leaves, roughly torn, and toss gently, taking care not to break them up. Squeeze over a little lemon juice, then place on a warm serving plate.

Slice the beef very thinly, place on top of the courgettes, season with a little sea salt and serve. For 8.

# Rain and a gooseberry ice

## July 11

I wake to fat, pear-shaped raindrops and sky the colour of a church roof. The cool air is a relief. Mrs Lovell the greengrocer has gooseberries in a wooden tray and I take the lot. Crumble of course, but I want to make an ice cream too. For all its piercing tartness, the gooseberry submits all too easily in the presence of custard and sugar and can make a weak and indistinctive ice cream. Today I try using only half a litre of custard to a kilo of fruit and very little sugar. What results is a clean, refreshing ice.

What appeals about the gooseberry is not just its characteristic tartness, but also the fact that its flavour intensifies with the application of heat and sugar, unlike most other fruits, whose character diminishes once they meet the heat of the oven. Anyone who has suffered a strawberry cooked in a pie will probably know where I'm coming from.

The gooseberry is at the heart of some of my favourite things; it's one of my top two or three jams and the main ingredient in the ultimate fool. For a long time I have dreamed of making a gooseberry ice cream like this too, but had only eaten those whose fruit had been drowned by too much cream and sugar. The recipe that follows manages to retain the effervescence of the berry, an ice halfway along the line between sorbet and ice cream. I make it in an ice cream machine, because I genuinely believe the texture to be creamier and lighter than if I make it by hand, but you could do without if you wish. Just tip the mixture into freezer boxes and freeze for about five hours, stirring or, better still, beating, every hour, till almost frozen.

I make two batches, one with homemade custard, the other with a luxury brand of chilled, ready-made vanilla custard from the supermarket. As a cook who loves the gentle stirring of a pan

of vanilla-freckled custard over a low heat till it thickens, I would relish the chance to say how much better the texture and flavour of the homemade ice was. But it wasn't. Not only could we not tell the difference, the ready-made version was cheaper too.

## Gooseberry ice cream

gooseberries – 1kg                    custard – 500ml
caster sugar – 3 tablespoons

Top and tail the gooseberries, removing the stalks and tiny dried flowers. Put the fruit into a deep non-reactive pan (stainless steel or enamelled cast-iron), then add the sugar and a couple of tablespoons of water. Bring to the boil, then turn the heat down to a low simmer and leave for five to ten minutes, till the fruits have become opaque and started to burst. Remove the pan from the heat, lightly crush the berries with a fork or potato masher, then set aside to cool.

Stir the custard into the cool gooseberry mixture, then pour into the ice cream machine and churn till almost frozen. Serves 8.

# Beans and tomatoes

## July 12

I long ago gave up trying to please everyone. As a cookery columnist you soon realise that there are two sorts of cooks, those who are happy to use tinned cannellini or borlotti beans, and those who consider it to be utter heresy. To some, should you dare to suggest using beans from a tin, you are clearly not a good person, are not to be taken seriously and should certainly never be allowed to put pen to paper. On the other hand, there are those who will give you an exceedingly hard time for suggesting they might like to soak dried beans overnight, then boil them till tender. Then you have to deal with the pressure cooker crowd, who can't understand why you don't use the precious piece of machinery they swear by. In other words, whichever route you take, you get it in the neck from someone.

I'm not so black and white about things. I look at the matter differently. Sometimes I will open a tin of beans, other times I soak dried beans and boil them from scratch. What defines my choice is not a matter of pedantry or purist values; my choice is neither monetary nor is it time-sensitive. It is all down to how and when I intend to use them. During the week, I find it rather useful to tip ready-cooked beans from a tin, rinse them under cold water, then warm them in stock with onion, bay and peppercorns. Such dishes as the duck breast and cannellini beans in *Eat* are midweek lifesavers that actually eat better because of the slight softness of the tinned beans. But at the weekend, I might want to take a purist approach and cook dried and reconstituted beans for a long time, say in a deeply layered cassoulet-type recipe, or perhaps turn them into a rich and lovingly stirred purée.

The difference in flavour is negligible. Toss tinned, warm beans in a nice fruity olive oil and season them carefully and few will taste the difference. It is the texture of the beans that defines my choice. That duck breast dish I mentioned is much nicer with really soft beans, so I use tinned. Today, I am making a large salad of flageolet, cannellini and borlotti with chalk-white ricotta and cherry tomatoes. For a dish such as this, a slightly firmer texture is crucial. Soft, tinned beans wouldn't really cut the mustard.

An assortment of dried beans were tipped into cold water last night, where they stayed till this morning, when I drained them, covered them in fresh water, then boiled them with aromatics – onion, peppercorns, bay leaves – till they were nicely al dente. They have now been drained and tossed in olive oil, seasoned, and will soon be on the way to the table.

How we approach a recipe is dependent on several matters, such as how much time or money we have, how crucial is the exact texture or flavour of the end product and how much else we have on our plate that day. As a cookery writer you sometimes feel you can never win, but as an open-minded cook, you almost certainly can.

## Cannellini and ricotta salad

dried cannellini beans – 200g
dried borlotti beans – 200g
dried flageolet beans – 200g
bay leaves – 3
olive oil – 150ml, plus a little
  extra

rosemary – 4 sprigs
mixed tomatoes – 350g
parsley – a small bunch
ricotta – 200g

Soak the beans overnight in deep, cold water. The next day, tip them into pans of cold water and bring to the boil, removing the froth that rises to the surface, then add the bay leaves and turn the heat to a spirited simmer. Let the beans cook for about forty-five minutes, or until they are tender but not soft. After thirty minutes' cooking, you can salt them, but not before, as it seems to toughen the beans. Test regularly, as beans of different ages and harvests will take different

times to cook. Once tender, drain the beans in a colander and discard the cooking water. Tip into a bowl, trickle over a little olive oil, toss very gently and set aside.

In a large, deep pan, warm the 150ml of oil over a low heat with the whole rosemary sprigs, then add the tomatoes, cover with a lid and leave to cook for fifteen minutes, till the tomatoes are soft and just starting to burst.

Tip the drained beans, minus their bay leaves, in with the tomatoes and olive oil and fold the lightly crushed tomatoes into the beans. Chop the leaves of the parsley, not too finely, then toss with the beans. Transfer the salad to serving bowls.

Break the ricotta into pieces, add to the salad and serve. For 4–6.

# Summer cake

## July 17

I am reading Tove Jansson's *The Summer Book*. Her prose is spare, calm, soothing. I like the fact that nothing much happens. Even at eight in the morning, London is airless today; not a single leaf has moved since dawn. Even the gossamer petals of the Mutabilis rose, timid and light as duck down, are motionless. There is a heavy, wine-like smell in the garden from over-ripe loganberries and blackcurrants.

I want to make a simple cake for a summer's day, one that can be eaten warm, almost straight from the oven. The sort of cake Jansson might have Sophia and her grandmother take on a picnic to the island.

The loganberries, rambling across oak and iron frames by the yew hedge in the garden, need using, as do the blackcurrants. Their acidity and intensity would be perfect with sweet, unfussy cake.

This is not the day for buttercream, frosting or jam and I set about making a straightforward loaf cake, a layer of almond sponge – sweet and moist – then adding fresh berries and a dusting of thick, pebble-like crumble. We eat it even before lunch, warm from the oven.

*For the crumble crust:*
butter – 80g
plain flour – 80g
demerara sugar – 80g
a little water

*For the base:*
butter – 180g
golden caster sugar – 180g
eggs – 2

plain flour – 115g
ground almonds – 150g

*For the fruit:*
loganberries or raspberries
 – 150g
blackcurrants – 150g

You will need a couple of shallow cake tins, about 18cm x 12cm, lined with baking parchment.

Make the crumble mixture by rubbing the butter into the flour (done in seconds in a food processor, but a gentle pleasure to do by hand), then stirring in the demerara sugar. It should look like coarse, fresh breadcrumbs. Add a couple of teaspoons of water and firmly shake the bowl, to encourage the mixture to come together to form crumbs of varying sizes and therefore a more interesting texture.

To make the base of the cake, beat the butter and golden caster sugar together till light and fluffy. It should look like soft vanilla ice cream. This will take a good five minutes using an electric beater fitted with a flat paddle attachment. Beat the eggs lightly, then add them a little at a time to the mixture, followed, gently and briefly, by the flour and almonds.

Transfer the cake mixture to the lined tin and smooth it flat without compressing it. Scatter the berries over the surface, then add the crumble, loosely, letting it fall roughly over the surface without entirely covering it. Bake for a good hour, till pale biscuit-coloured and lightly firm.

Leave the cake to settle for a while, before cutting into thick slices. Makes 2 cakes.

# Hot roast chicken. Chilled sweet melon.

## July 18

Sometimes, most times actually, it is all about the juices. The herbal, deeply savoury liquor that collects in the pan of a roasting chicken, the sweet nectar that drips from a sliced, über-ripe melon. The magic that results from daring to mix the two.

It is too easy to let the juice of a roasting bird or joint of meat, the sweet liquor from ripe fruit, get away. They contain too much heart and soul to lose. In many ways they are the essence of our cooking, of our meat, fruits and vegetables at their best, and it would be heretical to allow them to be wasted. Gather them up, save them, use them.

Today I make a warm chicken salad for a blistering day, the cool of ripe melon pitched against the tender flesh of a roasting bird. It is, indeed, all about the juices.

## Warm roast chicken salad with melon

olive oil – a little
chicken breasts – 3
a small cantaloupe or
  Charentais melon
watermelon – 400g

*For the dressing:*
parsley – a large handful
olive oil – 80ml
sherry vinegar –
3 tablespoons

Set the oven at 200°C/Gas 6. Pour a little olive oil over the chicken breasts, then season them generously with salt and pepper and roast for about thirty to forty minutes, till crisp-skinned.

Whilst the chicken is roasting, halve the cantaloupe or Charentais melon and discard the seeds, then remove the flesh from the skin with a sharp knife and slice into thick, juicy pieces, putting them and

any juice into a large mixing bowl. Cut the watermelon into large chunks, removing the skin and as many of the seeds as you can, and add to the bowl.

Make the dressing. Blitz the parsley leaves in a blender with the olive oil and sherry vinegar. Remove the chicken from the oven, set aside to rest, then pour the dressing into the roasting tin, stirring to dissolve all the sediment and pan stickings from the tin. A little heat under the pan will help, but don't let the dressing boil. Season carefully.

Tear the warm chicken into large rough-edged pieces and add to the melon. Pour the warm dressing over and gently turn the melon and chicken to coat. Serves 6.

# Gazpacho

Ask forty cooks the correct way to make a classic recipe and you will get forty different answers. Many of them will go on to insist that their way, and only their way, is right. Indeed, some rather boorish individuals seem to have made a career out of it.

And so it is with gazpacho, that cooling red soup that seems so right on a baking summer's day. Spanish friends argue even within their own families as to the perfect mixture of tomatoes, green peppers and cucumber, the inclusion of bread and whether contemporary versions are fun or an aberration. Even the texture is up for heated discussion. And then I come along and change the green peppers to red because I don't like the green ones (more accurately, they don't like me).

I enjoy the fact that there are local or familial variations of a classic and no one single recipe. Indeed, not all gazpacho is even red, as some forms don't contain the tomato that one could assume lies at the heart of this chilled summer soup. White gazpacho, *ajo blanco*, originated in Málaga, and contains almonds and grapes, but no tomatoes. You start with shelled almonds, a clove or two of young garlic and salt, working them in a blender or with a pestle and mortar till finely ground. At this point you introduce bread that you have soaked in water then squeezed almost dry, olive oil in a steady stream whilst the motor runs or a friend pounds with the pestle, and then the vinegar, water and a few green grapes. The result, a smooth soup of palest ivory, is elegant. A few drops of olive oil on the surface is all the embellishment needed, though some add cubes of toasted bread.

The consistency of a gazpacho is down to personal preference and local tradition. Most teeter on the edge of a coarse purée, but it is rarely a smooth soup. No matter how much you chop and blitz the soup it is always more interesting for retaining a faint element of crunch from the raw ingredients, otherwise you might as well go the whole hog and turn it into a smoothie. Those that never see the inside of a blender can be particularly welcome, the tomatoes, peppers and cucumbers chopped very finely, giving more of a fine salsa than soup.

A version I like involves puréeing only two-thirds of the mixture, stirring in the remaining, coarse and crunchy third at the end.

In Spain, your gazpacho may come in a glass rather than a bowl, but I really like the chunky versions, and even more so when they include croutons. You can chop the ingredients finely instead or give them a brief ride in a food processor. If you intend to chop by hand, be prepared for a lot of juice to make its way off the chopping board on to the work surface.

Whether you take the rough route or the smooth, you will need a little vinegar in there. First choice is generally red, but a sherry vinegar is favoured by Moro, lending depth and mellowing the rawness of the peppers. Add it a spoonful at a time, tasting as you go. Sugar is altogether a more controversial addition, but one worth considering if the tomatoes call for it. A teaspoon or two is generally enough.

Bread, soaked in water, then squeezed out with your fist, is included in some recipes. Spanish friends, by which I mean James and his family, don't add it to theirs, but some insist it is essential. A few slices are a good way of padding out expensive tomatoes and using up a stale loaf, but it is also worth considering for the velvety texture it brings to the party. Some regard its presence as essential, others, like myself, unnecessary. We are, of course, all right.

# Gazpacho

I like to add a little Serrano ham to my soup at the last minute. Two or three cubes or a shredded slice or two is enough in each bowl.

| | |
|---|---|
| tomatoes, large, but not beefsteak – 6 | garlic – 2 cloves |
| red peppers – 3 | sherry vinegar – 2 tablespoons |
| yellow peppers – 3 | mild smoked paprika – 1 teaspoon |
| a red onion | olive oil – 1 tablespoon |
| half a cucumber | caster sugar – 2 teaspoons |
| spring onions – 3 | |

Cut a small cross in the end of each tomato, then put them into a heatproof mixing bowl. Put the kettle on and when it boils pour the water over the tomatoes and leave them for a minute or so. Lift them out one at a time with a draining spoon and slip off the skins. They should come away easily.

Cut each tomato in half, discard the seeds and core, then put them into a blender. Chop the peppers and add them to the tomatoes, together with the onion, peeled and chopped, and the roughly chopped cucumber. Remove most of the green shoots from the spring onions, then roughly chop the white and add to the tomatoes with the peeled garlic.

Blitz the mixture until it is the consistency you like. It's obviously up to you. Only you know how thick you like your soup. Now start to season it to taste with salt, the sherry vinegar, smoked paprika, olive oil and sugar. Start with the amounts in the list, then tweak to your own liking. Serves 6.

# Making mayo

## July 29

The sort that sits, glossy and quivering, in its bowl. The one that slides from your spoon like softly whipped cream. The shining pool. The trickle. The mayonnaise so thick you could cut it with a knife. The stuff that comes in a jar, just for emergencies. The rasping and the peppery, the one as smooth as a silk scarf, nutty or bland. And we probably shouldn't forget the mayo that you can squeeze from a tube.

There is a mayonnaise for every occasion. I tend to use a flavourless oil, adding a last-minute introduction of bright and fruity olive oil if it seems appropriate. The only time I use purely olive is in high summer, when the sun is high in the sky and we eat outdoors.

Mayonnaise makes a sleek dressing, especially when you let it down with a little cream, or even warm, but not hot, water. The mixture will become lighter in colour and can be spooned easily over fritters or a salad. Best of all, it can be spooned into fish soup to mingle with the brick-red juices.

Tonight I make a mint and coriander version, folding the roughly chopped herbs in at the last moment. It is to be used as a dressing for lamb, the meat being first grilled, then tossed with the herbed mayonnaise and eaten wrapped in vast curls of pale, crisp lettuce. Later, griddled Florence onions, the elongated variety whose bulbs are flushed with pink, piled on toasted open-textured bread, trickled with the same mayonnaise, its texture made more luxurious with the addition of cream.

# Lamb steaks, herb mayonnaise

You could do this with rump steak too. Or a chicken breast.

egg yolks – 3  
groundnut oil – 300ml  
lemon juice – a teaspoon  
mint and coriander –  
   10g total weight

lamb steaks – 4,  
   about 150g each  
lettuce – 12 large, crisp leaves

*To finish:*  
mint and coriander leaves

Make the dressing: place the egg yolks in a bowl, add a little salt and pepper, then slowly beat in the oil with a whisk, adding it drop by drop at first, then, as the mixture starts to thicken, as a thin trickle. When the dressing is thick, season with a little lemon juice, salt and pepper. Roughly chop the coriander and mint leaves, stir into the dressing and set aside.

Warm a griddle pan or overhead grill. Season the lamb steaks with salt and pepper, lightly on both sides. Cook the lamb under the grill or on the hot griddle, till crusted and brown on the outside and pink within, then leave to rest for five minutes in a warm place.

Slice the lamb steaks thickly, into finger-thick strips, then place in a bowl with half the herb mayonnaise and toss gently until the lamb is lightly coated. Place the lettuce leaves in deep bowls or plates, divide the lamb strips between them, and add a few sprigs of fresh coriander and some whole mint leaves. Wrap the lamb up in the lettuce leaves and eat. Serves 4.

# A question of balance and harmony

I want to make a blackcurrant ice. Cream tends to suffocate the wildly intense flavour of the blackcurrant. A sorbet made from it can overpower and pall after a spoonful or two. It is clear that if the ice is to have a velvety texture whilst keeping the glorious sourness of the fruit intact, then I must enter into a delicate balancing act.

After much tinkering (not to mention washing up), and with the ice cream machine begging for mercy, I settle on a mixture that includes sugar to soften the fruit's unremitting acidity, cream to introduce a pleasing texture and yoghurt to lend lightness to the proceedings.

Be it making a cup of coffee or putting together a salad dressing, preparing what we eat or drink will always be about balance and harmony. The ratio of one ingredient to another, and how they work together to be successful, pleasing and harmonious, is one of the great joys of a creative life. Sometimes I get it wrong. Today, for once, I think I got it right.

## Blackcurrant frozen yoghurt, warm crumble

blackcurrants – 250g
caster sugar – 4 tablespoons
water – 3 tablespoons
natural yoghurt (unsweetened,
    unflavoured) – 350g
double cream – 250ml

*For the crumble:*
plain flour – 70g
butter – 50g
caster or demerara sugar
    – 40g

Remove the currants from their stems, drop them into a saucepan with the caster sugar and water and bring to the boil. Leave to simmer for five minutes or so, until the sugar has dissolved and the berries have begun to burst. The syrup should be a deep, rich purple.

Remove the pan from the heat and set aside to cool. You can speed this up by tipping the hot berries and syrup into a bowl and dunking it in a sink of cold water.

Set the oven at 180°C/Gas 4. To make the crumble, tip the flour into a bowl, cube the butter and add it to the flour, then rub the butter into the flour until it resembles coarse breadcrumbs. Stir in the sugar. Lightly sprinkle the mixture with cold water, then shake the bowl in your hands till you have a mixture of coarse crumbs and small pebbles of dough. Tip the crumble on to a baking sheet in a shallow layer and bake for fifteen to twenty minutes or so, till the crumble is golden brown. Remove and set aside.

When the blackcurrants are cool, mix them with the yoghurt. In a cold bowl, lightly whip the cream until it just starts to thicken – it must not be thick enough to stand in peaks. Fold the cream into the yoghurt and blackcurrant mixture, then pour into the bowl of the ice cream machine and churn till almost frozen.

Scrape the frozen yoghurt from the churn, transfer to a freezer box and freeze till needed. It will get harder the longer it is frozen.

To serve, place scoops of ice cream in small bowls, then break up the crumble and scatter some of it over each one. Serves 4.

# A light fishcake for a summer's day

## July 31

I swear I can hear the courgettes growing. But then, in the silence of the garden at midnight, under a rare starry London sky, you could believe anything. If my pots of courgettes are indeed growing audibly, it could explain the fact that each morning I wake to find yet more have appeared where there were none when I went to bed.

The courgette's water content limits its use. No mash or soup worth making; grated, it will introduce sogginess to a salad. Salting, to extract some of the courgette's water, is worth it for the recipe that follows. If you skip the process, you may find your cakes are too wet and won't crisp appetisingly in the pan.

## Salmon and courgette cakes

| | |
|---|---|
| floury potatoes – 1kg | spring onions – 4 |
| salmon – 450g | a little oil and butter, |
| courgettes – 250g | for frying |

Set the oven at 200°C/Gas 6. Peel the potatoes and slice them into large pieces, then boil in salted water till tender. Place the salmon in an oiled baking dish, season lightly and bake for ten to fifteen minutes, till just done.

Coarsely grate the courgettes, ideally to the same matchstick thickness you would for a celeriac remoulade, then place them in a colander set on a plate or dish and add a generous sprinkling of sea salt. Leave for thirty minutes, till most of the juices have drained from them. (If you skip this step you end up with wet fishcakes.) Cut the spring onions into fine slices.

Drain the potatoes thoroughly, then mash smoothly with a potato masher or using a food mixer fitted with a flat beater attachment.

Squeeze the courgettes in your hands to remove any excess moisture. Using a little butter and oil, fry the courgettes, together with the chopped spring onions, till soft and golden, then fold into the potato. Gently fold in the fish, broken into large pieces, and check the seasoning.

Pat the mixture, using lightly floured hands if necessary, into six small cakes, then set them aside in the fridge for thirty minutes.

Warm the oil and butter in a shallow, non-stick pan, then place the fishcakes in the pan and leave them to cook, without moving them, until they have formed a thin golden crust on the underside. Turn carefully with a palette knife and let them cook for a further few minutes till golden. Lift them out and serve. For 3.

# AUGUST

## Grilling a squid

### August 1

The smell of fish on the grill, of ozone and salt, smoke and thyme. A smell of seaside and forest. But the outdoor grill has already returned to its home under the stairs till next summer. To be honest I couldn't wait to get it out of the garden. The griddle, a rectangular plank of ridged cast-iron, blackened by use and careless washing, is a good second best. And there's always the overhead grill inside the oven. OK, so you won't get the smoky flavours and charcoal smell of the barbecue, but the skin of a mackerel will crisp, the edges of a butterflied sardine will blacken, a squid will curl tantalisingly. There will be sizzle and crackle.

Some people prefer to griddle their fish without any oil, dressing it only when it comes off the heat. This method does cut out the plumes of smoke that fug up the kitchen and set off the fire detector, but it increases the risk of the seafood sticking. I oil mine lightly.

Cooking on a griddle or under a grill gives many fish a fine, brittle skin. The same skin you might normally scrape off and discard before eating suddenly becomes a delicacy, especially – and maybe this is just a personal thing – that moment when lemon juice hits the lightly charred edges.

# Grilled squid, pine kernels and parsley crumbs

Ask your fishmonger to prepare the squid for you. You need the body sac complete and the tentacles. When you get home, check carefully and rinse thoroughly.

olive oil – 6 tablespoons
anchovy fillets – 8
pine kernels – 50g
breadcrumbs – 100g
parsley – a good handful

the grated zest of a small
orange
squid, body sac and
tentacles – 500g
a lemon

Warm the olive oil in a shallow pan. Finely chop the anchovy fillets and add them to the olive oil. Roughly chop the pine kernels, toss them into the pan and let them colour lightly, then add the breadcrumbs. Let the crumbs colour lightly, turning pale gold, tossing them regularly so they don't burn. Roughly chop the parsley and finely grate the orange zest, then stir into the hot crumbs with a grinding of black pepper. Set aside.

Rinse the squid, then cut the body sacs into thin rings, leaving the tentacles whole. Heat a griddle pan, then, when it is really hot, cook the squid for a minute or two, till the flesh is opaque and the edges are very lightly singed. Transfer the hot squid to the breadcrumbs, toss gently and serve with a half lemon each to squeeze over. Serves 2 as a main dish.

# A good ribbing and the joy of crackling

## August 3

The garden table, a patchwork of zinc and recycled wood held together by rusty nails and love, can be a place of green tea and solitude or a riot of gluttony. Today it is all beer bottles and bones. An untidy pile of pork ribs gnawed clean, sticky-fingered paper towels and chatter.

The ribs were fatty ones, simmered then roasted and served with a thick slush of boiled-down tomatoes, vinegar and sugar. I put them on the table with a wooden board of crackling, crisp as meringue, mouth-numbing with Szechuan peppercorns and salt crystals the size of snowflakes. The assembled crowd shattered the crackling, sending shards of amber and black speckled pork skin over the table; they picked up the bones and tugged, gnawed and chewed. They chinked bottles of craft beer just short of frozen and told jokes that had me wincing as nearby homes closed their windows. You cannot, and probably shouldn't, eat pork ribs politely. Once beyond the initial attack, it is pointless to press on with knife, fork and good behaviour.

I cooked the ribs in an unusual fashion, poaching them first in a thick mixture of spices, mustard seeds, brown sugar and tomato, then roasting them. The initial simmering is as much about marinating as anything; the roasting giving them the necessary sheen and gloss, caramelising the adhering sugars and charring the edges in the way that all good ribs should be. The sauce is then boiled down to the point where it can, possibly, be described as a ketchup, a thick, sweet-sour glop that is as good with the sizzling, too-hot-to-handle ribs as it is the following day, in soft, porky wraps with soured cream, slices of avocado and pretty pink onions.

# Maple pork ribs with tomato chutney

You need big, plump pork ribs for this. Ask the butcher to remove and score the skin for crackling, and slice the belly into about eight ribs. You can cook the skin, slowly, glistening with coarse salt and crushed peppercorns, till it is as crisp as ice. Put it on the table with the ribs, or tuck it, in jagged strips, into your pork belly wraps.

| | |
|---|---|
| large onions – 2 | hot smoked paprika – |
| oil – a little | 2 teaspoons |
| garlic – 6 cloves | star anise – 3 |
| fennel seeds – 3 teaspoons | bay leaves – 3 |
| demerara sugar – | maple syrup – 8 tablespoons |
| 3 tablespoons | tomatoes – 2kg, chopped |
| mustard seeds – 3 tablespoons | pork ribs, large – 8 (2.5kg) |

Peel the onions, then roughly chop them. Warm a couple of tablespoons of oil in a very large, deep saucepan, then add the chopped onions and let them cook over a moderate heat, stirring from time to time. Peel the garlic, but leave the cloves whole, then stir them into the onions. Leave all to fully soften and turn pale gold.

Add the fennel seeds to the softened onions, then stir in the demerara sugar, mustard seeds, smoked paprika, star anise, bay leaves and 3 tablespoons of the maple syrup.

Roughly chop the tomatoes and add them to the onions and seasonings, together with a generous amount of salt and black pepper. Push the ribs down into the mixture, then bring to the boil. Lower the heat and leave to simmer for an hour.

Set the oven at 230°C/Gas 8. Remove the ribs and place them on a foil-lined rack over a roasting tin. Brush them with the remaining maple syrup and roast for twenty minutes, till sizzling and deep golden brown. (Check them regularly, they burn easily.)

Turn the heat up under the tomato and onion chutney mixture and leave to bubble, stirring regularly, until the liquid has reduced and the chutney is thick and rich. Check the seasoning and correct with salt and pepper. It should be sweet, sharp and slightly spicy. Serve with the roasted ribs. Serves 4.

# The joy of crackling

Crackling. The deliciously onomatopoeic name for something whose presence – light, translucent, crisp, salty and chewy – takes a Sunday pork roast trotting in the direction of perfection. And the lack of which epitomises the saying, 'Close, but no cigar.'

The skin of the shoulder, belly or loin of the pig, rubbed with salt and roasted till it can be shattered like ice on a pond, is as capricious as a soufflé, possibly more so. Its success, its presence even, depends upon the breed of pig (breeds that thrive outside, whose tough hide sees rain, wind and shine). On cooking, the skin should be dry if it is to crisp up nicely, so a night out of the humidity of the fridge will help. Give it a brave sizzle in a fierce oven for twenty minutes before the heat is turned down to the usual roasting temperature. And ensure that it is never covered in foil.

Crackling may be eaten hot, dipped into gravy or balanced on the fork with hot pork flesh, its roasting juices and a nugget of roast potato. But the crisped-up skin of the pig is good cold too, when it becomes jaw-achingly chewy, and especially when it is over-salted or dipped into wobbling, vivid yellow, mustardy mayonnaise.

# Szechuan crackling

It is worth noting that some people find Szechuan peppercorns can cause irritation in quantity. A few people may find they can send their mouth numb.

skin from the pork belly, from
page 309 (about 400g)
sea salt flakes – 3 tablespoons

Szechuan peppercorns –
2 tablespoons
celery seeds – 1 tablespoon

Set the oven at 160°C/Gas 3. Using a very sharp knife or box-cutter, score the outer side of the pork skin deeply, cutting almost through to the chopping board, at 1cm intervals. Turn it over so the fat side is uppermost and place on a foil-lined baking sheet.

Coarsely grind the salt, peppercorns and celery seeds in a pestle and mortar or a spice grinder. Rub the spice mix over the fat side of the skin, then bake for about forty minutes, till deep honey-gold and totally crisp.

# Pork wraps

I like to keep a piece of crackling back from the roast, smashed into long pieces of shrapnel, to tuck into soft, floury wraps of yesterday's pork with avocado, soured cream and pickled red onions. A lunch, yes, but also a solitary midnight feast of secretive salty joy.

## Pulled pork rib wraps

leftover pork ribs, from
   page 309 – 2
tomato chutney, from page
   309 – 2 tablespoons
a red onion
white wine vinegar –
   6 tablespoons
half a small cucumber
radishes – 150g

an avocado
tortilla wraps – 4
a lime
coriander leaves –
   a handful
a few thin strips of
   crackling, opposite
soured cream – 150ml

Cut or tear the meat from the rib bones. Discard the bones, then, using a couple of forks, tear the meat into large, rough pieces and place in a mixing bowl. (The texture is up to you. I don't like mine torn too finely.) Fold the chutney into the pork.

Peel and finely slice the red onion, put into a shallow bowl, then pour over the vinegar, toss gently and set aside for twenty to thirty minutes. The onion will become soft, more mellow in flavour and pale pink in colour.

Peel the cucumber, halve lengthways, scrape out the seeds and discard, then dice the flesh. Quarter the radishes. Toss together the drained onion slices, cucumber and radishes.

Peel, stone and slice the avocado. Place the tortilla wraps flat on the work surface, add some of the onion and cucumber salsa, a couple of spoonfuls of pork and its chutney, then a few slices of the avocado, a squeeze of lime and the coriander. Snap the crackling into short thin pieces and place on top of the avocado. Finally, a spoonful of soured cream. Roll or fold the wrap and serve. Serves 4.

# A berry tart

## August 7

I'm cooking for fun. I make a fruit tart. The crust is of crushed biscuits, part sweet oat, part almond. The filling comprises two layers, the first of creamed goat's curd, fresh and piquant. The second of whipped cream. The cargo, a veritable mound of bulgingly ripe, summer berries.

From blueberries and cherries to the first plums, from white currants to deep, crimson-black logans, this is the peak of the tart maker's year. Peaches on a frangipane base; damsons under a pebbly, oat and almond crust; plums sliced and layered on a sheet of fine, crisp puff pastry.

I am not sure it matters whether your tart is a flawless masterpiece or something more friendly, fun and wobbly-edged. What matters is the offering of something you have made simply for the pleasure involved, something made with a light heart. Good food that has come from a good place.

# Berry goat's curd tart

When goat's curd evades me, I use a soft, mild, fresh goat's cheese, creamed with a small amount of double cream.

| | |
|---|---|
| sweet oat or almond biscuits – 300g | blackberries – 200g |
| butter – 120g | cherries – 100g |
| double cream – 250ml | strawberries – 200g |
| goat's curd – 200g | icing sugar |

You will need a 24cm loose-bottomed tart tin.

Crush the biscuits to coarse crumbs. A food processor is the quickest tool for this, but crushing the biscuits in a plastic bag with a rolling pin works perfectly well. Melt the butter in a saucepan, tip in the biscuit crumbs and mix thoroughly with a wooden spoon.

Press the biscuit crumbs into the tart case, lining the base with them, then pushing the mixture up the sides with a spoon and pressing it into shape with your fingers. Chill in the fridge for twenty-five to thirty minutes, till crisply set.

Whip the cream in a chilled bowl till thick but not so firm that it will stand in peaks. It should just be able to hold its shape. Spread the goat's curd over the biscuit crust, followed by a layer of the cream.

Sort and trim the berries and cherries, removing stems, stones and leaves, then pile them on top of the tart. Dust with icing sugar, and eat soon after assembling. Serves 6–8.

# Ancient breads – two ways

## August 10

The dying embers of a fire have been used for centuries to bake bread. Flatbreads, the thin, scorched slippers of dough we tear to pieces and use to scoop up our food. The breads, mostly made from a straightforward mix of white flour, salt, yeast and water, are thin enough to feel the warmth of the meat through the dough and provide an edible mop for the sauce on your plate.

Smelling of yeast and charcoal, flatbreads are also split and stuffed after baking, often with salad leaves, meat from the grill and a trickle of mint-freckled yoghurt. The humble flatbread can also be stuffed before baking, so when the crust is torn, the hot filling oozes out. This latter method, the stuffed bread, is one I have taken to heart.

The garden sits ripe and sleeping. The air is heavy with the scent of plums from a neighbour's tree. I bake a batch of flatbreads to eat with lunch, but decide to cook them on the hob rather than in the oven.

The figs I had been keeping, hopefully for an almond frangipane tart, end up being chopped and mixed with blue cheese as one of the stuffings, the other filling being a silky-textured mixture of roast aubergine, olive oil and thyme.

I let my breads catch a little as they cook, blistering on the base of the cast-iron pan. The slight blackening introduces a smoky note that, it turns out, is appropriate with both the aubergines (expected) and the figs (not expected). I imagine that is how they would have looked after their time in the embers of a fire, rather than the pallid biscuit-colour flatbreads that so often appear in the shops.

I could have stuffed the breads with mozzarella or olive paste, fried mushrooms or any good melting cheese such as Fontina. But the still, parched air, now thick with smoke from a far-off garden fire, seems appropriate for a char-edged bread and ripe figs, thyme and aubergines. What I call parched earth flavours.

# A simple flatbread dough

| strong white bread flour – 500g | easy bake dried yeast – 10g |
| salt – 8g | butter – 180g |
| | water – about 300ml |

Warm a large, wide mixing bowl with hot water, then dry it. The warmth will help your dough get started. Put the flour into the bowl with the salt and the dried yeast. Cut the butter into small pieces and add to the flour, then, pouring in most of the water, mix with your hands, bringing the dough together. Gradually add as much of the remaining water as you need, or maybe a little more, till you have a soft but rollable dough.

Put the dough on a lightly floured board and knead it for five to ten minutes, until it feels smooth and silky. Place it back in the mixing bowl, cover with a warm tea towel and leave in a warm place to rise for at least an hour, until the dough has doubled in size.

Tip the dough on to a floured surface, fold repeatedly till all the air is knocked out of it, then tear into twelve equal pieces. Roll each piece into a ball.

# Fig and Gorgonzola flatbreads

Use a good ripe cheese.

| large, ripe figs – 3 | Gorgonzola – 200g |
| half the dough above | olive oil – a little |

Cut the figs into quarters. Make an indentation in the centre of each ball of dough and push a piece of fig and a similarly sized lump of Gorgonzola into it. Pinch the dough over the filling to seal it.

Continue till all six pieces of dough are filled.

Put a ball of the stuffed dough on a well-floured work surface and flatten with a rolling pin into a disc or oval about 16cm in diameter. Place on a baking sheet and continue with the others.

Put the baking sheet of flatbreads in a warm place for ten to fifteen minutes. Warm a heavy-based frying pan over a moderate heat. Rub very lightly with a little olive oil, then place two or three flatbreads in the pan and let them cook for about three to four minutes. Once they have started to darken here and there, turn them over and cook the other side. A little blistering is good. Remove and eat immediately. Makes 6.

## Aubergine and thyme flatbreads

You could grill the aubergines instead of baking them. It's up to you.

| | |
|---|---|
| a medium-sized aubergine | thyme – a few sprigs |
| olive oil | half the dough opposite |

Set the oven at 200°C/Gas 6. Cut the aubergine in half from stalk to tip. Place the halves in a baking dish, cut side up, and slash a criss-cross of cuts into the flesh, reaching almost down to the skin. Trickle or brush over a little olive oil, then bake for twenty-five minutes, or until completely soft. Remove from the oven and use a teaspoon to scrape the flesh out of the aubergine shell into a mixing bowl. Chop the thyme leaves and stir them, with a little salt and black pepper, into the aubergine.

Make an indentation in the centre of each ball of dough, then put a couple of heaped teaspoons of the aubergine mixture into the hollow and pinch the dough over to seal. Carry on with the remaining pieces of dough.

Place a ball of the stuffed dough on a well-floured work surface and flatten with a rolling pin into a disc or oval about 16cm in diameter. Place on a baking sheet and continue with the others.

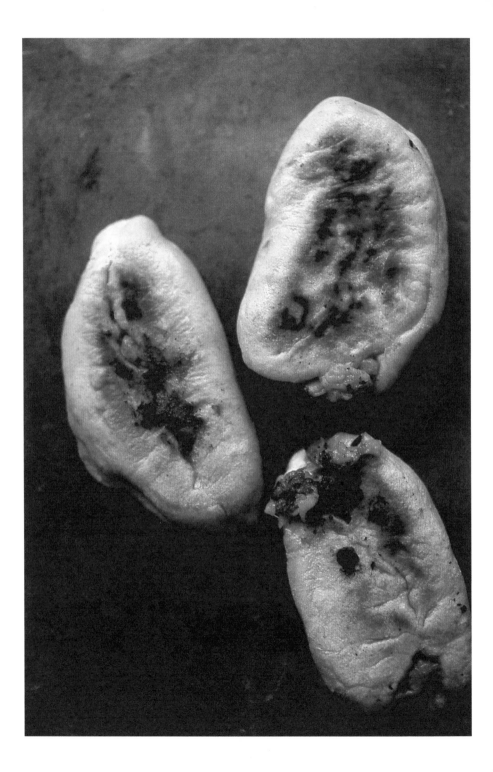

Put the baking sheet of flatbreads in a warm place for ten to fifteen minutes. Warm a heavy-based frying pan over a moderate heat. Rub very lightly with a little olive oil, then place two or three flatbreads in the pan and let them cook for about three to four minutes. Once they have started to darken here and there, turn them over and cook the other side. A little blistering is good. Remove and eat immediately. Makes 6.

# Grilled langoustines, salty, buttery juices

I like messy food. Juices that drip, ooze and dribble. And bones and shells that beg for fingers rather than forks. The signal crayfish, or the slimmer, more expensive langoustine, fits the bill well enough. You buy a pile of them, allowing anything from four to eight per person depending on your generosity, the state of your wallet and whatever else you may be eating with them.

## Grilled langoustines, Parmesan butter

Parmesan – 50g

butter – 175g

mild smoked paprika –
2 teaspoons

a medium, hot red chilli

langoustines – 8

Grate the Parmesan into a bowl and mash most of it into the butter with the smoked paprika. Halve, seed and finely chop the red chilli, then stir into the butter.

Slice the langoustines in half lengthways and place them cosily, cut side up, on a baking sheet. Spoon the butter generously over the surface of the langoustines. Preheat the oven grill.

Scatter the remaining Parmesan over the langoustines, then place them under the hot grill and let them cook for five or six minutes, till the butter is melted, the langoustines are lightly cooked and the crust is sizzling and golden. Eat whilst they are hot (fingers rather than forks), sucking the buttery, salty shells as you go. Serves 2.

# A scarlet granita. Getting the texture right.

Never buy a watermelon bigger than your head. They take up far too much room in the fridge. I have bought too generous a wedge, so we eat as much as we can in a salad, then make the rest into sorbet. A sparkling scarlet water ice flecked with emerald-green basil and mint sugar, to be precise.

The water ice is technically a granita, a twinkling mound of frozen granules rather than a smooth sorbet. No machine required, just the patience to take the mixture from the freezer every hour and carefully bring the frozen crystals from the edges into the liquid centre, until you have a grainy, shimmering pile of ice crystals. I prefer this slow method, which entails an extra bit of vigilance.

A quicker way is to freeze the purée and sugar into a block, then scrape the surface with a fork, as if you were scraping ice off a windscreen with your credit card. It works, but your ice will lack the larger, deeper-coloured grains achieved by the slow method and will be more like crushed ice.

## Watermelon granita, herb sugar

*For the sugar syrup:*
caster sugar – 4 tablespoons
water – 4 tablespoons
watermelon – 1.5kg

*For the basil mint sugar:*
caster sugar – 50g
basil leaves – 7g
mint leaves – 7g

Make the sugar syrup by bringing the caster sugar and water to the boil in a small saucepan. Lower the heat and simmer till the sugar is completely dissolved, then remove from the heat and leave to cool.

You can speed the process up by lowering the saucepan into a sink of cold water.

Remove the green and white rind from the watermelon and discard – you will end up with about 1kg of flesh. Roughly chop the watermelon, remove the seeds, then process to a thick slush in a blender or food processor.

Stir the sugar syrup into the crushed watermelon, then pour into a stainless steel or rigid plastic freezer box and freeze for an hour. Using a fork, gently bring the frozen edges of the granita, the crystals of frozen mixture that lie around the edges, into the middle, then return to the freezer. The crucial point is not to let the granita freeze into one vast ice cube. Instead, encourage the crystallisation by this regular, gentle mixing.

Continue like this, gently stirring the frozen crystals into the scarlet liquid, every hour, until the granita is entirely, but lightly, frozen into millions of tiny crystals. The process should take about four hours.

To make the herb sugar, pour the caster sugar into the bowl of a food processor and add the basil and mint leaves. Process the herbs and sugar for a few seconds, till you have a fine, brilliant green sugar.

To serve, pile mounds of the granita into small bowls and scatter over a little of the mint and basil sugar. Serves 6–8.

# A soup to celebrate the (early) arrival of autumn

## August 17

Sunday morning, a sky the grey and white of a pebble beach, the first 'pullover day' of autumn. A walk down the garden path reveals a garden in a state of early autumn decay, a tangle of nasturtiums, fallen apples, stinging nettles the height of a small child. Amongst the chaos, marigolds, the old-fashioned single sort known as Indian Prince, shine brightly in shades of piercing orange and dried blood. I should weed, trim and tidy but instead decide to go back to the kitchen and make soup.

Inspired by those marigolds or, more likely, by what needs using up, I make a soup of carrots and tomato. The result is sweet, with less piquancy than I had hoped, brought about by using over-ripe tomatoes. You can get round this by adding a teaspoon of red wine vinegar as you correct the seasoning, but instead I crumble feta cheese into the soup at the table. Fat, jagged pieces of salty sheep's-milk cheese that lift the sweetness of a carrot soup in the way a slice of Parma ham does a wedge of ripe melon.

## Carrot, tomato and feta soup

The success of a bowl of soup is as much about the texture as it is about flavour. My habit of blitzing only two-thirds of a pot of soup, leaving the remainder chunky and whole, works splendidly with this soup, albeit using a slightly different method. Choose carrots that are large and firm, rather than the fine early finger-thick carrots that tend to make a watery soup.

a large onion
groundnut or vegetable oil
  – 5 tablespoons
carrots – 400g

vegetable stock – 1.5 litres
tomatoes – 500g
feta – 200g

Peel the onion, roughly chop it, then let it cook, over a moderate heat, in a large pan with half the oil. Roughly chop the carrots. When the onion is soft and translucent, add the carrots and let them colour very slightly, for about ten minutes, stirring regularly.

Pour in the stock, bring to the boil, then lower the heat to a simmer. Let the soup cook for about thirty minutes, with the occasional stir, on a low to moderate heat.

Chop the tomatoes, put them into a shallow pan over a medium heat with the remaining oil and let them cook down to a soft, slushy consistency.

Blend the soup to a smooth texture in an electric blender or food processor. Stir in the cooked-down tomato, and season with salt and black pepper.

Divide the soup between bowls, then crumble the feta and add to the soup. It will soften, but not melt. A pinch of sour saltiness with your sweet soup. Serves 6–8.

# Pork, and a gift of blackberries

## August 20

London is starting to resemble a ghost town in a western. Everyone is away. Friends are like tumbleweed. There are virtually no cars in the lane (except, of course, when the painters need to park their van), the restaurant James and I visit today in Hackney is almost empty despite the food being awesome (kid faggots and garlic mash, pig's trotters on toast) and halfway through lunch the rain starts pissing down.

August has changed since I was a lad. Memories are of long, sunny days, endless walks till dusk through dusty fields of stubble, and everyone as brown as a berry. Now, late August is autumn. The leaves on the horse chestnut trees in the lane are crisping copper and yellow, curling and falling in the wind; the home-grown plums have all but disappeared from the market; the garden is sodden. To add to the sense of lost summer, the shops are already selling their autumn/ winter clothes collections.

A friend drops round with a basket of wild blackberries. A *Kinfolk* moment. The delight and gratefulness wears off as soon as she leaves, and I realise the fruit is exceedingly ripe and needs using lickety-split.

A couple of years ago I included a recipe on one of my television programmes where I baked a large lump of pork with a glut of blackberries, keeping the dish savoury with red onions and stock. Initially wary of how it might be received, I was chuffed to get several rather jolly emails about it, with initially sceptical viewers happily making it for a second time and serving the purple-rimmed meat cold the following day.

My diary notes for the recipe instruct me to 'stand in the fridge overnight covered in squashed blackberries'. There is a tiny part of me that feels that following the instructions to the letter might be fun, but instead I marinate a rolled shoulder of pork in the crushed

fruit until the outside of the meat has turned pink, then bake it, covered with a lid, and make an onion and blackberry gravy the colour of garnets.

## Pork and blackberries

| | |
|---|---|
| rolled pork shoulder, tied | olive oil – 2 tablespoons |
| – 1.5 kg | plain flour – 2 tablespoons |
| blackberries – 800g | vegetable or chicken stock |
| a red onion | – 500ml |

Place the pork in a large stainless steel or glass bowl and pierce the meat all over with a skewer or meat fork. Tip the berries over the pork, then crush them with your hands, squashing them all over the meat. Try not to squeeze them to a jam, leaving some whole or lightly crushed. Cover with clingfilm and leave in the fridge overnight.

The following day, set the oven at 160°C/Gas 3. Transfer the pork and berries to a roasting dish or casserole and roast for about an hour and forty minutes. Test the meat for doneness, then remove the meat from the dish to a warm, heatproof plate, cover with foil and let it rest. While the meat is cooking, peel and finely slice the onion and let it soften in the oil in a large, deep pan over a moderate heat. Stir in the flour, continue cooking for four or five minutes, then set aside.

Place the roasting dish, together with its berries and any juice, over a medium heat, then pour in the hot stock. With the heat at a moderate level, scrape at the dish with a wooden spatula, dissolving any crusted sediment from the meat into the liquid. Set the onion pan over a medium heat, tip in the berries and stock, then bring to the boil, stirring regularly. Season with salt and pepper, then carve the resting meat and serve with the sauce.

I like to brown the crust of the pork by slipping the whole joint, fat side up, under the grill, just before I carve. Serves 4–5.

# A mysterious sauce

I wake, early as ever, but at my lowest ebb. The long summer days have been a torture to me, the fetid summer haze. The ugly light. The vicious colours. The fermenting air. I long for crisp autumn and winter dawns, the air once again pure and icy, the light clean and Nordic.

Once out of bed, my mood changes. There are yet more signs of a shift in the season, a hint that autumn is well and truly here. The chestnut trees in the lane outside are changing to a mottled gold, the dahlias are out and the greengrocer has plums, baskets of Victorias and a wicker box of greengages.

Yes, there are more interesting plums than the Victoria, sweeter, thinner-skinned and more Sauternes-like. But Vics are good all-rounders, providing rivers of sweet juice. They make a serviceable jam. There are few finer ways to start a winter's day than with frost, and sourdough toast with plum jam. And anyway, if you let a Victoria soften to the point of translucence, it will have something of a honeyed sweetness and is good enough to eat as a dessert fruit.

Today is a summer's day lived whilst thinking of a winter night, a day for making good things for later in the year. Jam of course, jolly pots of jewel-hued fig and plum, but this year something different too. I have always loved the Chinese plum sauce that comes with crisp-skinned duck and soft, warm pancakes. It has something of the night about it. Mysterious, dark, intriguing. You imagine the recipe to be secret, written in Chinese characters on browning parchment, the result of centuries of kitchen alchemy.

Truth is, plum sauce is simply plums and sugar, simmered with aromatics then darkened with soy and dark brown sugar. As mine bubbles on the hob, the scent of star anise climbs the polished wooden stairs, an ancient smell, like that of an old apothecary. A glossy linctus

for roast duck, for pork, for a ploughman's lunch. A jagged shard of crackling dipped into a bowl of plum sauce is a magical thing indeed. Happiness is restored.

## Chinese plum sauce

Bottled and refrigerated, this sweet-sharp sauce is one for duck pancakes, but also for spreading on a roast chicken sandwich, or serving as an accompaniment for roast pork.

plums – 800g
red wine vinegar – 400ml
dried chilli flakes –
  1 teaspoon
star anise – 4
Szechuan peppercorns –
  1 teaspoon

garlic – 4 large cloves
ginger – a thumb-sized knob
salt – 1 teaspoon
dark soy sauce – 80ml
soft brown sugar – 125g

Wipe, halve and stone the plums and put them into a wide, deep saucepan. Pour in the red wine vinegar, and add the dried chilli flakes, the star anise and the Szechuan peppercorns.

Peel and slice the garlic and add to the plums. Peel the ginger, slice it into thick coins and add it to the plums, together with the salt, then place over a moderate flame and bring to the boil. Lower the heat so the mixture simmers gently and leave for about forty minutes, stirring occasionally, till the plums are soft.

Place a large sieve over a bowl or clean saucepan, pour the plums and their liquid into it, then push as much as you can through the sieve. Return the mixture to the stove, add the soy sauce and the sugar and simmer, with the occasional stir, until the sugar has dissolved. Simmer for five minutes, taking care that the mixture doesn't burn. It should be very dark and glossy.

Taste the sauce – it should be sour, sweet and salty and a little more fruity than the commercial variety. Pour through a funnel into a sterilised bottle and store in the fridge. Makes enough for 2 medium bottles.

# A jam of figs and plums

## August 23

I like my jams softly set. You know that. A slow ooze rather than a wobble. The downside is a preserve that doesn't stay on your toast or stay put in a sponge cake. The upside is a conserve of softly glistening joy, a pool of jam whose texture is poised between quiver and trickle.

The texture of jam depends on the ratio of fruit to sugar and the time for which they are boiled, but just as crucially on the level of pectin present in the fruit. High pectin fruits are crab apples, quinces and gooseberries. Low pectin, and those that are a bugger to set, are cherries, apricots, raspberries and strawberries.

This morning I make a jam whose texture is almost soft enough to eat from a spoon, like the spoon-sweets of the Mediterranean. Left overnight, it sets more firmly, but not so much that it would be good in jam tarts or as the filling in a Victoria sponge. If sponge it must be, then I would serve a little pot of the ruby-coloured preserve on the side (as you might for scones), for the recipient to dip their cake in as they eat.

If it is a firmer set you are after, then take the boiling fruit and sugar right up to 105°C on a sugar thermometer and check its progress by dropping a teaspoon of the hot jam on to a fridge-cold saucer. If the surface of the jam wrinkles after a minute or two, you will have what jam bores call 'a good set'. Which, in my book, means a jam too solid.

**Afternote**. My plum jam glows like a box of jewels, the fruit on the point of dissolve yet very obviously plum. The real joy for me lies in the figs, which have kept their shape, but fall effortlessly to purée as I spread them on my breakfast toast. A jam that shines in the morning light, full of the essence of the fruit, that first breath of autumn.

# Soft-set plum and fig jam

plums – 1kg          figs – 400g
water – 300ml        granulated sugar – 1kg

Wash the plums, removing any leaves and stalks as you go. Halve each plum and remove the stones, reserving four. Tip the plums into a wide, deep pan – stainless steel, enamelled cast-iron or copper – and add the water and reserved stones. Bring to the boil, then turn the heat down so the fruit simmers gently and continue cooking for about twenty-five minutes, till the fruit is thoroughly soft.

Slice the figs in half. Tip the sugar into the plums and bring to the boil, then add the halved figs, letting the fruit bubble for about ten minutes until it reaches 105°C on a kitchen thermometer (there is often a jam-setting point marked on these).

Test the jam for setting. An easy way to do this is to pour a teaspoon of the syrup on to a chilled saucer, leave for a minute, then tip the saucer back and forth to see if the jam has set. If a skin has formed and the jam barely moves, it is ready. If the jam is still liquid, continue cooking and retest after five minutes.

Ladle the jam, still hot, into sterilised jars, then tightly seal and allow to cool. Makes 4 medium jars.

# Smoke without fire

In autumn, I like the idea of slices or strips of sausage on my pizza. Not breakfast sausage, which somehow feels plain wrong, unless of course you are the sort of person who eats pizza for breakfast. No judgement. Thickly sliced salami or maybe slices of chorizo are exceptionally good. Better I think is the sausage I used this week, a chubby salsiccia, spiced with black pepper, fennel and chilli, which you can often pick up at Italian delicatessens.

## Smoked mozzarella and salsiccia pizza

You can use fresh mozzarella if you can't find smoked, but I like the effect the smoked cheese brings to the crisp dough. If the spicy Italian sausages evade you, use a herby sausage instead.

rosemary – 8 sprigs
thyme – about 20 sprigs
olive oil – 3 tablespoons
half the dough on page 68
(250g)

*For the top:*
mushrooms – 150g
olive oil
smoked mozzarella (scamorza)
– 300g
Italian salsiccia sausage – 200g

Get the oven hot and if you have a pizza stone, place it in the oven. I suggest 230°C/Gas 8. Strip the leaves from the rosemary and thyme. Pour the olive oil into a blender or food processor, add the rosemary and thyme leaves and process till the herbs are finely chopped. Keep a little of the herb oil back, then knead the remainder into the dough, making sure it goes in evenly. Return the dough to the mixing bowl, cover with clingfilm and set aside in a warm place to prove once more.

While the dough is proving, slice or quarter the mushrooms depending on their size, then cook them in a little oil in a shallow pan, for eight to ten minutes till they are golden brown.

After half an hour or so, roll the dough into two large discs, the exact size depending on how thin you like your crust. Place them on a baking sheet. Slice the smoked mozzarella and divide it between the two pizzas, leaving a gap around the edges. Add the mushrooms, then the sausage, torn into small pieces, tucking it amongst the mushrooms and cheese. Trickle a little of the reserved herb oil over the top.

Bake the pizza for fifteen minutes or so, till the sausage is golden, the cheese melted and the base and edges crisp. Eat immediately. Makes 2.

# Little parcels of mushrooms and garlic

## August 27

Mushrooms, garlic, butter and thyme. I can hardly think of a better double date. Even more satisfying, I think, is when there is some sort of crust involved to soak up the mushroomy, garlicky butter. Toast will do as long as it is thick enough, or you could add a lid of fresh, white breadcrumbs.

I take the pastry route. Shortcrust, rolled thicker than is the habit, and used to form a pasty around the mushrooms and aromatics. I use a particularly rich shortcrust so that it crumbles as you break the pasties open. Pastry soaked in garlic butter being one of the world's better ideas.

## Mushroom and garlic pasties

If you prefer, make these with puff pastry. You will need a 375g sheet, and expect to have a little left over.

*For the pastry:*
plain flour – 175g, plus extra
  for rolling
baking powder – half a teaspoon
fine salt – half a teaspoon
butter, cold, cut into small
  cubes – 100g
an egg yolk

milk – a little
a beaten egg

*For the mushroom filling:*
assorted mushrooms – 250g
thyme – 4 sprigs
butter – 50g
garlic – a single clove

Put the flour, baking powder and salt into a mixing bowl, add the butter, cut into small pieces, and rub into the flour till it resembles coarse

343

breadcrumbs. Mix in the egg yolk and enough milk to make a soft but rollable dough. Pat into a ball and chill in the fridge for thirty minutes.

Cut the mushrooms into halves and quarters depending on their size. Strip the thyme leaves from their stalks – you need a couple of teaspoonfuls. Melt the butter in a shallow pan, crush the clove of garlic flat, then add to the butter (you want the merest whiff of garlic). Add the mushrooms with the thyme and let them cook for five minutes or so, till golden. Ideally, they will be a little sticky on their cut sides. Salt and pepper them and set aside.

On a generously floured board, roll the dough out to 1cm thick. Fold it in by thirds, then roll and fold again. Chill for a further thirty minutes. Roll the dough into a square measuring roughly 24cm, then cut that into four equal squares. Set the oven at 200°C/Gas 6.

Divide the mushrooms between the squares of pastry, piling them in the centre, then brush a little beaten egg around the edges. Bring the opposite corners of the squares together and seal loosely along the edges. It is good to do this loosely, so the seals break here and there to reveal the mushrooms within. Transfer to a parchment-lined baking sheet. Brush the outside of the pastry with beaten egg, and bake for about forty minutes, till golden. Allow to cool a little before eating. Makes 4.

# SEPTEMBER

## Using up the herbs

### September 2

The fine, delicate leaves of the tender herbs – coriander, basil, dill and mint – are often used to lend a fresh, green, vibrant edge to a dish. Added near the end of the cooking time you get every drop of their essence, an invigorating, energising hit. But what about the stems?

The stems of fresh green herbs, the fragile ones that are just as suited to a salad as they are to the cooking pot, can hold almost as much flavour as their leaves and fronds. Any of these soft-stemmed herbs can be processed or pounded to a paste for pesto or a herb or spice mix. Not so parsley, thyme or oregano, whose tough stems are better in the stock pot, or rosemary, which would be rather like chewing your way, goat-like, through a gorse bush.

I make a coriander paste, fresh, lively and green as a spring lawn, by processing the leaves and thinnest stems with toasted cashews, basil stems and leaves and a generous splash of lime juice.

The brilliant jade herb paste will keep for a day or two in the fridge, its surface covered with a film of olive or groundnut oil, but is brighter tasting when used as soon as it is made. You could make the paste by hand if your wrists are up to it, pounding the nuts and leaves using a pestle and mortar. A food processor does the job in seconds.

Tonight, several heaped spoonfuls of the paste find their way into a straightforward lamb and coconut milk curry. Warm and sweet with coconut, illuminated by coriander, lime and basil, this is a dish we couldn't stop eating. Spoons were needed, as the sauce is unthickened, and we served it with warm Indian-style flatbreads.

# Coconut and coriander lamb

A mild and creamy lamb casserole given a heady green freshness with a coriander herb paste. Aromatic rather than hot.

a large onion
garlic – 3 or 4 cloves
olive or groundnut oil
lamb shoulder or leg, cubed
 – 500g
coconut milk – 500ml

*For the herb paste:*
cashews – 80g
a bunch of coriander – 50g
basil – 50g
lime juice – 5 tablespoons
 (2 limes)

Peel and roughly chop the onion and garlic. Pour two tablespoons of oil into a deep, heavy-based pan, add the onions and garlic and let them cook, over a moderate to high heat, for fifteen minutes or so, till soft and pale. They should not colour beyond a pale honey tone.

Whilst the onions are cooking, make the spice paste. Put the cashews into a dry, shallow pan and toast till golden. Tip them into the bowl of a food processor, add the coriander leaves and stalks, the basil and the lime juice, and process to a rough paste, then set aside.

Remove the onions and garlic from the pan and set aside. Return the pan to the heat, add a further tablespoon of oil, then add some of the lamb, without crowding the pan, and brown lightly and evenly on all sides. Remove the pieces as they brown and add them to the onions. Continue with the remaining lamb.

When the last of the meat is browned, add the coconut milk and let it heat through, scraping at any tasty, crusty bits on the surface of the pan and stirring them into the coconut milk. Return all the meat and onion to the pan, then leave to simmer for a good ten minutes, seasoning with salt and pepper as you wish.

Stir in three heaped tablespoons of the spice mix and continue to simmer, gently, for a further ten minutes. Serve, with warm flatbread or rice as you wish. For 3.

# Time on my floury hands

I have eaten an apple virtually every day of my life. A tiny, white- and rose-fleshed Discovery for an autumn breakfast; a lazy, anonymous apple eaten as I vacuum; a Cox in October still bright and sharp, all crunch and foaming juice; a rare Ribston Pippin straight from the tree.

I like cooking with the sweeter varieties, using the oversized 'cooking' apples only for the traditional baked apple, whose wide shoulders and sharp buttery froth rises to the occasion. The sweeter the apple the more it seems to keep its shape as it cooks, useful in a neatly laid open tart, and good for apple fool too.

I'm baking, not bread, but a focaccia with rosemary and goat's cheese. Some leftover dough allows for some play. I open the fridge and gaze blankly, uninspired by fennel salami and Parmesan, black grapes and Japanese pickles. I'm sure olive paste would make a splendid addition, but doubt the pickled herrings would do the olive oil dough many favours.

I have baked a couple of sweet focaccia before, one of blackberry and another of dark, bloom-freckled grapes. Both were good (they can be found in *Tender II*), the fruit being dotted through the dough, the juice bleeding into the crumb of the loaf.

What results from a little time on my hands is an apple focaccia made with the Cox's left in the fridge, a soft-textured bread sticky with maple syrup and freckled with salt flakes. I knead a handful of shelled pecans through the dough, a toothsome crunch amidst the soft apple and smoky syrup. Something to be eaten warm.

# Apple and maple syrup focaccia

strong white bread flour – 450g
easy bake dried yeast – 1 sachet
  (7g, 2 teaspoons)
sea salt – 1 teaspoon
olive oil – 1 tablespoon, and
  a little more for trickling
caster sugar – 1 tablespoon

warm water – 350ml

*For the topping:*
large, sweet apples such as
  Cox's – 3
shelled pecans – 150g
maple syrup – 150ml

Put the flour and yeast into a large bowl and add the sea salt, finely crushed, then the oil, sugar and warm water. Mix thoroughly, then turn the dough out on to a well-floured board and knead lightly for five minutes or so. Nothing good will come from too heavy a knead.

As soon as the dough feels elastic, put it into a lightly floured bowl, cover with a cloth or clingfilm, then leave it in a warm place to rise. Once it has doubled in size – about an hour or so – gently press it down with your fist, knocking some of the air out. Chop and core the apples, peeling them if you wish, then knead them into the dough, with the pecans, leaving a few for the top. Put the dough into a shallow 28cm tin. Set the oven at 220°C/Gas 7.

Cover the dough once more and return it to a warm place to rise. Once it has expanded to almost twice its size, trickle a little olive oil over it (you won't need much), scatter over the reserved pecans and bake for thirty-five to forty minutes, till well risen, golden brown and crisp on top. It should feel springy when pressed. Spoon the maple syrup over the top and let it soak in. Leave to cool a little before tearing apart. Serves 6–8.

# Dumpling squash

## September 5

I buy four dumpling squash today, each one round as a cricket ball, dragged and stippled like 1980s wallpaper. Chubby little things they are, ripe and begging to be stuffed. There are two distinct types of squash: the hard-skinned, orange-fleshed 'keepers' that will last you through the winter, and the green varieties like marrows and these plump dumplings that have a thin, soft skin and won't last more than a week or two.

The tomatoes are so good at the moment you can smell them the moment you walk into the greengrocer's. The result, I imagine, of late summer sun. Tomatoes that are sweet and sour at the same time bring a piercing fruitiness to squash of all sorts, but particularly the green-fleshed summer varieties that would otherwise be like eating warm, wet cucumber.

I hollow out the squash, chuck the seeds and woolly core on the compost and fill the deep cavities with tomatoes, a fat pinch of dried chilli and some basil leaves as warm and heady as black pepper. To introduce some substance – this is dinner, after all – I tip in a can of butter or judion beans. The smell, as they bake, is the essence of late summer. Rich and scorched, that faint backnote of warm summer herbs. I put a ridiculous amount of salt on them, which, with the sweet sharpness of the tomato, stings my lips like sunburn.

# Stuffed summer squash with tomatoes and butter beans

Light, fresh-tasting yet deeply satisfying.

dumpling or other small
squash – 4
small or cherry tomatoes
– 350g
olive oil – 3 tablespoons,
and a little more

a dried chilli
butter or judion beans –
a 400g tin or jar
large basil leaves – 10–12

Set the oven at 180°C/Gas 4. Slice a lid from each dumpling squash and set aside. Using a teaspoon, scoop out and discard the seeds and fibres from the centre of each squash.

Chop the tomatoes, put them into a shallow pan and let them soften with the olive oil over a moderate heat. When they are soft enough to crush with a fork, add the chilli, finely crumbled (remove the seeds for a less spicy filling), the drained and rinsed butter or judion beans and a little salt and black pepper. Mix well, then add the whole basil leaves.

Fill each hollowed-out squash with the tomato and bean stuffing, packing them into a baking dish or roasting tin. Trickle a little oil over and bake for about an hour, till the squash is soft. Serves 4.

# Blackberry way

## September 8

The sides of the lane that lead to the location house, where we are filming a new series, is home to sloe bushes and brambles. There are cobnuts too, raided already by the squirrels. I return with enough blackberries to send purple ripples through my breakfast stewed apples, to colour the Bramleys for the mother of all pies and to wolf straight from the bowl into which they were picked.

I decide to use the remaining handful in shortbread, a crumbly, hazelnut version that smells of autumn. I have never bumped the ratio of butter to flour this high before, and together with the ground, roasted hazelnuts, it produces a shortbread worthy of the name. It is indeed the shortest I have ever made and the tender, crumbling biscuit requires more than a little care to lift it from the tin.

In theory, the more butter you add, the softer and more crumbly your shortbread will be. But then comes the point of no return, when the ratio is unbalanced and the dough becomes unworkable. It works the other way of course – when you add too much flour to butter you get a dry, hard biscuit and no fun.

This seemed like a chance to push the envelope, not only adding enough butter to increase the shortbread's tenderness but intro- ducing ground nuts too, which add both flavour and moistness. The trick is to find the balance; a recipe that holds together but remains so fragile you can barely lift it to your mouth without it collapsing. The blackberries bring their own autumnal joy.

# Blackberry hazelnut shortbread

shelled hazelnuts – 75g  
butter – 125g  
icing sugar – 50g  
salt – a pinch  
plain flour – 75g  

vanilla extract – a few drops  
the zest of a lemon  
blackberries – 125g  
a handful of whole, toasted  
hazelnuts, to finish  

You will need a shallow, square 20cm cake tin, its base lined with baking paper.

Set the oven at 160°C/Gas 3. Toast the hazelnuts in a dry frying pan, almost constantly moving them around the pan so they colour easily. (I would toast a handful for decoration at this point too, then remove them and set aside for later.) When the rest are an even colour, grind them finely in a food processor.

Using a food mixer fitted with a flat paddle attachment, mix the butter and icing sugar till soft and fluffy. Sift in the salt and flour, then stir in the ground hazelnuts, a few drops of vanilla extract and the lemon zest.

Bring the dough into a ball, then press into the cake tin. Dot the top with the blackberries, pushing them down a little into the dough. Finally, scatter the surface with the whole toasted hazelnuts and bake for about thirty minutes. Cool slightly before lifting out and breaking into uneven pieces. Enough for 8.

# Giving dal a kick

Dear dal, how I love thee. Aromatic, ochre-hued, velvet-textured slush that you are. I love the sound of you. The gentle tattle-tattle of the lid as you putter away on the hob. Your scent, the way you make the kitchen smell of home. I love the way you are neither soup nor stew, sauce nor purée. Indeed you hold a texture all to yourself, soft, soothing, silken. A little nubbly sometimes.

You heal more rapidly than arnica. You put the world to rights even before you reach the table. Earthy and aromatic, as you simmer; the air steamy with cumin, garlic, black pepper. I don't need to dilute you with rice as others do. To me you are enough, just as you are.

There is little that could be more nourishing, satisfying or frugal than a bowl of yellow split peas, boiled till soft enough to crush between the fingers, then stirred into slow-cooked onions and garlic and spiked with paprika and turmeric. Of all the dried beans and lentils from which it can be made, the yellow split pea is the one that works best for me, breaking down just enough to give a texture poised between soup and mash. Others work too.

Good as the pure, classic method is, today I fire things up, adding both freshness and a teasing punch. This time, I give the earthy note of the spiced split peas a dash of homemade coriander and basil paste. The result is spoon after spoon of warming, golden dal and the occasional flash of brilliant green herb paste. Food to comfort and hug, yes, but also to dazzle. Love indeed.

# Split peas and coriander

yellow split peas – 250g
a medium-sized onion
garlic – 4 cloves
groundnut or vegetable oil –
  2 tablespoons
ground turmeric – 1 teaspoon
paprika – 1 teaspoon
ripe tomatoes – 500g

coriander – a handful

*For the herb paste:*
cashews – 80g
coriander – 50g
basil – 50g
lime juice – 5 tablespoons
(2 limes)

Rinse the split peas, then cook them in deep, unsalted boiling water for about thirty minutes, till soft and tender.

Make the herb paste. Put the cashews into a dry, shallow pan and toast till golden. Tip them into the bowl of a food processor, add the coriander leaves and stalks, the basil and the lime juice and process to a rough paste, then set aside.

While the split peas cook, peel and roughly chop the onion and peel and finely slice the garlic. Warm a couple of tablespoons of oil in a medium-sized saucepan, then add the onion and garlic and cook over a moderate heat till deep gold and translucent.

Stir the ground turmeric and paprika into the onions, then roughly chop the tomatoes and stir them in. Let the mixture cook, over a low to moderate heat, for about fifteen minutes, then stir in the cooked split peas and five heaped tablespoons of the herb paste. Stir in the coriander leaves. Serves 4 generously. The spare paste will keep in the fridge, covered, for a day or two.

# A Thai curry to make your heart pound

## September 19

I generally mix my own spice pastes, be they Thai, Indian or Korean. I like the vibrancy that comes from freshly blitzed lemon grass, ginger, garlic and chillies. I successfully introduce salty, sour notes using a spoonful of seriously aromatic shrimp paste and some Thai fish sauce. My paste also gets the merest pinch of sugar, just as it would in Thailand. Something I find British cooks are generally reluctant to do. They will happily eat a cupcake smothered in buttercream, but ask them to add a pinch of sugar to a curry and they will run screaming.

Today, as part of an episode of *Eating Together*, the series we are currently filming for the BBC, I visit a well-established Thai food shop in a smart part of West London. It's generously stocked with authentic Thai produce and I don't know why I haven't been there before, even though I have passed it a hundred times. Once the cameras are turned off, I take advantage of being there and do some shopping, stocking up on my favourite brands of fish sauce and chilli paste. Out of curiosity, I buy three sachets of ready-mixed red spice paste.

Back at home, the prettily packaged paste, a stiff, brick-red purée, is darker and finer than the one I usually make, and, once in the gently sizzling oil, I can smell that it is hotter too. My eyes sting as the steam rises. The sourness that is so much part of the red curries of Thailand is more pronounced than it is in my homemade version, and somehow more reminiscent of the curries I have eaten at midnight in Chiang Mai's night market.

During this evening's cooking I decide to have a go at a red curry with some duck legs I found at the butcher's. I like the effect that the sweet coconut milk and hot spice paste have on the dark, sweet meat of the duck and its fat. The meat takes the extra hot spices well and the richness of the meat and its fat means that you don't need a large amount to satisfy, one leg being quite enough for each person.

Rather than adding noodles to this, I introduce thin-stemmed broccoli, and no thickening, keeping the duck in a pool of rust-coloured, tongue-tingling broth for which we all need soup spoons.

## A Thai-inspired duck curry soup

duck legs – 2 whole
groundnut oil – 1 tablespoon
Thai red curry paste –
  2 tablespoons
curry powder – 2 teaspoons
chicken stock – 250ml
coconut milk – 400ml

Thai or Vietnamese fish sauce
  – 2 teaspoons or more
lime juice – 1 tablespoon,
  to taste
palm or caster sugar –
  a good pinch
tenderstem broccoli – 200g

Cut each of the duck legs into two, to give four pieces, then season with a little black pepper and some salt. Warm the oil in a deep casserole, then add the duck pieces and let them brown to a pale honey colour on all sides.

Add the Thai curry paste and stir over a low to medium heat for a couple of minutes. Add the curry powder, then the chicken stock and coconut milk, and bring to the boil. As soon as it comes to the boil, lower the heat so the duck simmers gently, cover with a lid and leave for about twenty minutes, until the duck is tender.

Stir in the fish sauce, the lime juice and palm sugar to taste. Trim the broccoli and cut into short lengths. Add to the pan and continue simmering for four or five minutes, till the broccoli is tender but still retains a little crispness in the stalks. Serves 2.

# The ice cream of angels

## September 22

Dining at Lyle's restaurant in Shoreditch we consume a succession of intimate delights: cod's tongues, duck's hearts, pig's cheeks. Eating out nowadays one learns to tick these things off, like conducting a delicious autopsy. We finish with an ice cream made from fig leaves. The flavour, as if you snapped a fig leaf from its branch and caught and froze the milky sap, is soft, green and powdery. If heaven tastes of anything it is probably this.

My fig leaves are currently turning and not, I suspect, supple enough to make an ice with. But there are figs aplenty, dusky with bloom, flesh the colour of dried blood. I make them into an ice cream the hue of a Peace rose and scatter it with petals.

## Fig ice cream

| | |
|---|---|
| figs – 10 | vanilla custard – 200ml |
| caster sugar – 150g | double cream – 150ml |
| water – 300ml | |

Skin the figs and chop the flesh. Put the sugar into a saucepan with the water and bring to the boil. As soon as the sugar has dissolved, add the figs, lower the heat, and leave to simmer gently for fifteen to twenty minutes, till the fruit is translucent and jammy. Set aside and allow to cool.

Stir half the cooled fruit mixture into the custard. Gently whip the cream till it will sit in soft folds, then stir into the custard. Churn the mixture in an ice cream machine till smooth and thick. Fold in the remaining fruit mixture. Transfer to a freezer box, cover and freeze. Serve, scattered, if you wish, with petals. Serves 6.

# Grilled langoustines at the garden table

## September 25

Even now, simple things take me by surprise. Langoustines, split in half and grilled, their shells glistening, their juices mixed with nothing more than butter and the chopped needles of a few sprigs of rosemary, did that today. Eaten outside, at the garden table, a little feast of shells to crack and suck, snowy flesh to chew, buttery, salty fingers to lick and the smoky, resinous scent of warm rosemary.

## Langoustine with herb butter

Make sure everyone gets plenty of warm, herb-infused melted butter and sea salt.

| | |
|---|---|
| langoustines – 12 | rosemary – 5 sprigs |
| butter – 200g | thyme – 8 sprigs |

Split the langoustines in half from head to tail and place them, cut side up, in a shallow roasting tin. Season them generously with salt, pepper and a little melted butter. Place under a hot overhead grill and cook for seven to eight minutes, till just cooked. The flesh should be opaque and juicy.

Remove the langoustines from the roasting tin and place on a large serving plate. Place the tin over a low to moderate heat, add the butter, the sprigs of rosemary and thyme and allow to sizzle for a couple of minutes, till the butter has taken in the flavour of the herbs. Pour some of the butter and herbs over the langoustines, then pour the rest into a small jug and pass round at the table. Serves 6.

# The heady warmth of garam masala

## September 28

The idea that something is always the same – predictable, reliable, guaranteed – is often of less interest to me than that which brings with it the possibility of discovery or maybe even a little excitement. And that includes recipes.

I am reminded of this every time I pick up a packet of garam masala, the subtle, earthy spice mix whose heat and pungency will vary according to the whim of the person or company that mixed it. I have bought a blend in Kerala, sold in a twist of blue paper, that was softly heady with cloves and pepper; a slightly less fragrant commercial mix in cellophane; and hotter, more chilli-infused mixtures in resealable foil here in Britain. Each will bring its own qualities to our supper.

The exact recipe varies according to cook, location and what it will be used for but the essence of garam masala – literally hot mixture – is generally one of warmth rather than heat. Yes, there is a pungency to most brands, but rarely more than a hint of chilli. Cardamom, black and white peppercorns, cumin, nutmeg and cinnamon are the most commonly met spices in a commercial pack, but it is not unusual to find star anise, fennel seeds, turmeric and mustard too. Part of the charm lies in the looseness of the recipe, and the fact it will vary from region to region. Pedants take note. In my experience, the further north you venture, the hotter spice mixes seem to be.

I use a bought mix rather than make my own, even though the idea of a rainy afternoon spent in the company of spice jars and a grinder appeals. Sometimes I like to bow to the expertise of others who do something day in day out, other times I think I can do my own version just as well. For now, I'm happy to let others do it.

The most common way of using garam masala is to add it as a base note with the onions at the start of cooking and sometimes again at the end, so the finer and most fragrant notes are not lost. Adding it early on in the recipe lays down a deep, almost smoky backnote of pepper and cumin. A last-minute addition will leave the more ephemeral notes of cardamom, cinnamon and clove intact.

Stirring a teaspoon or so of garam masala into a pan of cooked, buttered rice on the hob imbues it with a homely, fragrant headnote. I cook white or brown basmati till the water has evaporated, drop in a thick slice of butter and a teaspoon of garam masala and stir over a low heat until the grains are glistening. The smell is as comforting as the flavour.

## Chicken, tomatoes, garam masala

I used fat, free-range thighs for this, but drumsticks would work nicely, as I hope would joints of rabbit too.

chicken thighs – 6 large
garlic – 4 cloves
ginger – 50g
a small to medium-sized onion
red chillies – 2 small hot ones
groundnut or vegetable oil –
  3 tablespoons
brown mustard seeds –
  1 teaspoon
cumin seeds – 1 teaspoon

ground turmeric –
  half a teaspoon
ground coriander –
  1 tablespoon, lightly heaped
tomatoes – 5 medium-sized
  (600g)
water – 100ml, from the kettle
garam masala – 3 teaspoons
the juice of a lime
coriander – a small bunch

Season the chicken with salt and ground pepper and set aside. Peel the garlic and crush to a coarse paste. Peel the ginger, grate or crush finely, then mix with the crushed garlic. Peel and finely chop the onion. Deseed and finely chop the chillies.

Warm the oil in a wok or non-stick frying pan, add the seasoned chicken and fry on both sides till the skin is pale gold. Lower the heat, cover with a lid and leave the chicken to cook for ten to twelve minutes, until it is almost cooked through. To check its progress, pierce the thickest part of the meat with a metal skewer – if the juices that run out are clear, then the meat is ready. If there is any sign of blood, continue cooking for a few more minutes. When the chicken is ready, remove it to a plate with a draining spoon and discard the oil, but do not wash the pan. (There is much flavour stuck to the bottom.)

Return the pan to the heat and add the crushed garlic and ginger paste, stirring to prevent the mixture burning and to mix in the tasty pan-stickings from the chicken. Add the mustard and cumin seeds, the finely chopped chillies, turmeric and coriander and fry briefly, then add the chopped onion and leave to cook over a moderate heat, with the occasional stir, for five minutes or so.

Finely chop the tomatoes, losing as little of their juice as you can. (I find cutting them one at a time, putting each one into the pan immediately it is cut, helps.) Add the chopped tomatoes to the pan, simmering over a moderate heat and stirring from time to time. Leave for five minutes before adding the water from the kettle, the garam masala and a little salt. Bring back to the boil, stir, and leave to simmer for a couple of minutes before returning the chicken to the pan. Simmer for five minutes or so, till the chicken is hot, then add the lime juice and chopped coriander. Serves 3.

# The luxury of steak, the comfort of broth

## September 29

A damp day. The garden, a mess of fallen, blackening leaves, over-flowing water butts and treacherous, slippery paths, continues to fill me with guilt. A day that calls for a clear broth, light but sustaining, deeply savoury, to be prepared with as little fuss as possible.

I could, given an hour or two, roast beef bones, onions and carrots in the oven, then tip them into my most capacious pot and simmer them with water to make a broth. I could clear it by constantly skimming and sieving. I could make something almost as beefy by soaking dried porcini in hot water. Instead I buy a ready-made beef broth from the butcher. He makes his own. I also like the instant gratification of the ready-made sachets in the supermarket. Much has to do with the time available, and today I need to feel better, quickly.

The skirt steak I am adding to the broth is the butcher's secret. So few seem to display it, and it is almost unheard of at the supermarkets. Skirt comes from the belly of the animal, sandwiched between the brisket at the front and the flank at the rear. A flat cut with a coarse grain, it often ends up in the mincer. A rather ignominious end, I always think, for a cut that is better flash fried and served with fried onions, or braised with beer, softened shallots and sliced field mushrooms.

The meat, with the deep spoonfuls of Madeira-coloured broth, are as much medicine as they are sustenance. A meal to restore, to heal and put you back on the road. Sadly, it does nothing for the guilt.

# Skirt steak, herbal broth

large shallots – 2
olive oil – 1 tablespoon
thyme – 6 small sprigs
sage leaves – 3
beef stock – 500ml
skirt steak – 400g

butter – 40g
parsley, chopped –
2 tablespoons
chives, chopped –
2 tablespoons

Peel and thinly slice the shallots and put them into a deep, wide pan with the oil and the leaves pulled from the sprigs of thyme. Stirring regularly, cook the shallots over a moderate heat till they are soft and palest gold. Add the shredded sage leaves, then pour in the stock and leave to simmer gently.

Lightly oil and season the steak. Warm a shallow, non-stick pan over a moderately high heat, add the steak and brown briefly on both sides. Add the butter to the pan, let it melt and start to fizz, then continue cooking the steak, constantly basting the meat with the butter, till it is cooked to your liking.

Remove the meat from the pan and let it rest, covered lightly with foil, in a warm place. Put the meat on a chopping board and slice it into finger-thick strips, then divide between two large soup bowls. Add the chopped chives and parsley to the broth, then ladle over the steak, spooning in the shallots as you go. Serves 2.

# A surprising whiff of orange blossom

## September 30

Buy a slice of candied orange peel, cut through its frosted coating and inhale. Sugar, yes, but also a faint whiff of orange blossom, of a sweet, ripe citrus. Compare that to the gravel-textured nubs sold as candied peel in plastic tubs that end their days lost in Christmas cakes, where no amount of sugar can hide their dry bitterness.

Wedges of citron, lemon and orange peel are tricky to track down. Upmarket food halls are a good hunting ground, as are Italian delicatessens at Christmas, where they sometimes hang from the ceiling wrapped in cellophane bags. You have to cut them yourself, but it is hardly what you might call a chore, and the scent on a winter's day is romantic, uplifting even.

Last week I came home with a huge slice of crystallised orange peel, glowing translucently in its crackly bag. It now seems too precious to tumble into a cake mix with currants and sultanas. There is a crispness to its sugar coating, like frost on a windowpane, and then a sticky softness to it under the knife, that demands it be celebrated rather than hidden.

I have served wedges, barely thicker than a pencil, on a saucer with tiny cups of Brazilian coffee; dipped pieces of it into dark chocolate and scattered it, in glistening crystals, over the top of a glossy iced chocolate cake. This afternoon, I use this sweetmeat, in tiny pieces, in friands. Charming, airy cakes for serving with bowls of green tea. You'll love these.

# Orange and chocolate friands

I use a whole piece of crystallised orange peel for this, and chop it finely. You can sometimes find it in Italian delicatessens at this time of year. If it proves evasive, you could use ordinary candied peel, but the effect won't be quite as moist and perfumed.

crystallised orange peel – 60g

dark chocolate – 60g

butter – 180g

plain flour – 50g

icing sugar – 180g

ground almonds – 100g

orange zest – 1 teaspoon

egg whites – 5

Set the oven at 200°C/Gas 6. Lightly butter twelve shallow bun tins.

Finely chop the crystallised orange peel and the chocolate and set aside. Put the butter into a small pan and melt over a moderate heat, then watch it carefully until it becomes a dark, nutty gold. Take great care not to let it burn. Leave it to cool a little.

Sieve the flour and icing sugar into a large mixing bowl, then add the ground almonds. Grate in the orange zest, then add the chocolate and crystallised orange peel. Beat the egg whites to a soft, moist and sloppy foam – they shouldn't be able to stand up.

Make a well in the centre of the dry ingredients and pour in the egg whites, together with the melted butter. Mix lightly but thoroughly, then pour into the buttered bun tins.

Bake for ten to fifteen minutes, then take out of the oven and leave to settle before carefully removing from the tins with a palette knife. Makes 12.

# Autumn
# eats

# Stir-fried marinated tofu

tofu, garlic, red chilli, chestnut mushrooms, sugar snap peas, pak choi, light soy sauce

Cut **350g of firm tofu** into large bite-sized cubes and put them into a mixing bowl. Finely chop **2 plump cloves of garlic** and stir them into **6 tablespoons of groundnut or vegetable oil**. Halve, seed and finely chop **a medium-hot red chilli**, add to the oil with the cubes of tofu and set aside for a good 30 minutes.

Slice or roughly chop **100g of chestnut mushrooms**. Pour the marinade into a hot wok, leaving the tofu behind, and let it sizzle, then fry the mushrooms until golden and tender. Add **150g of whole sugar snap peas**, then **200g of chopped pak choi**. Stir and fry for a few minutes, until the greens have wilted a little and the peas are crisp, then add **a splash of light soy sauce**, cook briefly, and tip on to two warm plates or into bowls.

Wipe the wok with kitchen paper, return it to the heat, and when it is hot add the cubes of tofu and any oil clinging to them. Fry for a couple of minutes, until golden on each side. Tip on top of the stir-fried vegetables and serve immediately. Enough for 2.

### &

Tofu has a habit of breaking up in a stir-fry, so cook the cubes separately at the end. It only takes a minute or two at most. As with all stir-frying, keep the pan as hot as possible and move the ingredients round quickly, so they do not burn. Wipe the wok rather than washing it. That way it will develop a good non-stick patina.

### &

I like to add a few shakes of sesame oil at the end. You could also add a tablespoon of fish sauce if you like a more piquant result. You could include a handful of fresh egg or rice noodles, or a shake of chilli sauce.

# Chermoula aubergine

coriander, preserved lemon, red chilli, green chilli,
cumin seeds, coriander seeds, ground ginger, paprika, cayenne,
ground saffron, lemons, olive oil, aubergines

Put **30g of coriander leaves and stems** into a blender or food processor. Slice **30g of preserved lemon** and add to the coriander together with **a red and a green chilli** (seeds removed if you are worried about the heat), **a tablespoon of cumin seeds, a teaspoon each of coriander seeds, ground ginger** and **paprika**, and **a pinch of cayenne and ground saffron**. Squeeze in the juice of **2 fresh lemons** and add **100ml of olive oil**, then process to a fairly smooth, loose paste.

Peel **2 medium-sized aubergines**, then cut deep slits into the flesh in four places, taking care not to slice right through. Place the aubergines in a sealable plastic food bag and pour over the marinade paste, turning the aubergines to cover the outside. Leave to marinate for at least an hour, two or three if you can, rolling the aubergines over in the marinade from time to time.

Heat the oven to 200°C/Gas 6. Tip the aubergines and their marinade into a shallow baking dish and cook in the oven for about 45 minutes. Baste the aubergines now and again until they become dark and soft. You may need to cover them with tin foil. Ideally, your aubergines should have a slight brown crust on the surface. Carefully lift on to plates and cut each one into thick slices, like a steak. Serves 2.

# Lamb steaks, creamed cannellini

spinach, chicken stock, tinned cannellini beans, lamb steaks,
garlic, double cream

Trim and wash **100g of spinach leaves**, then cook them in a lidded pan for a minute or two until they wilt. Drain them and squeeze gently, then put into a food processor or blender.

Warm **200ml of chicken stock** in a deep pan. Add **2 drained 400g tins of cannellini beans** and let them warm through over a moderate heat for 5 minutes. Then add them to the spinach in the blender, together with the stock, and process for a minute or so.

Season **two 250g lamb steaks**. Warm **a little butter and oil** in a shallow pan, add **3 peeled and lightly squashed garlic cloves**, then brown the lamb nicely on both sides. When the lamb is cooked to your liking, remove from the pan and keep warm under a piece of kitchen foil.

Add the spinach and bean purée to the pan, stir in **100ml of double cream or crème fraîche** and heat thoroughly. Check the seasoning and serve with the lamb. Enough for 2.

&

Resting the lamb for 5 minutes while you continue with the sauce gives a juicier result. Rinse the beans and discard the salty, starchy liquor. Avoid including the spinach stalks unless they are very fine, otherwise they will make the purée stringy.

&

This is very good when done with butter beans instead of cannellini and a small rump or rib-eye steak rather than lamb. I see no reason why you couldn't do it with a chicken breast if you wish. If you fancy something more herbal, include fresh tarragon leaves with the beans when you warm and purée them. A dab of Dijon mustard in the purée is a very good idea indeed.

# Quick fish chowder

onion, new potatoes, milk, bay leaves, salmon, cod,
smoked haddock, sweetcorn, spring onions, parsley

Peel and roughly chop **an onion**, put it into a large deep pan with
a little oil and fry till golden. Scrub **400g of new potatoes**, then
halve or quarter them depending on their size. Add them to the
onion then pour in **500ml of water** and **500ml of milk**. Bring to the
boil, with a coarse grinding of pepper and **a couple of bay leaves**.
Lower the heat so the liquid simmers and, when the potato is soft,
introduce **400g of mixed fish, such as salmon, cod and smoked
haddock**, cut into large cubes, and continue to cook on a low heat
for 10 minutes.

Slice **the kernels from a head of sweetcorn** and drop them
into the pan. Roughly chop **2 spring onions** and **a small bunch of
parsley** and stir them into the soup carefully, without breaking up
the fish. Serve as soon as the corn is tender. Serves 2.

&

You could use one of the ready-prepared assortments of fish meant
for fish pie if it is more convenient. The soup is a calming, delicate
version, but sustaining enough to be a light main dish. It is important
not to stir the chowder too much as it cooks, which would result in
the fish breaking up.

&

I sometimes like to add a handful of mussels or clams to the soup
once the fish has almost reached tenderness. Finely sliced leeks can
work well instead of the onion. To give the soup a sweeter note, cook
the onion or leek in a little butter and oil until it is soft, before adding
the milk. You could stir a little tarragon or dill, finely chopped, into
the soup near the end of the cooking time.

# Pork chops with mushrooms

pork chops, banana shallot, anchovy fillets,
button mushrooms, parsley

Lightly brown **a couple of pork chops** in **a little sizzling butter** in a shallow pan. When the fat is golden, remove the chops and set aside. Peel and very finely chop **a banana shallot**, then add it to the pork chop pan and let it soften in the butter and pork fat, without much colour. Finely chop **6 anchovy fillets** and add them to the shallot.

Quarter **200g of button mushrooms**, unless they are very small, in which case halve them. Add them to the pan and continue cooking, adding more butter if necessary, and cook until sticky and golden.

Roughly chop **a handful of parsley**, stir into the shallots and mushrooms, then return the chops to the pan and continue cooking until they are hot, juicy and tender. Serve the chops with the relish. Serves two as a main dish.

&

Once the chops are lightly browned on both sides, put them on a warm plate, covered with an upturned bowl to keep them warm.

&

Use lamb steaks. Sun-dried tomatoes, very finely chopped, can be added instead of the anchovy. Red onion works if you don't have shallots.

# Pappardelle with leeks

### leeks, butter, thyme, pappardelle, Gruyère

Cut **3 large leeks** in half lengthways and then in half again, and wash them thoroughly under cold running water. Melt **100g of butter** in a pan (this sounds like a lot, but the pasta soaks it up later), then add the leeks to the pan and let them stew slowly in the butter until they are soft and tender.

While they are stewing, remove the leaves from **10 sprigs of thyme** and add them to the leeks. Season lightly. Cook **250g of pappardelle** in generously salted, deep boiling water until al dente, then drain lightly and toss with the buttery leeks.

Scatter over **100g of Gruyère** slices, letting them melt in the warmth of the butter and leeks. Serves 2.

### &

Leeks like butter rather than oil, and a low heat in which to cook. To prevent them from becoming brown and bitter, place a piece of greaseproof paper over them as they cook. This will encourage them to cook in their own steam and will lessen the risk of them colouring.

### &

Any ribbon-shaped pasta will work here – especially the slimmer tagliatelle. The juice of half a lemon, added at the end of cooking, will add a fresh note. Swap the thyme for tarragon if you like aniseed, or use basil, which works surprisingly well with leeks. A few green olives, stoned and roughly chopped, are worth considering as an addition – especially if you have chosen to use the lemon juice.

# Lentils with couscous

small green lentils, couscous, stock, dried apricots, raisins, dill,
pine kernels, lemon, olive oil, walnut oil

Put 125g of small green lentils (such as Puy lentils) to cook in deep,
unsalted boiling water. As they come to the boil, lower the heat so
that they cook at an enthusiastic simmer for about 20 minutes. They
should be tender but still retain a bit of bite. Put 75g of couscous into
a bowl and pour over just enough stock to cover it. Set aside for a
good 10 minutes, until the stock has been fully absorbed.

Thinly slice 50g of dried apricots, then toss them into a bowl with
100g of raisins. Chop a handful of dill fronds and add them to the
apricots and raisins. Lightly toast 50g of pine kernels in a shallow
pan, then, as they turn golden brown, tip them out and roughly chop
them. Stir them into the apricots.

Make a simple dressing with 2 teaspoons of lemon juice, 2
tablespoons of olive oil, a dash of walnut oil and some salt and
pepper. Drain the lentils, mix them with the dressing, then add to
the couscous using a fork and toss lightly with the dried fruit mixture.
Serve warm or at room temperature. Enough for 4.

&

Small, dark lentils need constant checking during cooking. They are
probably best with a little bite left in them. I find they are generally
perfect after about 15–18 minutes, but the exact time will vary
according to the age of the lentils.

&

For a more substantial version, use brown basmati rice instead of the
couscous. Change the raisins for dried cherries or cranberries and
swap the apricots for dried figs. A little pomegranate molasses can be
added to the dressing in place of the lemon juice. You could leave the
walnut oil out altogether, or use hazelnut oil if you prefer.

# Black pudding, cabbage and mustard

red cabbage, white cabbage, red wine vinegar, black pudding,
double cream, grain mustard

Coarsely shred **300g of red cabbage** and **200g of crisp white cabbage**. Warm **4 tablespoons of olive or groundnut oil** in a deep pan, then add the shredded cabbage and let it sizzle briefly. Lower the heat, cover with a lid and cook for about 7–8 minutes, occasionally shaking the pan, until the cabbage is approaching tenderness.

Pour in **2 tablespoons of red wine vinegar**, let it sizzle and spit, then cover with a lid and continue cooking for 2 minutes. Crumble **250g of black pudding** into large pieces and add it to the cabbage, letting it fry until lightly crisp on the outside. Season with salt and black pepper, then divide between two plates.

Pour **200ml of double cream** into the pan and warm until it starts to bubble, stirring to loosen any crusty bits of black pudding that may be left on the base of the pan. Season with a little salt and black pepper and **1 tablespoon of grain mustard**, then pour over the cabbage and black pudding. Enough for 2.

### &

Once the cabbage goes into the pot, stir it regularly so that it wilts rather than crisps. Cut the black pudding into thick chunks and break it into fat pieces. It will crumble naturally as it cooks. As you add the cream, scrape gently at the bits of black pudding stuck to the pan, and stir them into the sauce.

### &

Swap the black pudding for a plump, herby breakfast sausage. Ditch the cream if you prefer something less rich. Add juniper berries, lightly crushed, or a little grated nutmeg to the cabbage as it cooks. Introduce some diced apple, adding it once the cabbage has started to soften.

# Lamb and bacon stew

cubed lamb shoulder, onion, smoked bacon, new potatoes,
rosemary, chicken stock, soured cream

Season **300g of cubed lamb shoulder or leg** with a little salt and black pepper, then brown lightly on all sides in **2 tablespoons of olive oil**. While the lamb is colouring, peel and roughly chop **a large onion**. Finely dice **6 rashers of smoked bacon**. Remove the lamb from the pan and transfer it to a small bowl, then add the onion and the bacon, cut into small pieces, to the pan and cook for 10 minutes or so, till golden.

Halve **250g of new potatoes**, add them to the onion and bacon with **3 sprigs of rosemary** and **500ml of chicken stock**, then return the lamb to the pan. Let everything simmer gently for 30 minutes, or until the lamb and the potatoes are tender, then check the seasoning. Spoon in **150ml of soured cream**, stir and leave to warm through, without boiling. Serves 2–3.

&

The cooking time is quite short, so use a tender cut of lamb for this, such as fillet, shoulder or leg. Brown the lamb thoroughly so that all sides are well coloured. The residue that is left in the pan after browning the meat forms an essential part of the sauce. It is probably best not to let the sauce boil after you have added the soured cream.

&

Introduce tarragon leaves, roughly chopped, or chervil fronds to the sauce at the same time as you add the stock. Add blanched green beans, cut into short lengths, fresh peas, or in-season, cooked and skinned broad beans to the lamb 15 minutes before the meat is ready. Use diced chicken instead of lamb if you wish.

# Baked potatoes with aubergine and cream

baking potatoes, aubergines, coriander seeds, cardamom, garlic, double cream, lemon

Bake **4 large potatoes** at 200°C/Gas 6 for 45 minutes to an hour, until crisp-skinned and fluffy inside. Slice **a couple of medium-sized aubergines** in half and score the cut sides in a lattice pattern, almost through to the skin. Place the aubergines, cut side up, in a roasting tin.

Using a pestle and mortar, crush **a teaspoon of coriander seeds** to a fine powder, then split the pods of **4 green cardamoms**, tip out their little black seeds and crush them, too. Peel and finely crush **2 cloves of garlic**, then mix with the spices. Scatter the ground spice and garlic mixture over the aubergines, then spoon **2 tablespoons of olive oil** over each.

Bake the aubergines for about 35 minutes, until soft, then remove from the oven and cut them into thick slices. Place over a gentle heat, season with a little salt, then add **100ml of double cream**. Finish with **a little lemon juice**. Slice the potatoes in half, divide the aubergine filling between them, and serve. For 4.

&

Wash the potatoes, leaving the skin slightly damp, prick them here and there with a fork, then roll them in sea salt flakes. This will give a lovely crisp skin.

&

You can use sweet potatoes instead. The aubergines can be seasoned with ground cumin instead of cardamom. If you are using sweet potatoes, try a little ground cinnamon instead of coriander.

# Chickpea, courgette and pepper stew

red onion, yellow onion, Romano pepper, courgettes,
tinned chickpeas, basil, sourdough bread

Peel **1 red and 1 yellow onion** and slice them as finely as you can. Warm **a couple of tablespoons of olive oil** in a large, deep frying pan, then add the chopped onions. Cut **a large Romano pepper** into bite-sized pieces, removing any seeds and the core as you do it, then add to the onion and leave it to soften over a moderate heat.

Cut **1 large green and 1 large yellow courgette** into slices not much thicker than a pound coin, then add the courgette to the onion and pepper in the pan and cook for 15 minutes or so, until soft. Rinse the contents of **a 400g tin of chickpeas**, then stir into the vegetables and season carefully with salt, pepper and **8 basil leaves**. When all is warm and bubbling, serve in deep bowls, with a trickle of oil over the surface of each, and eat with chewy **sourdough bread**. Serves 2.

&

If your courgettes produce too thin a juice, turn up the heat and let the liquid reduce by half. It won't thicken, but the flavours will concentrate. Good though this is with sourdough, I rather like it piled on to toasted focaccia or ciabatta.

&

It is the sweet pan juices that make this dish worth making. Intensify them with a little garlic, a trickle of balsamic vinegar, a few capers or thyme leaves – or perhaps you would prefer a spoonful of basil pesto. You can also use this as a rough and ready pasta sauce, and fold in a few handfuls of cooked penne.

# Lamb kofta

minced lamb, ground ginger, ground coriander, thyme, rosemary,
parsley, anchovy fillets, sesame seeds

Put **500g of minced lamb** into a large mixing bowl and add
**2 teaspoons of ground ginger, a teaspoon of ground coriander,
2 teaspoons each of chopped thyme and rosemary leaves**, and **a
tablespoon of chopped parsley**.

Roughly chop **6 anchovy fillets** and add to the lamb. Tip
**2 tablespoons of sesame seeds** into a dry frying pan and toast over
a moderate heat till pale gold. Tip the seeds into the lamb, then
season generously with salt and pepper.

Divide the seasoned lamb into nine, then roll each piece into
a small, squat sausage, like a large wine cork. Gently push a long
wooden skewer lengthways through the centre of each one and set
aside for 20 minutes in the fridge.

Get a grill or griddle pan hot. Place the kofta on the griddle and let
them brown nicely, then carefully turn and cook the other side. They
will probably need about 10 minutes. Serve hot. Makes 9. Serves 3.

### &

Don't skip the resting of the meat in the fridge. Once the lamb is on
the grill, try not to move it around. Let the meat form a light crust
before you attempt to turn it over, otherwise the kofta may break up.

### &

Good as these lamb kofta are on their own, they're even better with
a herb dip. To make it, mix a handful of chopped dill and another of
chopped mint leaves with 4 tablespoons of yoghurt, and serve with
the lamb.

### &

You need not use lamb – minced beef will work instead, as will
minced pork.

# Chicken, haricot beans and lemon

chicken breasts, tinned haricot beans, thyme, chicken stock,
lemon, parsley

Using a heavy knife, cut **2 bone-in chicken breasts** in half and season them with salt and black pepper. Warm **a little olive oil** in a sauté pan, add the chicken and let it brown on both sides. Drain **a couple of 400g tins of haricot beans** and add them to the pan together with **8 little sprigs of thyme, 500ml of chicken stock** and **the juice of a lemon**. Bring the stock and beans to the boil, then lower the heat and simmer for 10–15 minutes. Stir in **4 tablespoons of chopped parsley**, check the seasoning and serve. For 2.

&

Keep the heat low to moderate in order to give the chicken plenty of time to cook through to the bone. Regularly baste it with the cooking juices to keep the meat moist. Use a good-quality ready-made chicken stock. Most supermarkets and butchers have them in the chilled section.

&

Use other members of the bean family, such as butter beans, flageolet or cannellini. Try adding tarragon to the stock instead of thyme, as it works beautifully with the chicken stock and lemon. To make a really fast version of the dish, use boned chicken breast pieces instead of bone-in breasts. You can make a similar recipe with duck breast, too, but omit the lemon and add a dash of Marsala instead.

# Black pudding, potato and egg

### small potatoes, black pudding, eggs

Cut **400g of small potatoes** into thin discs. You can peel them if you wish, but I don't really see the point if the skins are thin. Pile them into a deep baking dish. Thickly slice or crumble **200g of black pudding** and tuck it in among the potatoes. Trickle over **4 tablespoons of olive oil**. Bake for 45 minutes to an hour in an oven at 180°C/Gas 4, until the potatoes are golden and tender and the black pudding is toasted.

Remove the dish from the oven, make four shallow hollows in the potatoes, then break **4 large eggs** on top and return it to the oven for a couple of minutes or longer, depending on how you like your eggs. Serves 2.

&

Keep the slices of potato thin, about the thickness of a £2 coin, which will ensure they cook right the way through. So that the eggs cook neatly, make four small hollows within the potatoes to crack them into, otherwise they will spread untidily.

&

Chorizo has become a little ubiquitous, but that doesn't stop it being a perfect alternative for black pudding in this dish. The softer and more crumbly the chorizo, the better. There is no reason why you shouldn't swap the potatoes for parsnips if you wish, though I would be tempted to introduce a little butter with the oil.

# Mackerel and broccoli gratin

broccoli, smoked mackerel, tomatoes, béchamel sauce,
breadcrumbs, Parmesan

Bring a large saucepan of water to the boil. Break **200g of broccoli** into large florets, then lower into the boiling water and leave to cook for 3 or 4 minutes, until bright and still a little crisp. Drain and cool under cold running water, then set aside. Set the oven at 180°C/ Gas 4.

Remove the skin from **375g of smoked mackerel** and break the flesh into large pieces, removing any stray bones as you go. Halve **a couple of large tomatoes**, then cut each half into four. Put the smoked mackerel, drained broccoli and tomatoes into a shallow ovenproof dish or baking tin.

Pour over **500ml of béchamel sauce**, then scatter over **4 handfuls of soft, fresh breadcrumbs** and **4 tablespoons of finely grated Parmesan**. Bake in the preheated oven for 45 minutes or so, until crisp and bubbling. Serves 4.

### &

Make your own béchamel sauce by cooking 40g of butter with 20g of plain flour until pale biscuit colour, then stirring in 425ml of warm milk seasoned with a bay leaf, peppercorns and salt. Continue to cook for 20 minutes over a gentle heat, stirring regularly. Alternatively, use a ready-made Italian besciamella sauce from an Italian deli or supermarket, improving it by a short simmer with bay leaves, a pinch of ground mace and a little cream.

**&**

Cauliflower makes a good substitute for the broccoli. Instead of tomatoes, fry a couple of handfuls of sliced mushrooms in a little butter. Introduce an extra layer of flavour with a seasoning of thyme leaves, finely chopped. Add a little sliced garlic, slowly fried in butter or oil.

**&**

In place of the smoked mackerel you could use kipper fillets, hot-smoked salmon, or smoked haddock. (Cauliflower works better with smoked haddock.) Some chopped tarragon or even basil would work nicely here too, torn and folded into the béchamel.

# OCTOBER

## The burger.
## Getting to grips with texture.

October 1

It's about the meat (lean but not too lean), the fat content (more than you might think), the seasoning (almost invisible), but, crucially, the stand or fall of a burger is about its texture.

I like to start from scratch. Easy though it is to buy the meat ready minced, I prefer to choose a whole piece and prepare it myself. Not that there is anything wrong with the mince you will get from a family butcher, it is just that I like to know the whole story.

The point of making your own mince is not only knowing exactly what it is made from, but having the chance to make it as coarse or as fine as you wish. I prefer a mince that is rough and open in texture, despite the fact that my burger will probably crumble a little on the grill.

You can mince pretty much any cut of meat you like for a beef patty. Butcher's mince is economical and will vary according to what he has around to use up. It often makes the most interesting product of all, using cuts we might not often see on display. Although I have used everything from rump to topside, I prefer, after years of tinkering, a burger made from chuck or skirt. I like a bit of fat in there too, though not so much that it smokes everyone out if you decide to slap your patties on the barbecue.

I will often cook a burger without any seasoning other than salt and pepper. Even more so if it is going to be one of those hip, heroic towers of meat, bacon, pink pickled onions, mustard mayonnaise and pan drippings. Occasionally I will introduce a single herb such as rosemary, very finely chopped, or a little thyme. But the beef burgers I grilled tonight got a spike of extra heat from a shredded chilli and

401

smoky notes from a sun-dried tomato, an ingredient I use rarely. Like tomato purée, the sun-dried tomato is a schoolyard bully. The hot, smoky notes just felt right on this occasion, and worked neatly with a salad of thickly sliced avocado, basil leaves and lime.

## Beef, chilli and sun-dried tomato burger

steak (skirt, chuck, rump, etc.) – 400g
a medium-sized red chilli
sun-dried tomatoes in oil – 6
chives – 6 long ones

*For the salad:*
avocados – 2
basil leaves – 6 or 7
a lime

Very finely chop or mince the steak. Halve the chilli lengthways, discard the seeds and chop the flesh very finely. Drain the sun-dried tomatoes, chop them almost to a pulp, then toss them with the steak mince, chilli and a generous seasoning of salt. Finely chop the chives and stir in. Roll a tablespoon of the meat into a small patty, then cook briefly on both sides in a little oil in a shallow pan. Taste, then alter the seasoning of the remaining mixture to taste. Shape the remaining mixture into four thick patties.

You can fry or grill the burgers. I prefer them on the grill, but they need to be turned carefully as they cook, so they don't fall apart. Let them cook for four or five minutes on each side, turning until they are fully browned on both sides.

Halve the avocados, remove and discard the stones, remove the skins, then slice the flesh. Tear or finely shred the basil leaves and stir into the juice of the lime. (You will get more juice from the lime if you warm it a little first, then roll it hard on the table with the palm of your hand.) Dress the avocado with the lime and basil. Makes 4.

# A couscous to love

## October 2

I can't really *love* couscous. I eat it, a fine, soft grit with which to pad out a stew, in order to fill myself up. It does the job admirably, but I'm not sure one can ever really love couscous the way one can potatoes, pasta, bread or rice.

But there is a better, bigger couscous. Mograbia. The most popular name for those plump, rounded beads of 'giant' couscous of which I have recently become extraordinarily fond. Balls of starch that soak up the gravy of a tagine, the precious juices of chicken or beef, whatever you have in your roasting tin. Within seconds of your first taste, you feel you have known them all your life.

Also called maftoul, mograbia takes slightly longer to cook than the fine variety. I like mine as I like my pasta, cooked al dente, that is, with a satisfyingly chewy interior, but it's up to you. You cannot pretend it is anything more nourishing than starch. The only real excuse for eating it is to fill you up or to slurp up blissful quantities of the meat juices from a roast or the caramelised liquor of roast vegetables.

Soft, bobbly and texturally intriguing, there is nothing else quite like this modish 'grain'. Though, like regular couscous, it is not a grain at all, but fine wheat flour rolled and part-cooked. (I ate couscous for years before I knew it is partially cooked and dried before it is packed.) There is something of the texture of commercial gnocchi about these fat grains, which is no bad thing, and they are every bit as resilient and chewable.

I boil the little balls of starch in deep, salted water, as you might conchiglie or penne, then toss with olive oil, lemon and roasted, caramelised shallots. I make the couscous feel at home with a handful of chopped green olives and mint. (I sometimes use them with preserved lemon too, the pulp removed and the skin chopped finely.) We need bright, piquant flavours in a monochromatic salad such as this.

Water is a perfectly sound medium for cooking any starch destined to be served cold, but I prefer to use stock if I have it. The carbohydrates sponge up the aromatic cooking liquid, making your salad a whole lot more interesting. If I'm using the traditional and more accessible fine couscous, I pour hot chicken stock and lemon juice over, cover it tightly with a lid and let the magic happen.

I'm not sure you have to dress these grains when they are warm, as you might potatoes, which allows us to cook them in advance. A roll in olive oil will stop the beads sticking to one another. This also means they make worthwhile additions to a packed lunch. You can include the dressing separately if you wish, in a tiny tightly lidded pot, and stir it at your desk.

## Mograbia, shallots, lemon

I pick mograbia up, in large bags, generally from Middle Eastern grocers, whenever I see it. Some of the larger supermarkets have it too.

| | |
|---|---|
| mograbia – 200g | mint – a large handful, |
| olive oil – 3 tablespoons | shredded |
| small shallots – 6 | olives – 150g |
| cornichons – 10 | the zest and juice of a lemon |

Cook the mograbia in deep, salted boiling water for about twenty minutes, till tender. It should retain a little bite. Drain and refresh in cold water, then tip into a mixing bowl and toss gently with a tablespoon of olive oil.

Peel the shallots and halve them. Pour a thin film of olive oil into a shallow pan and cook the shallots till golden and sweetly caramelised, turning them regularly so they colour evenly. When they are soft and glossy, add them to the mograbia.

Halve the cornichons lengthways and add them to the mograbia. Shred the mint leaves finely. Mix the olive oil left in the shallot pan with the lemon juice and zest, the chopped olives and the shredded mint. Gently toss all the ingredients together. Serves 3.

# Eating little birds

A little feast. A partridge each. Plump as cherubs, grilled till their skin has crisped and darkened, their legs charred black at the tips. We eat them with neither knife nor fork. Just our hands, tearing the legs first, then winkling the breasts from the carcass with our thumbs. We suck, we tug, we gnaw, we chew. Crisp skin, scented with clementine zest and thyme, pink flesh the colour of the last rose of autumn.

## Grilled partridge, orange and lemon marinade

plump partridges – 2
lemons – 2
clementines – 4
rosé or white wine – 250ml
red wine vinegar –
  2 tablespoons
thyme – 6 sprigs

butter – a thin slice

*For the kale:*
kale – 100g
butter – 30g
olive oil – 2 tablespoons
golden sultanas – a handful

Using a heavy kitchen knife, slice the partridges down their backbones and open them out flat.

Grate the zest from the lemons and two of the clementines into a large mixing bowl. Squeeze in the juice of both the lemons and all four of the clementines. Pour in the wine and the vinegar, then add the thyme sprigs and a generous seasoning of sea salt and coarsely ground black pepper. Push the partridges down into the marinade and set aside in a cool place for a good hour or two, longer if you have it.

Place the birds, skin side up, in a roasting tin. Trickle a tablespoon or so of the marinade over each bird, then cook under the oven grill,

a good 10cm away from the element, for ten minutes, till the skin is nicely crisped and the flesh is still pink and juicy within.

Pour the rest of the marinade into a small pan and reduce to half the volume over a moderate to high heat. Whisk in the butter and check the seasoning.

Shred the kale finely, cook in the melted butter and oil in a shallow pan for three minutes, tossing it gently, then add a little salt and the golden sultanas. Serve the kale underneath the spatchcocked partridges, with some of the reduced cooking juices. Serves 2.

# Sweet fruit, golden onions.
# An experiment.

## October 5

The autumn leaves have been exceptional this year. Most striking of all has been the Winter Nelis pear, whose foliage has turned a glowing crimson in the cold snap. The sprawling fig tree, whose yellow leaves fall in one great swoosh that sounds like a landslide, has held its leaves for longer than usual.

A brief trip to Norway has brought home the need for more autumn colour in my own garden. Not so much a Vermont-style patchwork of russets and ochres, pleasing though that can be, but one colour in particular. Gold. The trees throughout Oslo and Bergen shone as if illuminated by candlelight, even in the endless and beautiful autumn rain. Here and there a burning scarlet and maroon bush against a dense patch of deepest green, but wherever I walked, clusters of golden-leaved trees shone under the streetlights.

Golden leaves work well in this garden because of the solid black-greens of the ivy-clad walls and yew hedges. They shine like torches on a dark night. The clearest, brightest golden foliage right now is on the sprawling medlar, the spindly damson that is just about hanging in there, and the vast canopy of the fig that overshadows the terrace. There is a plate of its fruit on the table now. Deepest purple-black figs on yellow leaves. Few things could be more beautiful.

Today, a short experiment, the marriage of soft, buttery onion, cooked down to an amber marmalade, and dark figs, baked as small, sweet pastry tarts. The result is so good I cannot imagine why it hasn't occurred to me before. We eat the crumbly tarts warm, the scent of sweet figs and caramelised onions hanging in distinctly nippy autumn air.

# Fig and red onion tartlets

I have used sweet pastry here. It works perfectly with the onions and figs. Use a plain shortcrust if you prefer, but you will be missing a sweet savoury treat.

| For the pastry: | For the filling: |
|---|---|
| plain flour – 180g | red onions – 2 large |
| butter – 90g | butter – 40g |
| an egg yolk | figs – 200g |
| caster sugar – 1 tablespoon | crème fraîche – 200ml |

You will need six loose-bottomed tart tins that are 8cm wide and 3cm deep.

Make the pastry: put the flour into a food processor, add the butter and process for a minute or so till you have coarse crumbs. Add the egg yolk and sugar and about two or three tablespoons of water, then continue processing to a moderately firm dough. Remove from the machine, knead very briefly on a floured board, then pat it into a round, wrap it in clingfilm and let it relax in the fridge for half an hour.

Set the oven at 180°C/Gas 4. Peel the onions, slice them thinly, then let them cook over a low to moderate heat in the butter, till very soft. Give them time, so they become jammy and glossy, then remove them from the heat. Chop the figs into small dice, then stir into the onions with the crème fraîche and season gently.

Roll the pastry out thinly and cut six discs measuring roughly 15cm. Use the discs to fill the tart tins, then add a ball of screwed-up kitchen foil to each one – it will prevent the pastry sides from shrinking. Bake for about fifteen minutes, till pale biscuit-coloured, then remove the foil.

Into each baked tartlet case place a couple of spoonfuls of the filling. Bake for about forty minutes, then cool for a few minutes and remove from the tart tins. Serve warm. Makes 6.

# Grilling mussels

## October 7

Back to texture. The underestimated importance of the crisp, the soft, the coarse, the smooth, the infinitesimal details of how something feels in the mouth. Sometimes it is a question of purity, an ingredient you enjoy for what it is, unburdened by the tinkering of the cook; on other occasions it is a thoughtful partnership of one texture with another. Something crisp and soft in the same mouthful perhaps (the everlasting success of the ice cream cornet), or a dazzling combination of textures assembled in a much more complex and exciting manner. The more adventurous stars of the Michelin guide can be very good at this.

Back to basics. The mussels I bought this morning are fat nuggets of juice-filled flesh, the colour of sand. They taste of the sea. My inclination to eat them raw is thwarted only by the tightness of their shells. I cook them briefly, in a stainless steel pan with a tight-fitting lid, the vast one I normally keep for stock. I need them to cook for the shortest possible time, till the second their shells open. They clatter out of the pan into a bowl and I twist and snap off the uppermost, empty shell from each.

Lined up like naval cadets ready for inspection, each mussel is placed on a baking tray, crowned with a spoonful of butter whose flavour and texture has been plumped up with coarse crumbs, finely grated Parmesan, lemon juice and thyme leaves. I grill them, just until the first crumb of bread turns gold, until the cheese has started to glisten, until the butter has formed a pool surrounding each fat morsel in its pearlescent shell.

# Grilled mussels with thyme and Parmesan

Mussels are cheap, sustainable (look out for hand-gathered and farmed ones) and curiously filling. When I feel I have had enough of chucking them into a pot with a glass of white wine and some tarragon, I grill them under a coating of buttery breadcrumbs.

large mussels – 24
a glass of white wine

*For the herb butter:*
butter – 120g
parsley – 4 bushy sprigs
thyme leaves – 2 good
  tablespoons

a clove of garlic
a medium-sized, hot chilli
a little lemon juice
white breadcrumbs –
  5 tablespoons
grated Parmesan – 3
  tablespoons

Put the butter into a mixing bowl. Finely chop the parsley leaves, thyme, garlic and seeded chilli. Mash into the butter with the lemon juice, crumbs and Parmesan. Season with salt and black pepper.

Put the prepared mussels (thoroughly cleaned and scrubbed, and checked for broken or dead ones) into a deep pan over a moderate heat, pour in the white wine, then cover tightly with a lid. Let them steam for a minute or two until their shells open.

Lift the mussels out of the pan, pulling off the top shells as you go. Lay the mussels in their bottom shells flat on a baking sheet or ovenproof tray. Spread a teaspoon or so of the butter over each mussel, then cook under a preheated grill till bubbling. Enough for 2.

# A duck leg dinner

## October 10

Confit de canard, where the whole leg of the duck has been preserved under a snowy veil of its fat, is probably one of the most popular autumn and winter dinners in this house. The reason for this is obviously its crisp skin, tender brown leg meat that falls apart in strings, and of course the sumptuous fat. Crisped in a hot oven, duck confit ranks number one in the easy dinner list when I come home tired and hungry.

But a whole duck, or even a boned breast, is a rare treat. Truth told, I find roast duck a messy meal to cook, and the bird itself awkward to carve. Boneless duck breasts, about as appetising as a pair of old slippers, grab me only occasionally, when I cook them with fat butter beans or white haricots. Duck legs, packed in pairs, are at last becoming easier to find. Supermarkets have them, some butchers too.

Duck legs, raw rather than confit, can be used in pretty much the same way as chicken but they respond to stronger, richer ingredients, such as dried fruits and nuts. They take well to fortified wines such as Marsala and port, and are happier in the company of walnuts and fruits such as cranberries and dark grapes than chicken is. The sweet meat also likes a little acidity in the form of bitter marmalade oranges, lemon juice, vinegar and verjuice.

With this in mind, I tuck three browned duck legs into a deep casserole with ingredients that, if I'm honest, feel more like Christmas than October. The juices, shiny with port and prunes, are balanced with a little sherry vinegar and brought back from too sweet an end with some cubes of smoky pancetta.

# Duck, prunes and red cabbage

In a recipe such as this, where duck is cooked in a deep casserole with port and dried fruit, it is best to use meat on the bone.

groundnut oil or duck fat –
2 tablespoons
duck legs – 3
prunes, stoned – 250g
port – 250ml
chicken, duck or vegetable
stock – 250ml

smoked pancetta or bacon
– 200g
a small red cabbage
sherry vinegar –
2 tablespoons

In a deep-sided casserole, warm the oil and lightly brown the pieces of duck, turning them as necessary to get an even colour. Remove the duck as each piece browns and set aside.

In a bowl, soak the prunes in the port, turning occasionally, for thirty minutes or so. Tip as much of the fat as possible from the casserole, then return the pan to the heat and add the port and soaked prunes, stirring at any tasty sediment left by the browning of the duck and letting it dissolve in the bubbling liquid. Once the port has boiled for a minute or two, pour in the stock, bring to the boil, lower the heat to a simmer, then return the pieces of duck to the pan. Season with salt, cover with a lid, and leave to cook on a low to moderate heat for about forty minutes.

Cut the pancetta or bacon into small cubes and brown evenly in a casserole or medium-sized saucepan. Halve and coarsely shred the red cabbage, then add to the pancetta and toss briefly in the melted fat. As the cabbage brightens, pour in the vinegar, add a little salt and pepper, let it sizzle briefly, then cover with a lid and leave to simmer for about fifteen minutes, till the cabbage is soft.

Serve with the duck and prunes on top. For 3.

# Smoke and crunch

## October 15

Some recipes are just downright useful. A light lunch. A first course. Something to eat with drinks. A bit of dinner. Well, that's smoked mackerel remoulade.

## Smoked mackerel celeriac remoulade

celeriac – 300g
a lemon
radishes – 8
Dijon mustard – 2 tablespoons
grain mustard – 2 tablespoons

capers – 2 teaspoons
cornichons – 8
a whole smoked mackerel
  or 2 large fillets
butter – 60g

Cut away and discard the celeriac's tough, whiskery roots, then peel it. Slice the white flesh into large pieces, then shred them coarsely, into the same matchstick-thin shards you would for a classic remoulade. Squeeze the lemon juice into a mixing bowl, then tip in the shredded celeriac and immediately toss to prevent it from discolouring.

Trim the radishes, removing any leaves and stalks, slice them thinly and add to the shredded celeriac. Stir the two mustards, a little salt and the capers into the celeriac and radishes, then finely slice and add the cornichons.

Remove and discard the skin of the smoked mackerel, then break the flesh into large, thick pieces and add to the bowl, gently tossing the ingredients together. Pack the mixture down into a clean bowl or glass storage jar and smooth the surface quite flat. Melt the butter in a small pan, then spoon over the surface of the remoulade. Grind over a little black pepper, then leave to chill and refrigerate overnight. Serve with hot toast. For 6.

# A plate of autumn

## October 18

A golden afternoon and someone has lit a fire in their garden. The smell of leaves collected and burned may be romantic but makes no sense to a gardener who worships the soft, tobacco-coloured treasure that is leaf mould. Still, there are few better smells on an autumn day than smoke from a garden fire.

If I were a forager, I would be down in the woods with my wooden-handled mushroom knife and a trusty guide. But foraging is something I confine to picking blackberries, chestnuts (found, looking like little green hedgehogs, hidden in the long grass) and cobnuts from the woods or sloes from the hedges in the lanes around where we have been filming. I am not sure I trust myself to pick and cook my own mushrooms.

And yet there are days at this time of year when there is nothing I would rather eat. Those days are usually ones when the air is damp, maybe a little cold, when the horse chestnut leaves pile up on the grass verge outside the house, begging to be kicked, and the garden smells like the sweetest muscat.

It is then I want two vast field mushrooms, cooked slowly in a shallow pan, butter spooned over them as their velvety gills cook. I want a clear broth, the colour of amber, with straw-like Japanese mushrooms afloat on the surface or perhaps a round tart the size of a side plate, all flaking pastry, sliced chestnut mushrooms and roast garlic and parsley butter.

Today, it's mushrooms cooked in red wine with twiggy herbs in the style of a boeuf bourguignon, all inky wine and mushrooms cooked to the texture of silk. It's satisfying, but I still serve it with a golden mash of butternut squash. A little plate of deepest autumn.

# A mushroom bourguignon

I like to add a little triangle of fried bread dipped in chopped parsley to each portion too, as a nod to the original boeuf bourguignon. Steaming, rather than boiling, the butternut will produce a drier, more fluffy mash.

onions – 2
olive oil
garlic – 3 cloves
small carrots – 2
shallots, small ones – 8
tomato purée – 2 teaspoons
plain flour – 2 tablespoons
vegetable stock – 500ml
sugar – a pinch or two
   (optional)
balsamic vinegar – 1 teaspoon

*For the marinade:*
king oyster mushrooms – 250g
brown chestnut mushrooms
 – 250g

button mushrooms – 250g
coriander seeds – 2 teaspoons
black peppercorns –
   2 teaspoons
bay leaves – 3
thyme – 6 sprigs
rosemary – 2 sprigs
red wine, such as a Pinot Noir
   – 500ml

*For the mash:*
butternut squash – 2
butter – 50g

Slice the largest, thick-stemmed mushrooms into pieces the thickness of a pound coin, then put them into a large, wide mixing bowl. Quarter the chestnut mushrooms, add them to the others, then drop in the whole button mushrooms.

Crack the coriander seeds and black peppercorns using a pestle and mortar, or grind them very coarsely in a spice mill. Tuck the bay leaves, thyme and rosemary sprigs amongst the mushrooms and add the ground spices. Pour the red wine over the mushrooms, cover with a lid or clingfilm, then leave for a good hour to marinate.

Peel the onions, cut them in half, then slice each half into six segments. Put a couple of tablespoons of the olive oil into a deep, heavy-based casserole, then add the onions and let them cook over a moderate heat, stirring from time to time, till they are soft and golden. You can expect this to take a good fifteen to twenty minutes.

Peel and thinly slice the garlic and stir into the softening onions. Scrub the carrots and cut them into small dice, then stir into the softening onions and garlic. Peel the shallots, leaving them whole, and add them to the onions.

Stir the tomato purée into the onions and leave to cook, with the occasional stir, for five minutes. Remove the mushrooms from the bowl and let them cook with the onions, allowing them to colour a little. The mixture should be gold and brown and woodsy.

Scatter the flour over the surface and stir in, let it cook for a couple of minutes, then pour in the red wine marinade and the stock, mixing well but gently (don't break up the slices of mushroom), and bring to the boil. Season with salt and pepper and leave to simmer gently for about twenty minutes, till all is dark, rich and glossy. Use a pinch or two of sugar and a teaspoon of balsamic vinegar to correct the seasoning.

To make the mash, peel, deseed and roughly chop the butternut squash and steam over boiling water for twenty minutes or so, till tender. Add the butter and crush using a potato masher or fork till light and fluffy. Serve with the mushrooms. For 4.

# A memorable train journey

The train from Oslo to Bergen. Headphones in. (Bonobo, Mitsuko Uchida, Throwing Snow, Pantha du Prince.) Leaning back, watching the rain. Silver needles falling on black fjords. Dense forests of dark firs line the track, here and there golden birches, their leaves clinging on, shimmering with each gust of piercing Nordic wind.

At Myrdal, swirling mist. By the time we reach Finse there is snowfall and hot chocolate in paper cups. There are wood-clad cottages on the horizon, plumes of smoke drifting lazily from their chimneys. I imagine wooden bowls of oat porridge on the table and something in the wood-fired oven, a pot roast maybe, plodding towards tenderness.

In Bergen I eat well: a bowl of lamb and barley broth with shredded cabbage; roast potatoes with bacon and Norwegian cheese; an apple crumble with cinnamon ice cream. The vegetable that reoccurs throughout my stay is the Jerusalem artichoke. First roasted, then in soup and finally as a smooth and pepper-freckled purée.

The rain has been endless on this trip. Beautiful rain, from soft grey skies, under a voluminous tangerine umbrella. I want a pot roast, possibly in one of those wooden cottages that line the hillsides. A roasted game bird, with smoked bacon, tufts of woody thyme with flowers the colour of heather, and artichokes, gold and ivory.

# Pot roast pheasant with artichokes and bacon

a little groundnut oil
a plump, oven-ready pheasant
baby shallots – 300g
Jerusalem artichokes – 300g
smoked streaky bacon – 8
   rashers

garlic – 4 cloves
rosemary – 4 large sprigs
thyme – 6 sprigs
apple juice – 250ml

Warm a couple of tablespoons of oil in a deep casserole over a moderately high heat, then brown the pheasant on all sides. Remove the bird and set aside. Set the oven at 180°C/Gas 4.

Peel the shallots, keeping them whole if very small, halved if large, then peel the Jerusalem artichokes and halve them lengthways. Cut the bacon rashers into pieces roughly the size of a postage stamp, then add them to the casserole and let them colour lightly. Add the shallots and artichokes, leaving them to turn gold in the bacon fat.

Add the whole peeled garlic cloves to the casserole, together with the rosemary and thyme sprigs and the apple juice. Bring the liquid to the boil, return the pheasant to the pan, then cover with a lid and bake for thirty minutes.

Remove the bird from the pan and leave to rest for ten minutes, covered in foil. Taste and season the juices, reducing them a little over a moderate heat if necessary. Serve cut in half, together with the vegetables from the pan, spooning over any pan juices as you go. Serves 2.

# Inspiration from the forest

## October 25

Scandinavia on my mind. I am making mushroom pies. Chestnut mushrooms, sliced and cooked with soft onions, thyme and butter in a crumbly shortcrust. I slice the onions and let them stew in oil and butter till they soften and turn a clear gold. Once the thyme is scattered in, and the mushrooms have browned a little round the edges, the mixture smells like a damp autumn day in the forest. Bosky, sweet, mellow.

It is not, at least in my mind, a big jump from mushrooms to berries (isn't that what we were going to survive on when, as children, we planned to run away and live in the woods?), and I find myself looking round for small, sharp blackberries to add to the filling (there are none) or (ideally) the lingonberries so beloved of Swedish cooks. I settle for blueberries and find myself surprisingly happy with the result.

The rowan jelly that accompanies roast venison; the blackberries we squash into the gravy for a loin of roast pork; those lingonberries that appear in a ruby puddle with Swedish meatballs and mashed potato, and the cranberries with the Christmas turkey. Berries have a traditional place in savoury dishes, so why not in my mushroom pies.

The blueberries burst a little in the heat, sending drops of deep purple juice rippling through the sizzling mushrooms. The smell is fruity and warm and fungal, like a forest on a humid autumn afternoon, and just asking to be wrapped in crumbly pastry.

# Mushroom pies

*For the pastry:*
plain flour – 175g
baking powder – half a teaspoon
fine salt – half a teaspoon
butter – 100g, cubed
an egg yolk
a little milk
an egg, beaten

*For the filling:*
onions – 2 medium
groundnut oil – a little
butter – a thin slice
1 tablespoon thyme leaves
chestnut mushrooms – 350g
crème fraîche – 150ml
blueberries – 125g

Make the pastry. Put the flour, baking powder and salt in a mixing bowl, then add the butter and rub into the flour till it resembles coarse breadcrumbs. Mix in the egg yolk and then enough milk to make a rollable dough. Pat into a ball and chill for thirty minutes.

Set the oven at 200°C/Gas 6. Roll the dough out to 1cm thick, fold it in by thirds, then roll and fold again. Chill for a further thirty minutes.

For the filling, peel and slice the onions. Warm a little oil and the butter in a casserole or large saucepan and add the onions, letting them cook over a moderate heat till they are soft and pale gold. Stir in the thyme leaves, together with salt and pepper. Slice the mushrooms thinly, add them to the onions and continue cooking, the heat quite low, till they are nut brown. Stir in the crème fraîche and blueberries, continue cooking briefly, then remove from the heat.

Roll the dough into a square measuring roughly 24cm, then cut that into four equal squares. Divide the mushrooms between the squares, piling them in the centre, then brush a little beaten egg around the edges, bring the opposite corners of the squares together and seal loosely along the edges. It is good to do this loosely, so the seals break here and there to reveal the mushrooms within. Transfer to a baking sheet. Brush the pastry with beaten egg, then bake for about forty minutes, till golden. Allow to cool a little before eating. Makes 4.

# Blue cheese and an apple

## October 26

The extraordinary partnership of blue cheese and apple can be celebrated with a jagged shard of Roquefort and a rough-skinned Blenheim Orange; a salad of frisée, wedges of Christmas Cox and crumbled Stichelton; or perhaps a tart of Cashel Blue from Ireland and slices of Ashmead's Kernel.

For me at least, blue cheese and an apple is an autumn rite of passage and this afternoon I have my own little celebration (life should be full of them) with a hunk of leaf-embalmed Spanish Picos and a quivering mound of amber-hued apple jelly.

Earlier in the summer, I made some pastry dumplings stuffed with crushed stewed apple and Stilton and I make them again today. They come from the oven like plump cushions, the apple hot and sweet, the cheese piquant and oozing. I bring them to the table now, as I did then, with an acid-edged pickle of rose-pink onions and golden sultanas.

## Apple and Stilton dumplings

| | |
|---|---|
| *For the filling:* | Stilton – 250g |
| apples – 3 large | an egg, beaten |
| water – 3 tablespoons | nigella seeds |
| puff pastry – approx. 325g | |

Peel the apples, quarter, core and roughly chop them, then put them into a pan with the water and simmer over a moderate heat till soft. Stir the apples occasionally, then crush them with a fork and set aside.

Cut the pastry in half lengthways. Set the oven at 200°C/Gas 6. Roll each piece of pastry into a large sheet, about 32cm square, and set one aside. Cut the other square of pastry into eight squares, then

divide the apples between them, placing a spoonful in the centre of each piece of pastry. Break the Stilton into large pieces and divide between the pastries, placing it on top of the apple.

Brush some of the beaten egg around the edge of each square. Cut the second piece of pastry into eight similar squares, then place them on top of the apple-filled pastries and seal the edges firmly. Transfer the pastries to a baking sheet and brush them all over with some of the beaten egg. Scatter lightly with the nigella seeds and bake for twenty minutes, till golden brown. Serve warm, with the pickle below. Makes 8.

## Onion pickle

red onions – 2
lemons – 2
caster sugar – 1 tablespoon
white wine vinegar –
  3 tablespoons

cloves – 5
cinnamon – half a stick
golden sultanas –
  a handful

Peel and thinly slice the red onions, put them into a stainless steel or other non-reactive pan with the juice of the lemons, the caster sugar and the vinegar, then tuck in the cloves and the cinnamon. Bring the mixture to the boil, lower the heat to a simmer, then cover with a lid and continue cooking for ten minutes. Add the golden sultanas and set aside to cool.

# Offal made luxurious

## Chicken liver ragout with potatoes and chive oil

The double cream is entirely optional, but does lend a velvety finish to the chicken liver ragout.

potatoes – 1kg
smoked streaky bacon –
  6 rashers
olive oil – 7 tablespoons
chestnut mushrooms – 150g
a banana shallot
chives – 10g

milk – 400ml
butter – 100g
chicken livers – 200g
Marsala – 4 tablespoons
double cream – 1 tablespoon
  (optional)

Peel the potatoes, quarter them, then boil in deep, lightly salted water till tender to the point of a knife. Meanwhile, dice the bacon and cook till almost crisp in 2 tablespoons of the olive oil. Quarter the mushrooms, add to the bacon and continue cooking. Peel and chop the shallot, then add to the pan and cook until soft.

Blitz together the chives and the remaining olive oil till you have a brilliant emerald oil. When the potatoes are cooked, drain them, then tip into the bowl of a food mixer. Warm the milk and butter in a small pan, then beat enough of the liquid into the cooked potatoes to produce a thoroughly soft mash, almost sloppy in texture.

Add the chicken livers to the pan of mushrooms and fry briefly. (I like mine pink in the middle, no matter what the food police say.) Pour in the Marsala, cook for a minute or two until the livers are done, then (if you wish) stir in the cream. Check the seasoning, and serve with the mashed potato and chive oil. Serves 2–3.

# The death of All Hallows

## October 31

The old Hallowe'en, when hollowed-out pumpkins glowed ghoulishly from darkened windows, was a night I rather enjoyed. Walking along London's Georgian streets, the occasional candlelit gourd to speed us on our way home to drink pumpkin soup and watch a crackly black and white Frankenstein movie, was something I looked forward to.

Nowadays it's all screaming groups in fancy dress ringing on doorbells. Trick or treat has become little more than licensed harassment. Parties bang on into the night. Crassness and commercialism have replaced the magic of a night where spirits were free to haunt. In my house at least, All Hallows' Eve is no more.

But that still leaves us with the sodding pumpkin to deal with. A cinnamon-scented pie aside, pumpkin only really works for me when it is accompanied by a savoury element, such as bacon or pancetta perhaps, onions, spice, mustard or cheese. Best of all is when the squash's sugary flesh comes glowing from the oven, sticky with the caramelised juices of a piece of roast pork.

Which is why I roasted a loin of crackling-encased pork on top of thick slices of pumpkin tonight, the piggy juices trickling down through the segments of golden squash. A glowing reminder of a night when, once upon a time, our imagination and candlelight were enough.

## Roast pork and pumpkin

I don't serve any gravy with this, but if you wish, pour off the fat from the roasting tin, then deglaze over a moderate heat with a little white wine or cider, scraping at the encrusted pork and pumpkin juices on the tin. Season carefully and serve with the pork.

Ask the butcher to score the pork skin. Leave the meat, uncovered, overnight, so the surface dries. That way lies crisper crackling.

a pumpkin, small to
  medium-sized
olive or groundnut oil –
  2 tablespoons
butter – 50g

pork loin, rolled and tied
  – 1–1.25kg
thyme sprigs – 6–8 sprigs
rosemary – 6 sprigs

Set the oven at 230°C/Gas 8.

Remove the skin from the pumpkin or squash. The best way to do this is to cut a slice from the top and base, so it stands firm on the chopping board, then remove the thick skin by peeling down the sides with a large, heavy cook's knife. Slice the pumpkin into five large segments, then pull out and discard the seeds and fibres from the middle.

Place the peeled and seeded segments of pumpkin in a large roasting tin, trickle with oil and add knobs of butter.

Check that the pork skin is dry to the touch. Wet pork will not crisp appetisingly. Put the loin on top of the squash, brush the skin with a little oil, just enough to allow the seasonings to adhere, then rub in a generous amount of sea salt. Grind over a little black pepper.

Tuck the sprigs of herbs on top of the pork and amongst the squash, roast in the preheated oven for twenty minutes, then lower the heat to 180°C/Gas 4 and continue roasting for sixty minutes.

Remove the pork and pumpkin from the oven, lift the pork out and put it somewhere warm to rest. Check the pumpkin for tenderness. It may need turning over and returning to the oven. Let it roast till truly tender and glowing.

Once the pork has rested for twenty minutes, carve into thick slices, together with its crackling, and serve with the pumpkin. Serves 4–5.

# NOVEMBER

## An old-fashioned pie.
## A modern crust.

### November 1

There is never enough crust. The layer of puff, shortcrust or toasted crumbs seems plentiful till you bring your homemade pie to the table. It is only then, as plates are passed round, that you realise your handiwork has its shortcomings, and the beloved layer of pastry, its topside crisp and dry, its underside soaked with gravy, is inadequate.

I tackle the problem today by making almost twice the amount it would normally take to cover a beef pie, and baking the excess alongside. The pie, seasoned with Marsala, thyme and tiny shallots baked in a small cast-iron dish, shares a baking sheet with a piece of extra crust, shaped and cut into wedges and fork-pricked like a round of shortbread, ready to be offered to those who understand the glory of the crust.

Instead of the usual butter and flour shortcrust, I exchange some of the weight of butter for blue cheese, and introduce a handful of chopped herbs. The resulting dough, fragile, cheese-marbled, is rolled a little thicker than is usual, creating a Stilton and thyme shortbread so good it could be eaten, in crumbly wedges, on its own.

# Steak, Stilton and thyme pie

The cut of beef is up to you. It gets a good couple of hours' cooking, so could be a cheaper cut such as shin, or one of the less expensive of the steaks, such as rump. Many butchers and supermarkets sell usefully ready-cubed meat especially for such recipes.

groundnut oil – a little
beef, cubed – 1kg
small shallots – 10
carrots – 300g
a rib of celery
plain flour – 2 tablespoons
Marsala – 200ml
beef stock – 1 litre
thyme – 8 sprigs

*For the shortbread crust:*
plain flour – 250g
butter – 75g
parsley – a large handful
Stilton – 80g
thyme leaves – 1 teaspoon
egg yolks – 2
water, to mix

Warm a couple of tablespoons of oil in a deep casserole dish over a moderately high heat, add a third of the beef and brown on all sides, then remove and continue with the rest of the meat. By doing it in two or three batches you avoid crowding the pan, allowing the meat to brown more effectively.

Peel and halve the shallots, roughly chop the carrots, then add both to the pan, with a little more oil if needed, browning gently and evenly. Slice the celery into thin pieces and add to the pan, but don't let it brown.

Return the beef to the pan, together with any juices that may have escaped. Scatter over the flour, continue cooking for a minute or two, then pour in the Marsala and the beef stock and bring to the boil. Season with salt and pepper, tuck in the thyme sprigs, then lower the heat and simmer, very gently, for almost two hours, till the beef is tender. Leave to cool a little whilst you make the crust.

For the crust: put the flour into a bowl, add the butter, then rub together until you have the texture of coarse, fresh breadcrumbs. Chop the parsley roughly. Add the crumbled Stilton, the chopped parsley and thyme leaves to the flour and butter and rub gently to fine crumbs. Mix in the egg yolks and enough water to make a soft but rollable dough. Set the oven at 200°C/Gas 6.

Cut the dough in half. Roll one half to the diameter of the casserole dish, then place on top of the beef. Cut a hole or small slit in the centre to let the steam out. Shape the other half into a 20cm disc, place on a baking sheet, prick the surface with a fork, then score into six segments, as if you were slicing a cake.

Bake the pie and the separate crust for twenty-five to thirty minutes, till golden brown. (Keep an eye on the disc of crust – you may need to remove it before the pie is ready.) Serve the pie with wedges of the extra crust for those who want it. For 4.

# Smoke and warm rice

## November 4

I have lit the fire. Seeing the flames dancing amongst the logs and twigs appeals to the pagan in me. I do so for the heat (there is no central heating in the main part of the house, so a fire is necessary as much as it is beautiful) but also for the scent of the smoke. Snow aside, woodsmoke is my favourite smell in the world.

The last time I visited a country smokehouse, the smell from the tar-blackened walls and rows of bronze fish hanging inside stayed with me for days. (I swear I can still detect it on the jacket I wore that day.) The whiff of smoked foods, be it a ham hock or a pale and elegant haddock fillet, is one I particularly like: woodsy, ancient and tarry.

Smoked fish seems more appropriate on a golden autumn day than at the height of summer. I sometimes wrap fillets of smoked mackerel in bacon and grill them; tuck fat chunks into a potato dauphinoise or crumble them into a potato salad (with chives and a thin mayonnaise). I stir smoked haddock, the pale un-dyed sort, into risotto with young spinach and butter or crush it in a retro pâté and spread it on pieces of hot, brown toast.

And then there was the pilaf that I made with a whole smoked haddock, the small ones from Arbroath known as smokies. I could have used mackerel instead. I tossed dried fruit, a mixture of golden sultanas and cranberries, into the onion mixture to stir through the cooked rice. Dried vine fruits are surprisingly good with oily fish, as anyone who has stuffed a rolled fillet of mackerel or sardine with raisins, pine kernels and orange, in the Sicilian style, will testify.

Yes, a dish of warm rice, scented with cinnamon, dill and smoke.

# Smoked haddock pilaf

I used an Arbroath smokie here, the whole smoked small haddock whose flesh is mild. Smoked mackerel would work too.

white basmati rice – 150g
whole black peppercorns – 6
cloves – 3
a cinnamon stick
bay leaves – 2
banana shallots – 2 medium
  (or 1 large)
butter – a thick slice

dried cherries or cranberries
  – 4 tablespoons
golden sultanas – 4 heaped
  tablespoons
finely chopped dill – 25g
Arbroath smokies – 2
  (or 400g smoked haddock)

Put the rice into a large mixing bowl, cover with warm water and rinse gently by moving it around. Pour off the water, then repeat twice. This will, in my experience, stop the rice from sticking. Transfer to a saucepan, add the whole black peppercorns, a little salt, the cloves, cinnamon stick, broken in two, and the bay leaves. Cover with water and bring to the boil. Lower to a simmer then cover with a lid and leave to putter away for ten minutes. Lift the lid and if the water is no longer visible, close the lid again and leave off the heat for ten minutes.

Peel the shallots and slice them very finely. Warm the butter in a saucepan, add the shallots and let them cook for a good ten minutes, till soft and golden, then add the dried cherries or cranberries and the sultanas.

Finely chop the dill. Remove the smokies from their skins – you should be able to prise the flesh away quite easily. Flake it into smallish chunks and add to the shallot mixture. Run a fork through the rice to separate the grains. Stir the shallot mixture into the rice and add the dill. Season generously, and serve. For 2.

# Getting rid of the pumpkin

## November 5

A savoury element can help to prevent the orange flesh of the pumpkin from cloying, as can be the case with a pumpkin risotto when it is made without the savoury notes of bacon or mushrooms. (I have had a few that could have just as easily been served as a pudding.) A handful of Parmesan in pumpkin ravioli, or a scattering over a gratin of butternut or other member of the squash family, will do the trick, successfully seeing off the overdose of sugar.

Mushrooms work well. Stuff the large field variety with mashed pumpkin, or add pieces of the flesh, steamed or sautéd, to a broth made from dried porcini. They are also often the answer, sliced and cooked with the shallots, to a squash risotto.

Mustard is another way to calm the sugar hit of an autumn pumpkin. The firmer varieties of the family, such as butternut, make a fine gratin, cooked in a slow oven with cream or crème fraîche and perhaps a little cheese. To contrast the softness of the long-cooked butternut I sometimes cover the gratin with a herb crust, often with chopped rosemary or thyme amongst the breadcrumbs. That way, it is suitable as a meatless main course.

# Butternut and red onion gratin

A main course if you wish, but this can also be served as an accompaniment. Try it with roast lamb.

red onions – 2
crème fraîche – 400ml
double cream – 300ml
bay leaves – 2
grain mustard – 3 tablespoons
butternut squash – 700g
  (weight after peeling and
  deseeding)

butter – a thin slice

*For the crust:*
ciabatta or other light bread
  – 100g
chives – a small bunch
olive oil – 4 tablespoons

You will need a gratin dish about 24cm in diameter.

Peel and thinly slice the onions, then put them into a pan with the crème fraîche and cream, the bay leaves and a grinding of salt and black pepper. Bring the creams to the boil, then turn off the heat and leave for twenty minutes. Stir in the mustard. Set the oven at 160°C/Gas 3.

Slice the peeled squash into discs about the thickness of a pound coin. Rub the butter around the gratin dish, spreading it thinly round the sides and base, then place a layer of butternut over the base of the dish, season, and add a layer of the softened onion. Continue, in layers of butternut and onion, till both are all used, then pour the seasoned cream over the squash, letting it run down through the layers. Tuck the bay leaves amongst the squash.

Bake for a good hour and a half, checking the progress towards tenderness with a skewer.

Reduce the ciabatta to crumbs in a food processor, then add the chives and blitz till the crumbs are pale green. Mix in the olive oil, then scatter over the top of the gratin and return to the oven for ten minutes, till the crumbs are lightly crisp. Serves 4, or 6 as a side dish.

441

# A salad that sorts

## November 8

The quiet joy of preparing the day's salad bowl is something of a ritual in this kitchen. Becalming, life-enriching, strangely grounding.

In this house, salad is eaten solely for the pleasure of something raw, a quiet celebration of vegetables, herbs and, occasionally, fruits that are consumed in their purest form. Rarely, if ever, is it eaten for 'health'.

Today, however, my salad is eaten as a cure. A bowl of leaves, spices and nuts that is clean, crisp and uplifting. To shredded red cabbage and carrots I add fat black grapes, the sort you have to pick the seeds out of, some toasted almonds, sizzling saltily from their hot pan, and grated ginger, whose hot citrus-scented flesh I regard as an ingredient that heals almost above all others.

Ginger, grown in tropical, humid regions, is celebrated as much as a healer as it is as a culinary ingredient in both Indian and Chinese medicine. The gingerol contained in the rhizomes is believed to contain therapeutic qualities by many natural health practitioners. Along with turmeric (it belongs to the same botanical family), ginger is prescribed for everything from colds to arthritis, migraines to nausea, and whilst the pharmaceutical industry obviously has a vested interest in rubbishing such claims, I am more than happy to go along with any long-established notion of food as healer. Food is always my first medicinal port of call.

The result of today's peeling, chopping, grating and toasting is a bowl of salad that crunches and crackles as you eat; a pile of jewel-coloured ingredients dressed with grated ginger to energise, uplift and generally straighten me out.

# A salad of red cabbage, grapes and almonds

half a medium red cabbage
carrots, skinny – 100g
olive oil
skinned almonds – 100g
fennel – a small bulb
black grapes – 120g
radish sprouts – a handful

*For the marinade:*
ginger – 25g
white wine vinegar – 100ml

*For the dressing:*
an egg yolk
Dijon mustard – 1 tablespoon
olive oil – 5 tablespoons

Finely shred the leaves of the red cabbage, discarding the tough bits of stalk. Slice the carrots finely lengthways, using a vegetable peeler, and toss with the cabbage.

Peel the ginger, then grate it very finely, almost to a purée, and stir it into the wine vinegar. Pour over the vegetables, toss them gently, then put them to one side, covered, for a good hour. Toss the vegetables occasionally to keep them wet with marinade.

Warm a tablespoon of olive oil in a frying pan, add the skinned almonds and let them toast till golden on both sides. It is probably best to do nothing else while the nuts are toasting, as they have a habit of burning as soon as you turn your back on them.

Halve the head of fennel, then slice each half thinly and add it to the dressed carrot and cabbage. Halve and seed the grapes.

Put the egg yolk into a bowl, stir in the mustard and a pinch of salt, and beat in the olive oil. Pour the dressing into the red cabbage and carrot, then add the grapes, almonds and radish sprouts. Serves 2–3.

# Of earth and smoke

November 10

Old garlic turns evil. A single clove will ruin your dinner. Acrid and bitter, there is little to do but hurl the entire head on the compost.

If I am to use garlic at all in winter, it will most likely be the smoked variety. Each head is beautiful, with its gold, papery skin and cloves the colour of old parchment. The smell is ancient, a mixture of log fires and potato dauphinoise, the scent of home and hearth.

The plump heads used to be something I picked up from fish smokeries, where adventurous proprietors, sensing the need to move on from kippers, had thrown a few in with the rows of shimmering mackerel. Now most supermarkets sell smoked garlic, as does my local butcher, in a bowl on the counter, the way Midlands butchers often sell pork scratchings.

The sky today is almost lavender grey. There are cold ashes in the grate. We are not warm. I peel potatoes. Fat floury ones, and tuck them into a shallow cast-iron pan. I pour in olive oil, throw in sea salt, a couple of sprigs of rosemary, and let the potatoes putter away, but spend a while now and again gently spooning the oil over them. There is a pan of warm milk on the other ring, infusing with cloves of smoked garlic.

As the dish progresses I realise it is more than the accompaniment I intended it to be. On a cold, bleak day such as today, this could be a meal in itself. A slice of air-dried ham on the side, a smoked mackerel in its golden mackintosh, a wispy mop head of frisée to clean the cream from my plate.

When the potatoes have sponged up most of the oil, and are on the verge of collapse, I pour the steaming, smoked scented cream over them and serve them in deep, warm bowls.

# Potatoes with smoked garlic

potatoes – 700g,
  medium-sized
olive oil
rosemary – 3 bushy sprigs
parsley – a small handful

*For the smoked garlic cream:*
double cream – 400ml
smoked garlic – 4 fat cloves

Peel the potatoes, slice them in half lengthways, then put them snugly, cut side down, into a high-sided frying pan, sauté pan or shallow casserole. Pour in enough olive oil to come a third of the way up the potatoes, then add enough water to lap the top of them. You do not need to completely cover the potatoes. Add salt and the sprigs of rosemary.

Set the pan over a moderate heat, bring slowly to the boil, then let them simmer for about forty minutes, turning regularly so they cook evenly through to the middle, letting them soak up as much of the rosemary-scented olive oil and water as possible. Test for doneness with the point of a knife – it should slide in easily.

While the potatoes are cooking, pour the cream into a saucepan, squeeze the smoked garlic from its skins, add to the cream, then bring to the boil. Remove from the heat and leave to infuse.

When the potatoes are almost cooked and the liquid has almost disappeared (a few tablespoons of liquid in the bottom is fine), pour the garlic cream over and continue to simmer for a further ten minutes. Serve in shallow bowls and offer spoons for the sauce. Roughly chop the parsley and scatter over the top. Serves 3–4 as a side dish, 2 as a main dish.

# The glow of maple syrup

## November 15

There is a sticky shelf in the pantry. Home to a leaky jar of molasses, several pots of set and liquid honey (lavender, local London Fields, a piece on the comb), golden syrup in a green and gold tin and a bottle of maple syrup. No matter how fastidiously one wipes them, the various jars and pots half full of liquid amber, gold and jet, always leave a syrupy ring on the shelf. A calling card in molten sugar.

Maple syrup has all the stickiness of golden syrup with the addition of the most glorious nutty, smoky notes. The syrup is made from the sap of black, red and sugar maples, but delve a little deeper, and we must, things start to get complicated.

Canada and America have, at the time of writing, different grading systems for quality, translucency and flavour of their syrups, whilst Vermont, the largest producer, has even more detailed codes. From extra light through medium and amber to dark, the labelling is strictly regulated. Grades within grades. It is all fascinating stuff.

I have always wanted to make a biscuit that tasted of maple syrup. A clear and frosty winter's day that smells of maple syrup biscuits has an element of fairy tale about it. And that is exactly what I do on this bone-cold afternoon, rolling the butterscotch-coloured dough into a log, slicing it thickly and baking biscuits that crumble softly as you eat.

These are just possibly the most delicious biscuits I have ever made. So I sit, drinking coffee, picking up maple-scented crumbs with a damp finger, breathing in soft notes of smoke and syrup.

# Hazelnut maple biscuits

skinned hazelnuts – 120g
butter – 225g
light muscovado sugar
 – 50g
dark maple syrup – 50ml
plain flour – 250g

salt – a pinch

*To finish:*
whole skinned hazelnuts
 – 20g

Set the oven at 200°C/Gas 6. Put the hazelnuts on a baking tray in a single layer and toast them till they are lightly coloured on all sides. Moving them around every now and again will aid even browning. Remove them from the oven and crush to crumbs using a food processor. They should be fine, but not as fine as commercial ground almonds. The nuts should feel a little gritty between the fingers.

Cut the butter into small pieces and put it into the bowl of a food mixer fitted with a flat beater attachment. Add the muscovado sugar and beat till pale and fluffy. Pour in the maple syrup, a tablespoon at a time, beating continually. If the mixture appears to curdle, don't worry, just keep beating. It will eventually become a smooth, soft mixture.

Sieve the flour and the salt, then fold in the nuts. Gradually incorporate the flour and nuts into the creamed butter, sugar and maple syrup. Roll the dough into a thick sausage about 3cm in diameter, then wrap in clingfilm or greaseproof paper and refrigerate for an hour. Don't be tempted to skip this step, no matter how impatient you are to get your biscuits baked.

Set the oven at 160°C/Gas 3. Unwrap the dough and slice it into about sixteen biscuits. Place them snugly on a baking sheet lined with baking parchment. Roughly halve the whole hazelnuts and put a few on top of each biscuit, pressing them gently down into the dough. Bake for twenty minutes. They won't look cooked at this point, but let them cool for a few minutes on the tray, then carefully lift off with a palette knife and cool on a wire baking rack. Makes about 16.

# Brightly shining leaves

They shine so brightly they could be made of emeralds and rubies. Glossy green leaves with red stems, perky as morning. It is not often I see beetroot with leaves in such fine fettle this late in the growing season.

You either like the earthy, mineral sweetness of beetroot or you don't. The root itself is currently a little over-used, popping up on menus as regularly as blood splatter in an episode of *Dexter*. Roasted, the root becomes especially sweet, though it's the very devil to time accurately. Depending on their age, beets (as they are called in the US) can cook in anything from thirty minutes to over an hour when wrapped in foil and baked.

Armed with latex gloves, the skin can easily be peeled from a cooked beetroot. A good clue as to whether the root is cooked is how effortlessly the skin can be slipped off. The leaves cook in a matter of minutes, the exact time being longer than spinach, less than chard. I keep them away from water, preferring to turn them repeatedly in butter and olive oil.

Tonight, dinner is cobbled together from those green and crimson leaves, a couple of potatoes and a can of chickpeas. A hotchpotch, yet the ingredients glow in the pan like a peep into a Victorian jewel box. I make the beetroot stems and their leaves smart a little with something acidic – lemon juice, but I could have used red wine vinegar – to balance their sugar and calm their mineral notes.

# Beetroot leaf sauté

large floury potatoes – 2
olive oil – 3 tablespoons
carrots – 2
garlic – 2 cloves
chickpeas – a 400g tin

beetroot stems – 50g
beetroot leaves – 150g
a small lemon
mint – a small handful

Cut the potatoes in half and then into small cubes. I really don't think it is necessary to peel them. Pour the olive oil into a wide shallow-sided pan, add the potatoes and leave them to cook over a medium heat.

Peel the carrots, cube them similarly and add to the pan. Peel and finely chop the garlic, add to the potatoes and carrots, season with salt and pepper, and continue cooking, stirring from time to time, till the vegetables are approaching tenderness.

Drain the chickpeas and tip into the pan. Let them warm through for ten minutes. Chop the beetroot stems into small pieces, then stir into the pan. Roll the beetroot leaves into a short cigar-like cylinder, then slice into ribbons and fold into the potatoes and chickpeas. Squeeze in the juice of the lemon, chop the mint leaves, stir in and serve. For 4–6.

# Fried chicken, lightly spiced

## November 29

It is not easy to find a bunch of coriander for sale with its roots intact. The long white tails are an important ingredient in recipes for spice pastes, particularly the green ones of Thailand. Chinese, South East Asian and Indian food stores have rooted bunches for sale as a matter of course, but I struggle to find them anywhere else and often make my pastes without them. (And then wonder why they are not quite right.)

The roots appear in my recipe for Thai fried chicken. I wouldn't say they are absolutely essential, but if you can find them, do use them. Their absence, however, is not a good enough reason not to make marinated fried chicken. Left for a few hours in a bath of garlic, ginger, sugar, shallots, lemon grass and fish and oyster sauces, the bony morsels of meat are then lightly dusted with flour and fried till crisp.

The pleasures are abundant. Scorching hot batter, thin, crisp and almost not there. Young chicken flesh that slips from the bone, soft cartilage to crunch, a bone to chew. Most of all, and this is what makes the recipe worth every second of your time, the spice paste – salty, sweet, deeply savoury – that is held in a layer just below the crackling crust.

# Thai fried chicken wings

chicken wings – 12–16,
  depending on their size
oil, for deep-frying
Thai basil leaves – 12
limes – 2

lemon grass – 2 stalks
coriander – a bunch,
  with roots
oyster sauce – 2 tablespoons
fish sauce – 2 tablespoons

*For the marinade:*
garlic – 3 cloves
ginger – a 2cm piece
small shallots – 2
salt – half a teaspoon
sugar – 1 level teaspoon

*For the batter:*
plain flour – 4 tablespoons
cornflour – 6 tablespoons
baking powder – 1 heaped
  teaspoon

Peel the garlic and drop the cloves into the bowl of a food processor. Peel and roughly chop the ginger and shallots, then add to the garlic. Add the salt and sugar, then peel the outer leaves from the lemon grass and discard. Chop the tender inner leaves and add to the ginger and shallot. Add the coriander roots – about twelve should be fine. Pour in the oyster and fish sauces, process to a thick paste, then scrape into a bowl large enough to fit the chicken.

Push the chicken wings down into the marinade, cover, then set aside in the refrigerator for a good four hours, or even overnight.

Make the batter: mix the two types of flour together, then add the baking powder. Warm the oil in a deep pan with plenty of room for it to bubble up without boiling over. (I can't tell you how important this is.)

When the oil reaches 180°C, toss the chicken wings in the flours and lower into the hot oil, taking great care as it tends to bubble enthusiastically. Let the chicken cook for about ten minutes, add the Thai basil leaves, then, as soon as they are crisp (we are talking seconds here), lift out and serve immediately, with the halved limes. For 2.

# DECEMBER

## Reflection and a fine dinner

### December 2

My butcher has some venison, dark red, neatly cubed, and I buy it on a whim. As I consider its fate – a sausage-rich stew, a softly crusted pie or a sauté with parsnips and, possibly, redcurrant jelly – I am reminded of a piece I wrote in my notebook last March in Japan.

'I go down early to breakfast, walking slowly, carefully, on the highly polished floors. There's a bowl of sticky rice, a tiny dish of pickles, a smoked fish and a bowl of buckwheat tea. I sit at the window, staring sleepily at the woods. The tea, clear and dark, tastes of smoke, and smells of the garden the morning after a bonfire. The woodland floor littered with pine needles and the winter's bronze leaves. There is a shallow brook with smooth, mossy rocks to one side, over which the flowing water laughs and babbles, on the other, the woods slope gently down to the water.

The stillness is broken by a sudden flutter of the twigs of a tree overhanging the brook. A spotted fawn, probably a young Sika deer, appears at the water's edge. I feel curiously uncomfortable, as if I shouldn't be here. As if I shouldn't be watching. The fawn looks round, ears up, then bends its neck and laps water from the brook. She – I feel sure it's a she – walks as if on tip-toe along the edge of the water, then disappears, leaving only a trail of trembling branches as witness.

A dish of steamed vegetables is brought to my table. Sansai, the wild greens the chefs have foraged from the mountain this morning. Warabi – fiddlehead ferns – caught in the process of unfurling. Two fukinoto, the open buds of the Japanese butterbur, and a pair of takenoko, the young bamboo shoots. There is a spear that I take to be wild asparagus. The waitress explains these are what the young chefs found this morning on the hillside. (There is a green caterpillar too, which throws me. I am not sure whether this is a delicacy, a gift from the kitchen or simply an oversight.) A dish of green shoots, nipped in their infancy, sweet asparagus, chrysanthemum greens, musky, pleasingly bitter butterbur, steamed and set in a row on a piece of local pottery. I drink water from the hotel's well.

It occurs to me that the deer and I have probably eaten the same breakfast.'

I read the piece twice, then decide to make a stew, with dumplings. My venison is from Scotland, where the deer live a different life. I have walked through their fields, and let them come, albeit gingerly, to investigate the latest trespasser. The farmed deer there live on grass in summer, hay and potatoes in winter. The young ones sleep indoors in hay barns when the weather is particularly icy. 'Farmed' is a bit of a misnomer really. Sadly, an ancient and proud word, a word with growing, nurture and care at its heart, has been degraded in recent years so that it is too often linked with the sinister world of factory farming. Living peacefully outdoors, munching on lush Scottish grass, the life of a 'farmed' deer couldn't be further from a world where thirty thousand chickens spend their entire life in a shed without natural light.

The flavour of venison is mild yet satisfyingly complex. It is not unlike beef. Wild venison is more hit and miss. It may be dry, strong and may occasionally have a bitter note. At its best, wild venison is magnificent.

We still eat very little venison in this country, and the wild deer population sometimes needs culling. Both wild and farmed deer are shot, rather than being transported to slaughterhouses like cattle. Few meats are more environmentally sound. Yes, most cuts of venison are unfortunately very lean, but we can get round that problem by cooking them with fat-rich meats such as pancetta or streaky bacon, or by letting it bubble slowly with sausages, herbs and stock.

# Port-braised venison with oat dumplings

You can use beef or lamb in place of the venison should you wish.
I used up half a bottle of port that had been haunting me for months
(a well-meant gift, but as I don't drink it I was glad to be rid of it), but
any fruity red wine would work in its place.

olive oil – a little
venison – 500g, cubed
shallots – 150g
parsnips – 200g
turnips – 200g
carrots – 150g
thyme – 4–6 sprigs
bay leaves – 3
smoked bacon – 150g
port – 400ml
water – 500ml

*For the oat dumplings:*
plain flour – 70g
fine oatmeal – 70g
baking powder – 1 heaped
  teaspoon
salt – 1 teaspoon
butter – 75g
water – 5 tablespoons

Warm a thin film of oil in a wide, deep pan, add the cubed venison,
let it brown evenly on all sides, then remove to a plate. While the
meat is browning, peel and roughly chop the shallots, parsnips and
turnips, then scrub and roughly chop the carrots and add them all to
the pan. Let the vegetables colour lightly, giving them the occasional
stir, then return the venison and its juices together with the whole
thyme sprigs and the bay leaves. Set the oven at 200°C/Gas 6.

Stir in the bacon, cubed, and continue cooking for a few minutes
before pouring in the port and water and bringing briefly to the boil.
Lower the heat, add salt and black pepper, cover with a lid, then
transfer to the oven and leave to cook for an hour and a half.

Make the oat dumplings: put the flour, oatmeal and baking powder
into a large mixing bowl with the salt and stir well to distribute the

raising agent. Dice the butter and add to the dry ingredients, rubbing it in with your fingertips until the mixture resembles coarse, fresh breadcrumbs. (You can do this in a food processor if you wish.) Spoon in the water and mix, adding a little less or more as necessary to give a firm, but not sticky dough.

Tear off lumps of the dough and roll each one into a small ball, using a very little flour if necessary. Remove the lid from the venison, lower the dumplings, not touching, into the liquid, cover, then continue baking for fifteen to twenty minutes, until they are risen. Serve the venison in shallow bowls, with the oat dumplings. For 6.

# A dazzling pickle

December 7

Ginger will provide the backbone, together with garlic and spring onion, for many a Chinese, Vietnamese or Thai recipe, but a piece of the root, pale-skinned and plump, is useful to finish a dish with too. Cut a small piece, stuff it into a garlic press and squeeze hard. The meagre raindrops of juice that emerge will brighten a piece of grilled chicken, a fillet of mackerel or, I found this week, a piece of raw salmon. You can grate it too, including it in a marinade for chicken or pork that is to be grilled or roasted.

My fridge is almost never without a sachet of sushi ginger, the ivory shavings of pickled root (it's a rhizome really, like galangal or the common or garden iris) that cure almost any craving, sweet or savoury. I made my own late last year, with the help of David Tanis's recipe, and his notion of adding a little beetroot. This time, I up the beetroot content considerably to give a pickle that is piquant, earthy and sweet. The colour is dazzling, the flavour exhilarating. A kind of sweet heat. It will keep, in a Kilner jar in the fridge, for two to three weeks.

## Pickled ginger and beetroot

caster sugar – 1¹/₂ tablespoons
sea salt – 1¹/₂ teaspoons
rice vinegar – 5 tablespoons

fresh ginger – 250g
raw beetroot – 3 thin slices
an orange

Put the caster sugar and salt into a large Kilner or screw-topped glass jar and pour in the rice vinegar. Stir or shake the ingredients in the jar until the salt has dissolved.

Peel the ginger, then slice it finely into strips or rounds, as thinly as you can. Ideally, each piece should be almost transparent. Submerge the ginger, as best you can, in the vinegar solution. Add the beetroot. Remove two 10cm long strips of zest from the orange, removing any white pith, then cut into the thinnest possible shreds and add to the jar, shaking it so that the ginger and beetroot are covered.

Leave, at room temperature, for a minimum of five hours, then refrigerate till needed. It will keep for two or three weeks in the fridge.

# Game pie. Parsnip crisps.

### December 16

Pigeons are to the urban gardener what rabbits are to the farmer. They peck the yellow crocus buds from the snow; make a lunch of our treasured cabbage seedlings; and in autumn leave elderberry and white splatters over the garden furniture. They can also strip a row of peas in minutes.

Whilst I will happily watch the wrens and robins that visit this garden for hours on end, and will listen enthralled to the woodpecker tapping away at the grey trunk of the robinia in April, I think pigeons are best observed simmering in a pot.

Of course, those birds we buy from the butcher are not the city pigeon and thank goodness for that. But even with that knowledge up my sleeve, there is still an element of 'serve you right' that accompanies the cooking of this particular bird.

I got my own back for the crocuses today by simmering a pack of pigeon breasts with mushrooms and a broth made from Marsala and dried porcini. The birds were bathed in a sauce as dark as a medieval wooden floor, mellow with dried and fresh mushrooms, and made festive with frozen cranberries. An element of crunch was introduced to the general softness with slices of parsnip cooked on top of the stew, their surface crisp, their underside chewy and soaked in blisteringly hot pigeon gravy.

# Pigeon, parsnip and porcini pie

A special pie for Christmas, with a soft, game and mushroom filling and topped with parsnip crisps.

dried porcini – 20g
water – 750ml
chestnut mushrooms – 250g
butter – 50g
olive or groundnut oil
pigeon breasts – 500g
plain flour – a heaped
   tablespoon

*For the top:*
a large parsnip
cranberries – 100g
butter – 80g
rosemary, chopped –
   1 tablespoon

Put the dried porcini into a heatproof bowl, then bring the water to the boil and pour over the porcini. Cover and set aside for fifteen minutes, to give a clear, golden brown broth.

Slice the chestnut mushrooms thickly, cook them, with some of the butter and oil, in a casserole or deep-sided frying pan till they are nut brown, then remove them and set aside.

Add a little more butter and oil to the pan and return to the heat. Season the pigeon breasts, then brown them nicely on both sides in the butter and oil. Return the mushrooms to the pan, scatter the flour over and cook briefly, then pour in 600ml of the porcini stock, stir well and add the porcini. Simmer gently for ten minutes, then set aside.

Set the oven at 180°C/Gas 4. Peel the parsnip and thinly slice into discs. Transfer the pigeon mixture to a large pie dish or shallow casserole. Scatter the cranberries over the surface. Melt the butter in a pan, add the finely chopped rosemary, then add the sliced parsnips and toss gently. Place the parsnips on top of the pigeon mixture, making sure they are all covered in butter, then bake for forty-five to fifty minutes, till the parsnips are crisp and the filling is bubbling. Serves 4–5.

# Dark chocolate and sugared fruits

## December 18

I decorated sheets of dark chocolate today, for snapping into jagged shards and serving with coffee. I scattered the liquid chocolate with segments of preserved clementines and crushed sugared rose petals, toasted almonds and chopped pistachios, letting the chocolate set till brittle.

## Chocolate fruit and nut slice

The sweetness of the rose petals and crystallised fruits means a dark chocolate is more appropriate here than a sweet, creamy milk version. It is, of course, up to you. I used an artisan-made 70 per cent dark chocolate.

| | |
|---|---|
| skinned hazelnuts – 100g | mixed crystallised fruits: |
| dark chocolate – 400g | pears, citrons, clementines |
| | – 400g in total |
| | a few sugared rose petals |
| | sea salt flakes – a teaspoon |

Set the oven at 180°C/Gas 4. Put the hazelnuts on a baking sheet in a single layer, then bake for fifteen to twenty minutes, watching them carefully, removing them when they are thoroughly brown.

Put a pan of water on to boil, with a heatproof glass or china bowl resting snugly on top. The bottom of the bowl shouldn't quite touch the water. Break the chocolate into small pieces and let it melt in the bowl over the hot water. It will melt more smoothly if you don't stir it, just leave it to melt, occasionally pushing any unmelted pieces under the surface.

Line a 32cm × 22cm tray with non-stick baking parchment. Pour the melted chocolate into the tray, and shake firmly to spread over the surface and into the corners.

Chop the crystallised fruits into small wedges or dice. I think a mixture of sizes looks best. Scatter the fruits over the chocolate. Break the rose petals into small pieces and distribute them between the fruits. Roughly chop the hazelnuts and scatter them over the chocolate. Lastly, add the sea salt flakes and leave in a cool place to set. The fridge is ideal for a short time, but don't leave the chocolate in there longer than an hour.

Snap into jagged pieces. Serves 10.

# A change of heart

## December 19

I didn't think I liked bread sauce. It turns out I simply hadn't had a good one. And by good, I mean one made with creamy milk in which bay leaves and whole peppercorns have been left to infuse. Where a few whole cloves have been floated on the surface of the milk as it shimmers towards the boil; and where an onion or shallot has been introduced as a backbone to the aromatics. What I had considered bread sauce was in reality little more than bread and milk.

I can think of few accompaniments that rely so heavily on their seasoning. Getting the balance of aromatics right is essential. In the right quantity, cloves give off a spicy floral note, as garden pinks do when caught on a warm breeze. In quantity, though, they will set your teeth on edge. You will need at least a couple of bay leaves, but any more than four and a bitter note can intrude. Black peppercorns, much gentler than the white ones, are crucial, as, I think, is the inclusion of shallot or onion.

James and I spend much of the morning developing recipes for our forthcoming series, *Eating Together*, and we both want to include a bread sauce recipe. In the series it is to go with pork and James has the idea of grating apple into it. I have long cooked apples with pheasant (see *Tender II*) and wonder if it would be a good accompaniment to a roast bird.

After much crumbling of bread, infusing of milk and grating of apples, we end up with a blissful bowl of sauce that brings with it the scents of warm bread and mulled cider. It has so many of the qualities of porridge, risotto, wet polenta, dal.

The moment when the pool of warm, bay-infused bread sauce on our plates merged with the roasting juices from the pheasant was the best Christmas gift of all. I just wish it hadn't taken me so long to discover I like bread sauce.

# Roast pheasant with apple bread sauce

pheasants – 2
banana shallots – 4
butter – a thick slice
olive oil – 2 tablespoons
streaky bacon rashers – 6

milk – 1 litre
bay leaves – 2
black peppercorns – 8
a cinnamon stick
white bread – 300g

*For the bread sauce:*
a shallot
cloves – 4
half an apple

*To finish:*
a whole apple
a little ground cinnamon

Set the oven at 180°C/Gas 4. Pull any stubborn feathers from the birds and wipe the skin gently to dry it, taking care not to tear it.

Peel the shallots and halve them lengthways. Warm the butter and oil in a roasting tin large enough to hold the shallots and the birds, then put the shallots in, cut side down. Let them colour very lightly over moderate heat, then turn them over and turn off the heat.

Lower the birds into the roasting tin, setting them side by side, so they roast evenly. Rub a little butter over the breasts and lay the bacon over the top, to keep them juicy. Roast them for thirty-five minutes, removing the bacon to the side of the birds for the last ten minutes.

To make the bread sauce, peel the shallot and pierce it with a couple of the cloves, then pierce the apple with the other two. Put the shallot and the apple into a fairly large, heavy-based saucepan, pour in the milk, then add the bay leaves, peppercorns and cinnamon stick. Bring the milk to the boil, turn off the heat and set aside for ten minutes.

Reduce the bread to coarse soft crumbs, then stir them into the milk. Grate some of the finishing apple into the sauce, then slowly warm through, stirring so the sauce doesn't catch. Spoon it into a warm bowl, grate over more apple and sprinkle with a fine dusting of cinnamon. Serve with the pheasant and its juices. For 4.

# A savoury pie for Christmas

## December 20

The ancient recipes for mince pies continue to intrigue me. With their stir-up of chopped dried fruit, beef and spices encased in pastry they sound both extravagant and extraordinary. Yet, in my kitchen, they remain something to read about rather than cook. The modern development, of brandy-soaked currants and raisins in a sugar-frosted, sweet-crusted tart, has only a freckling of suet to remind us of its origins. Even that is often left out now, suet having become the very devil itself.

In truth, I have never made the original meat-based filling. A recipe from cookery writer Eliza Acton sees the Victorian housewife stirring the minced meats (we are talking boiled and skinned ox tongue here) with grated apples, lemon zest, raisins, Madeira, sugar and candied peel, then seasoning it with mace, ginger and enough nutmeg to make you see Christmas fairies.

Whilst remaining perfectly happy with a modern, meatless filling for my mince pies, I am nevertheless fond of spiced meats sweetened with fruit. The pork terrine with figs in *Diaries II*, for instance. Fruited, spiced meat recipes seem especially appropriate for this time of year, possessing a suitably festive and luxurious note to them.

It crosses my mind that a sausage roll, sweetened with dried fruit, might go down well at Christmas. A sort of faggot with fruit and pastry. I set about stirring together minced pork, streaky bacon and a little liver with the sweetness of soft, stoned prunes and a little spice in the form of allspice, ginger and a dusting of nutmeg. A filling, in essence, not so far from the early mince pie recipes, it turns out to be one of the most delicious dishes of the season. Sweet, spicy, festive, and yes, a little intriguing.

# A Christmas sausage roll

sausage meat – 400g
medium banana shallots – 2
bacon – 4 rashers
garlic – 3 cloves, crushed
lamb's liver – 200g
prunes, soft-dried – 100g

ginger – 1 teaspoon
nutmeg – half a teaspoon
ground allspice – 1 teaspoon
puff pastry – 2 × 215g sheets
a little beaten egg

Put the sausage meat into a large mixing bowl. Peel and finely chop the shallots, then cook them, together with the bacon, cut into small pieces, and the crushed garlic, in a shallow pan till soft and golden. Let the bacon colour and crisp a little. Add the softened shallots and bacon to the sausage meat.

Finely chop the liver and add to the mixture, together with the roughly chopped prunes, the ginger, nutmeg and allspice, and a good seasoning of salt and black pepper. Mix thoroughly.

Set the oven at 200°C/Gas 6. Place one piece of pastry on a baking sheet and trim it on the longest sides, to give a slim rectangle roughly 18cm wide and 30cm long.

Pile the mixture down the middle and smooth into a low sausage shape, leaving a wide rim of bare pastry around the edges. Brush the edges with some of the beaten egg, then place the second sheet of pastry over the top, trim, and press the edges tightly to seal. Brush the pastry with beaten egg. If you wish, use the pastry trimmings to decorate the top of the pie with holly leaves and berries.

Score a series of cuts in the top of the pastry, so they will open a little in the oven, like Venetian blinds, allowing a peek at the meat within, then brush with more of the beaten egg.

Bake for about forty minutes, until risen and golden. Serves 6.

# The eve of the feast and
# a sweet Christmas pie

## December 24

I light the fire. Christmas is unthinkable without a fire in the hearth. I play carols, wallowing in them all, but waiting somewhat impatiently for 'Silent Night', the carol I love above all others. A carol that feels much older than its early nineteenth-century Salzburg origins. (I have asked that Franz Xaver Gruber's carol, set to Joseph Mohr's lyrics, be sung at my funeral, regardless of the time of year.)

This is the day I roast chicken wings and bones with which to make stock. The afternoon I roll, fill and bake mince pies. The evening I make stuffing for the bird with sausage meat, caramelised onions and thyme. It is the one day of the year, possibly the only day, I can call myself an organised cook. I love cooking, but also the art of being prepared. It is why I put the following day's clothes out every night before I go to bed. I like waking up knowing that what I will wear that day is already sorted. No thinking, just getting dressed.

Christmas is not the time for attempting new, untried recipes. Yet today I throw a spanner into my neat and tidy little Christmas by trying out a pie to serve with glasses of sweet Muscat later this evening. What I am trying to achieve, a sweet crusted pie tightly packed with dried fruits, part mince pie, part Christmas pudding, iced with a thin layer of crisp white icing, is so clear in my head I am not worried about sticking to my usual favourite recipes.

I include pistachio nuts in the filling. The effect, soft, crunchy, sweet and unmistakably festive, is not dissimilar to a panforte, the flat Italian fruit cake, though less chewy and with a loose, crumbly texture. I am exceedingly happy with this and will make it again next year. The lemon icing seems like overkill, but also curiously appropriate.

# Christmas pie

*For the pastry:*
butter – 140g
plain flour – 250g
icing sugar – 50g
a large egg yolk
a little beaten egg

*For the filling:*
dried cranberries – 100g
soft dried peaches – 200g
soft dried apricots – 200g
soft prunes – 150g
golden sultanas – 200g
pistachios, shelled – 100g
apricot jam – 150g

honey – 150g
ground cinnamon –
    1 teaspoon
ground allspice – 1 level
    teaspoon
ground cardamom – 1 level
    teaspoon
the zest of an orange
the zest of a lemon
Marsala – 125ml

*For the icing:*
icing sugar – 50g
the juice of a lemon

You will need a deep, 20cm cake tin with a removable base.

Make the pastry: rub the butter into the flour, either with your fingertips or using a food processor. Add the icing sugar and the egg yolk, then bring the dough together, press it into a round, wrap it in clingfilm and let it rest in the fridge for twenty minutes.

Set the oven at 180°C/Gas 4. Put the dried cranberries into a capacious mixing bowl. Chop the dried peaches, apricots and prunes into small pieces and add them to the cranberries, together with the sultanas and the pistachios, lightly chopped. If you use a food processor, mix only briefly, so the fruits stay in small pieces.

Add the jam and honey to the fruits, along with the cinnamon, allspice and cardamom, and mix gently, stirring in the finely grated zest of the orange and lemon as you go. Finally, stir in the Marsala and set aside.

Remove the pastry from the fridge, cut it in two, one half slightly larger than the other, then roll out the larger of the two pieces and use it to line the base of the cake tin, pulling the pastry halfway up the inside of the tin, pressing it firmly to the sides so it stays put.

Pile the fruit filling into the pastry case, smooth the surface fairly flat, then roll out the second piece of pastry and place over the top. Pinch the edges of the pastry together to seal, brush the surface with some of the beaten egg and pierce a couple of small holes in the top.

Bake the pie in the preheated oven for an hour and a half, then remove from the oven and leave to cool a little. Run a palette knife around the edge of the pie to loosen it from the cake tin, then carefully remove it from its tin.

In a small bowl, mix the icing sugar with enough of the lemon juice to make a runny icing. Trickle the icing over the pie, and leave for a few minutes to set. Serves 10.

# Christmas morning

## December 25

Its 5.30 a.m., and I should still be asleep. I pull the blinds, timidly, hoping for snowfall. Snow has fallen on Christmas Day in London just twenty-seven times since 1752 and only once since 1992. There is virtually no chance of seeing Mr Tumnus prancing through a lamp-lit garden blanketed in snow this morning.

I get up, have coffee, then make dough. The dough, a simple yeast bread base enriched with sugar and egg, sits near the Aga for a good hour while I potter around.

The dough is to form a crust for small, round buns, to be eaten warm, filled with a paste of marzipan and clementine zest. The dough is tricky to wrap around the filling, and I press hard to seal the edges together. Even then, they leak a little in their muffin tray as they bake, the almond paste caramelising slightly on the tin. It somehow makes them even more delightful, wobbly and welcoming.

They take two and a half hours from start to finish, which is asking a lot of any cook on Christmas morning. I suddenly realise that dusted with icing sugar they look like snowballs, which is of course what I was secretly hoping for when I pulled the blinds this morning.

# Warm marzipan buns

If you have time to play, these are the most wonderful little goods, eaten freshly baked.

*For the dough:*
strong bread flour – 450g
easy bake dried yeast – 7g
golden caster sugar –
 2 teaspoons
warm water – about 350ml
beaten egg, for glazing

*For the filling:*
marzipan – 400g
the zest of 2 clementines
chopped pistachios – 100g
flaked almonds, toasted – 75g
dark chocolate – 50g

Put the flour into a large bowl, sprinkle in the dried yeast and the sugar, then pour in enough of the water to make a soft but rollable dough. It should be a little sticky. Tip the dough on to a floured board and knead for a good six minutes, or use a food mixer fitted with a dough hook. Leave the dough in the bowl, in a warm place, covered with clingfilm for an hour, till well risen.

While the dough is proving, make the filling. Break the marzipan into small pieces and drop them into a mixing bowl or food processor with the grated zest of the clementines, the chopped pistachios and the flaked almonds. Chop the chocolate to the size of coarse gravel, then add to the marzipan and mix thoroughly. Set the oven at 220°C/Gas 7.

Tear the bread dough into fifteen pieces, then flatten and roll each into a small disc about 8cm in diameter. Brush the edge of one of the pieces of dough with beaten egg, then place a ball of marzipan in the centre. Bring the dough around the ball of marzipan, pressing the edges very tightly to seal. Place the ball of dough in a very lightly oiled muffin tin, then continue with the rest of the dough and marzipan mixtures.

Brush each ball of dough with some of the beaten egg, then pierce a tiny hole in the top of each and bake for ten minutes, till golden. Eat warm, while they are still oozing warm almond paste. Makes 15.

# The roast

## December 25

The roast is resting, those precious twenty minutes after the joint and its crackling are taken from the oven and left to sit quietly before we carve. The roasting tin may no longer hold the meat, but there is much treasure there to plunder. We could make a simple gravy, and I usually do, dissolving the good things left by the roast into wine, stock or Marsala. But today I use the roasting tin for something more substantial altogether.

What lies beneath the meat? Well, caramelised sugars mostly, sweet, gooey and firmly attached to the roasting tin. It is the concentrated essence of the meat, some charred herbs, sizzling fat, a sticky smudge of roasted garlic. A little magic perhaps. To waste it would be a crime.

I pour a straightforward batter, the egg, flour and milk type I usually use for a Yorkshire, into the roasting tin. It will take twenty-five minutes in a hot oven, time enough to rest the meat, to carve and pass round the plates and vegetables. But there is more to it than that. I have tossed some diced apple, softened first with a few thyme leaves while the meat was cooking, into the pan. The little cubes of apple sit in the batter, holding it down a bit (don't expect your usual cloud-like pudding), soaking up the juices and savour left behind by the pork.

It arrives at the table a little late, slightly eccentric-looking, but dark and golden, its surface all pits and furrows of batter and fruit, smelling of roast pork and herbs. I could have cooked the batter pudding separately, all spick and span like a clafoutis without the sugar, but that would be to miss out on the opportunity of using the good things left in the roasting tin. Of exploring what lies beneath.

# Pork belly with apple and thyme batter pudding

I am no butcher, so I ask my local one to leave the skin on the belly but to score it either in lines about 2cm apart or in a lattice pattern, whichever he thinks will produce the crispest crackling.

| | |
|---|---|
| belly pork – 1.5kg, boned weight, skin scored | olive oil – 3 tablespoons |
| | rosemary – 3 large sprigs |
| new potatoes – 500g | garlic – 4 cloves |

Set the oven at 230°C/Gas 8. Place the pork belly flat on the work surface, skin side down, then slice it horizontally, cutting almost all the way through, to give a large hinged flap. Season generously inside and out.

Put a pan of water on to boil and salt it. Wash the potatoes but don't feel the need to peel them. Cut each potato into three or four 'coins', then lower them into the boiling water. When the potatoes are tender to the point of a knife, drain them carefully and tip them into a bowl.

Pour the olive oil over the potatoes, then pull a few of the needles from the rosemary and add to the bowl with a grinding of salt and black pepper. Place the pork in a roasting tin. Lay the potatoes, as near as possible in a single layer, in between the two layers of pork. Tuck the remaining sprigs of rosemary and the cloves of garlic amongst the potatoes. Pull the top flap of meat over the potatoes, then place in the oven and leave to sizzle for about twenty-five minutes.

Lower the heat to 180°C/Gas 4, then leave the pork to cook for about an hour and a half, basting occasionally. During this time the potatoes will soften and soak up the juices and fat from the meat.

Remove the pork from the oven, check the potatoes are fully tender, then remove from the tin, cover lightly with foil and leave to rest in a warm place. Serve the pork as it is, carving in thick strips, or utilise the roasting tin and its fat with the recipe below. Serves 6.

# Pork dripping apple batter pudding

To serve with the pork. The sweet, dark crust left behind after the pork has been taken out is what gives this batter pudding its deep savour, but you can make it from scratch if you prefer. Use oil or lard, not butter, which would burn in the high oven heat, getting it very hot before you add the batter. Do make sure to cook the apples first – they should be soft and golden.

apples, such as Cox's – 3 large  
olive oil – 2 tablespoons  
half a lemon

*For the batter:*  
plain flour – 125g

eggs – 2  
milk – 150ml  
water – 150ml  
thyme leaves – a tablespoon

Turn the oven to 230°C/Gas 8. Halve and core the apples and cut them into small dice, roughly 1cm square. Warm the olive oil in a shallow pan, then add the apples and fry them, over a gentle heat, for about eight to ten minutes, till tender but not soft. They should be a nice even golden colour. Squeeze in the lemon juice.

Make the batter: tip the flour into a mixing bowl, add the eggs and the milk and whisk lightly. Nothing will come from beating too much. Beat in the water, thyme leaves and season.

Lift the apples from the pan with a draining spoon and into the roasting tin, then place in the oven for a few minutes to heat thoroughly. When the fat is warm and the apples are quietly sizzling, pour in the batter and return the tin to the oven for twenty minutes, by which time the batter will have risen and turned golden brown. Don't expect it to rise as high as a Yorkshire pudding, as the apples will prevent that.

Pudding ready and meat rested, serve either together, or the pudding a few minutes after the meat. Serves 6.

# Deep and crisp and even ...

December 26

## Walnut meringue with apples and custard

*For the meringue:*
caster sugar – 250g
egg whites – 6
cornflour – 1 tablespoon
white wine vinegar –
  2 teaspoons
shelled walnuts – 50g

*For the custard:*
milk – 600ml

a vanilla pod
egg yolks – 6
caster sugar – 50g
cornflour – 2 tablespoons

*For the apples:*
apples, sweet – 500g
butter – 50g
flaked almonds – a handful

You will need a shallow-sided baking tin roughly 32cm × 22cm.

Pour the milk into a non-stick saucepan. Split the vanilla pod in half lengthways, scrape out the black seeds with the point of a knife, and add to the milk, together with the empty pods. Bring the milk almost to the boil, then remove from the heat and set aside for the vanilla to scent the milk.

Mix the egg yolks and sugar together with a wooden spoon, then stir in the cornflour. Pour the warm milk over the egg yolks, stirring to combine, then return to the pan and place over a moderate heat. Stirring almost continuously, let the custard warm and thicken. Remove from the heat, pour into a cold bowl, then leave to cool. Refrigerate as soon as the mixture is cool enough to go into the fridge, to encourage it to thicken further.

Set the oven at 200°C/Gas 6. To make the meringue, scatter the sugar in a fine layer over a baking sheet and place in the oven for five minutes or so to warm.

Put the egg whites into a deep mixing bowl, preferably the bowl of a food mixer, then beat fairly slowly, till white and fluffy. I find the process works best with a food mixer and a whisk attachment, but a hand whisk will do the trick too.

Tip the warm sugar, a few tablespoons at a time, into the egg whites, beating all the time at a moderate to high speed. The sugar added, continue beating for a good five minutes, till the egg whites and sugar are stiff and glossy. They should be able to stand in stiff, shiny peaks. Mix in the cornflour and the vinegar.

While the eggs and sugar are beating, toast the walnuts in a shallow pan over a moderate heat till the skins darken. Rub the nuts in a tea towel to remove as much of the skin as possible (don't even try to remove all of it, a thoroughly annoying job), then put them back into the pan and toast till golden. Take care not to let them darken too much, as they can turn bitter. Chop them roughly.

As soon as the meringue has stiffened, add the toasted walnuts. Instead of mounding the mixture into individual meringues, line a rectangular baking sheet with baking parchment, then scrape the meringue mixture on to it and smooth level, pushing it right to the edges. Place in the oven and immediately turn the heat down to 140°C/Gas 1. Bake for forty-five minutes, till crisp and marshmallowy. Remove from the oven and leave to cool.

While the meringue cools, prepare the apples. Halve, core and thinly slice the apples, then fry them in the butter till soft, and just short of collapse. Toast the almonds.

When the meringue has cooled, using a large spoon, press the crust lightly to give six shallow hollows. Spoon the chilled custard into the hollows, then spoon over the warm apples and sprinkle with the almonds. Serves 6.

# Crumpkins and mufflets

## December 28

The patch between Boxing Day and New Year is something of a culinary no-man's-land. A time of making the best of what is left from the feast, a smorgasbord of pig's ears turned into silk purses and bouts of gentle invention. It is also a time to play. To spend more time than usual in the kitchen, cookbooks out, radio on – brioche perhaps, or to embark on a sourdough starter, a chance to master croissants. It is certainly the only time in the year I can devote an entire afternoon to making crumpets.

Well, I say crumpets. I started with a characteristically sloppy, ivory-coloured crumpet batter, but once I had made my mind up to introduce melted cheese and the trimmings from the Christmas ham they had lost their characteristic holes and resembled English muffins. Hmm. We then spent a good five minutes christening these yeast-risen hybrids that were neither crumpets, pikelets nor muffins. Crumpkins perhaps, or maybe pupplets or cruffets. My suggestion of mufflets was, probably wisely, overruled.

The mixture is little more than flour, water, yeast and a pinch of bicarbonate of soda. Unlike most British baked goods, the batter is pourable, rising up the moulds (I used pastry cutters, but you can buy non-stick crumpet rings at cookware shops) and developing bubbles on the surface, which then burst to form tiny holes. This is usually where I stop, slide a palette knife around the edge, wriggle the crumpet out of its ring and reach for the butter. But rather than play my usual game of how much butter will this thing hold, I dotted crumbled remnants of Stilton and shreds of ham on top, letting it melt, then turned them over to sizzle the cheese. The result was really quite wonderful.

# Ham and Stilton crumpets

Leave the batter to rest for a good hour and a half, until it has risen to twice its volume. Oil or butter both the pan and the crumpet rings, even if the ones you have are non-stick.

| | |
|---|---|
| skimmed milk – 175ml | bicarbonate of soda – a pinch |
| water – 160ml | Stilton or other blue cheese |
| plain flour – 225g | – 200g |
| salt – half a teaspoon | cooked ham – 100g |
| easy bake dried yeast – 7g | melted butter – a little |

Pour the milk and water into a small pan and warm to just about blood heat. It shouldn't be so hot you can't put your finger in it. Put the flour into a large mixing bowl, stir in the salt, dried yeast and bicarbonate of soda, then pour in the warmed milk and water and mix thoroughly to a thick, sticky batter. Beat for a full minute with either a wooden spoon or a flat whisk.

Cover the bowl with a cloth or clingfilm and set aside in a warm place for an hour and a half. The batter will rise to almost double the volume. Crumble the cheese into small pieces and finely chop the ham, then set aside.

Warm a heavy-based frying pan or griddle over a moderate heat. Brush the crumpet rings with melted butter and place them on the surface of the pan or griddle. Make sure the heat is on low, then pour a sixth of the batter into each ring. Let it slowly rise and cook for about ten minutes, occasionally checking the base of each.

When the top of each one is almost firm to the touch, scatter over the cheese and chopped ham. Continue cooking for a minute or two, then run a knife around the edge of each ring to release the crumpets.

Flip the crumpets over briefly so the cheese and ham start to colour a little. As soon as the top is golden brown, lift each one from the pan with a fish slice or palette knife and eat immediately. Makes 6.

# Another year

## December 30

The day ends as it so often does at this time of year, sitting around the kitchen table with a glass of sloe gin. Heg-pegs, slags, winter kecksies or sloes, the fruit of the blackthorn bush is the tiny, bitter fruit that gives sloe gin its glorious garnet hue. It is what brings the deep damson flavour to what has long been my go-to frosty night tipple.

This year, I failed to make my usual batch. One of the perils of this crazily busy life, my failure to put away good things for the future: pickles, chutney, jam and gin. This winter's stash is a commercial one, albeit the work of a small artisan maker. It is slightly less intense than my own, and less sweet, which is probably a good thing. I have taken to adding a splash to the occasional Negroni.

Finding the sloes is virtually impossible to an unconnected city dweller like myself. But they still line many of our country lanes, thick with a snowfall of white blossom in spring, the fruits dotted through the branches in autumn and winter like tiny purple bonbons.

Punctured by pin or rolling pin, the fruit is dropped into bottles with what seems like a frightening amount of sugar, then topped up with gin. The sugar, which is needed to soften the exceptional bitterness of the berries, will slowly dissolve, and regular turning of the bottles will help the colour and flavour permeate the spirit. Six to eight weeks later, when you have almost forgotten its existence, you will find a drink of glorious colour, nicely balanced between bitter and sweet, the colour of a papal robe.

Spirits, to my taste, are more appropriate in a glass than on a plate. Yet a brandy-fuelled fruit cake has a certain majesty. Feeding a fruit cake with booze being one of the better moments in a cook's life. I might draw the line at the notion of a tot in my porridge of a weekday morning, but this is one spirit I am happy to bring into the

kitchen and I use it tonight, to make poached apples, which will be served tomorrow, thoroughly chilled, their cheeks as pink as those of a child on a toboggan.

Needless to say, one or two are consumed whilst the fruit and its glowing syrup are still warm. A midnight feast that leaves me both deliriously happy and wracked with guilt.

## Apples in sloe gin syrup

Offer cream for those who wish it, but it will intrude on the quiet purity of the dessert.

| | |
|---|---|
| caster sugar – 200g | coriander seeds – 10 |
| water – 400ml | red or blackcurrant jelly – |
| small, sweet apples – 6 | 3 tablespoons |
| a tangerine | sloe gin – 150ml |
| half a cinnamon stick | |

Put the caster sugar into a heavy-based, medium-sized saucepan, pour in the water and bring to the boil. Peel the apples, but leave them whole. If they are more medium than small, peel and halve them (in which case you might as well core them too).

Lower the apples into the boiling syrup, then reduce the heat to a gentle simmer. Peel three wide strips of zest from the tangerine, then drop them into the syrup together with the cinnamon stick and the coriander seeds.

Stir in the fruit jelly, then add the sloe gin and let the apples continue to cook for fifteen to thirty minutes, depending on their variety and size, till they are tender.

Watch the progress of the apples carefully (they go from tender to a state of fluffy collapse in the blink of an eye). Serve the apples warm, with their syrup.

# Glorious, glorious goose fat

## New Year's Eve

The sixth day of Christmas, but I am not sure I would thank you for geese-a-laying. More interesting is their fat, snow-white and soft enough to spread on hot toast, freckled with flakes of sea salt and needles of rosemary.

I have a pot of goose fat in the fridge right now, drained from the baking tin of the Christmas roast, saved specifically for cooking potatoes but open to other ideas too. The lard-like whiteness made me wonder about using the fat in pastry, in particular a hot water crust, the sort you might use for a pork pie.

The fat that pours from a goose as it roasts is rather like duck fat, being relatively low in saturated fat at 28 per cent (beef dripping is 45, butter is 50), and present in the sort of quantity that will protect a bird from cold water. You can buy it from butchers and supermarkets, food halls and specialist shops, in jars and tins.

The pie worked a treat, but rather than one large one with high, hand-pulled edges, I made eight, each the size of a mince pie, and stuffed them with a tangle of softened onions, parsley and ham. A riff on the pork pie, but intended to be eaten hot, as indeed they were, with a crackling winter salad of shredded, blanched cabbage with a mustard seed dressing. Because of their richness, the eight little pies served four.

# Pork and onion pies with goose fat pastry

The pastry is very fragile – I use plenty of flour to roll it out.

*For the pastry:*
plain flour – 400g
goose fat – 200g
milk – 80ml
water – 80ml
beaten egg, for glazing

*For the filling:*
a medium onion
butter – a little

butcher's herby breakfast
   sausages – 2
cooked smoked ham – 100g
flour – 2 tablespoons
hot stock – 200ml
parsley – a few sprigs,
   chopped

*To serve:*
melted redcurrant jelly

Peel the onion and slice thinly, then let it colour in a little butter in a large, non-stick frying pan over a moderate heat. Remove the skin from the sausages, then add them, broken into small pieces, to the pan. Press them down with a palette knife and let them brown. Tear the ham into small pieces and add to the onion and sausage. Leave to brown lightly, add the flour and continue cooking for a minute or two, then introduce the stock and the parsley.

To make the pastry, season the flour with salt and black pepper. Put the fat, milk and water into a small saucepan and bring to the boil, then tip in the flour and stir briefly and firmly with a wooden spoon till you have a soft, smooth paste. Put a cloth over the pan and set aside for fifteen minutes to cool a little. The dough must not go cold.

Flour a wooden board or work surface generously (adding more as you feel the need), then knead the pastry, lightly, for a minute or two. Roll out the pastry, somewhat thicker than usual, roughly the thickness of two pound coins placed on top of one another. Using a cookie cutter or the rim of a tumbler, cut out rounds about 8cm in diameter (you will get 12–16 of them) and place half of them on a baking sheet lined with baking paper. Set the oven at 200°C/Gas 6.

Place two heaped tablespoons of the filling on each of the pastry rounds on the baking sheet, then brush a little beaten egg around the edge of each one. Place one of the remaining rounds of pastry on top of each, pressing the edges together either with your floured thumb or the tines of a fork. Brush with some of the beaten egg, pierce a small, single hole or slit in the centre of each little pie, then bake for thirty-five minutes, till nut brown and softly crisp. Leave to cool briefly, then serve warm rather than cold, with a pot of redcurrant jelly or cranberry sauce, lightly warmed. Makes 6–8 little pies, serving 3–4.

# Winter
# eats

# Meatball broth

celeriac, meatballs, spring onions, thyme, beef stock, Parmesan

Peel and grate **250g of celeriac**. Brown **250g of good-quality meatballs** in **a little oil** in a smallish, deep-sided pan. When they are sizzling and evenly coloured, add **4 spring onions**, roughly chopped, cook for a minute or two until the onions have softened, then add the grated celeriac and continue cooking briefly. Add **6 little sprigs of thyme**, then pour in **500ml of beef stock**. Bring to the boil, then lower the heat and leave to simmer for 15 minutes. Check the seasoning – it may need pepper and perhaps a little salt – then shake **40g of grated Parmesan** over the top. Place under a hot grill until the cheese starts to colour. Serves 2.

&

Get the oil hot before you add the meatballs, so they brown quickly, and move them gently round the pan as they colour to prevent them breaking up. Once the stock has come to the boil, lower the heat to a simmer so that the meatballs cook gently. If the liquid boils for too long, the meatballs will collapse.

&

You can buy ready-made meatballs from good butchers and supermarkets. If you want to make your own, use 500g of finely minced beef with a little salt, pepper and a pinch of ground mace. Use allspice if you prefer. Roll into balls about 2cm in diameter and leave for a good hour to firm up in the fridge before using. If celeriac isn't your thing, try parsnip, or even carrot.

# Feta with blood oranges and sesame

sesame seeds, runny honey, feta, blood oranges, olive oil,
white wine vinegar, spinach

Toast **3 tablespoons of sesame seeds** in a dry, shallow pan till golden, then remove from the heat. Brush **a tablespoon of runny honey** on the surface of a **250g block of feta**, then place the cheese flat side down in the sesame seeds and press gently. Turn the cheese over, brush the surface generously with more honey, then turn and pat down gently to cover with seeds.

Place the sesame-covered cheese on a piece of tin foil and place in a baking dish. Bake for 10 minutes at 200°C/Gas 6, until the cheese has started to soften.

While the cheese bakes, remove the peel from **2 blood oranges** with a very sharp knife, then cut them into thickish slices, about six per fruit. Squeeze a third orange into a bowl and add **30ml of olive oil, a tablespoon of white wine vinegar**, a little salt, some black pepper, coarsely ground, and the sliced oranges.

Wash **100g of spinach leaves** and dry in a salad spinner, then toss with the orange slices and their dressing. Divide the spinach and orange slices between two plates and spoon over some of the orange and olive oil dressing. Cut the warm feta in half, and place one piece on each of two plates. Serves 2.

# Crumbed lamb with Roquefort

lamb cutlets, white bread, thyme, parsley, egg,
Roquefort, double cream

Put **6 large lamb cutlets** on a chopping board and flatten them
slightly, using a cutlet bat or a rolling pin. They shouldn't be more
than a couple of centimetres thick.

Put **100g of white bread, crusts included**, into the bowl of a food
processor. Drop **a heaped tablespoon of thyme leaves** into the
breadcrumbs, add **a handful of picked parsley leaves**, then process
to coarse crumbs. Season with salt and black pepper.

Crack **an egg** into a shallow bowl or on to a plate and beat it lightly.
Place the chops, one at a time, in the beaten egg, turning to coat the
other side. Lift the chops from the egg and lower into the crumbs.
Press down firmly on the crumbs, then turn and coat the other side.
Warm **a little olive oil** in a frying pan over a moderate heat, add **a
slice of butter**, and fry the chops for 3 or 4 minutes on each side. Lift
the chops out and drain them on kitchen paper.

While the chops are cooking, mash **100g of Roquefort or other
soft blue cheese** with **150ml of double cream**. Serve with the
crumbed lamb. Serves 2.

&

The danger here is that the crumb coating cooks before the lamb is
ready, so make sure the lamb is no thicker than 2cm. Keep the heat
at a moderate level, so the crumbs don't colour too quickly.

&

This works well with pork steaks too – in which case the blue cheese
dressing could be replaced by something lighter, such as shredded
grated cucumber and yoghurt, or puréed poached rhubarb.

# Gnocchi dolcelatte

gnocchi, spinach, dolcelatte or Gorgonzola, double cream

Put a large pan of water on to boil. When the water is boiling, salt it lightly and add **500g of gnocchi**. Cook for 3 or 4 minutes, until the gnocchi rise to the surface, then drain.

Tip the gnocchi into a lightly buttered baking dish and set the oven at 180°C/Gas 4. Wash **150g of spinach** and, while it is still wet, put it into a deep pan, place over a moderate heat and cover tightly with a lid. Let the spinach cook in its own steam for a couple of minutes, then remove from the pan, drain and squeeze almost dry.

Tear the spinach into manageable pieces and tuck it among the gnocchi. Break **200g of dolcelatte or Gorgonzola** into large pieces and add to the dish. Season **300ml of double cream** with a little black pepper and pour over. Bake for 30 minutes, until bubbling. Enough for 4.

&

Take care not to over-salt the gnocchi's cooking water. The cheese will provide enough salt. Balance the richness of this dish by serving it with a crisp salad of bitter leaves, such as chicory, frisée and watercress with thick crunchy stems, to mop up the creamy, cheese-flavoured sauce.

&

Use steamed purple sprouting broccoli or lightly cooked Brussels sprouts in place of the spinach. Cover the surface with grated Parmesan and a handful of fine fresh breadcrumbs for a golden crust. Use penne or other pasta instead of gnocchi.

# Minced turkey chilli

onions, minced turkey, ground chilli, curry powder, chilli sauce,
tinned haricot beans, soured cream, coriander

Pour **a little olive or groundnut oil** into a shallow pan and warm
over a moderate heat. Add **a couple of onions**, peeled and roughly
chopped, and let them cook until soft and pale gold. Remove the
onions, then add **500g of minced turkey** to the pan and let it brown
lightly, stirring occasionally. Add **2 level teaspoons of ground chilli**,
followed by **a teaspoon of curry powder** and **a tablespoon of chilli
sauce**. Let the spices fry for a minute or so with the turkey, then
add **a drained 400g tin of haricot beans**. Let the mixture simmer
for a good 5–7 minutes, until thoroughly hot, then stir in a **few
tablespoons of soured cream or crème fraîche** and **a handful of
coriander leaves**. Serves 4.

&

Once you have added the minced turkey to the pan, leave it, without
stirring, to brown lightly. Constant stirring will mash the mince up
too finely and prevent it from browning, and the flavour will only
be deep enough if you brown the meat properly. As this dish has a
short cooking time, make sure the spices get a good minute or two
of cooking with the turkey before any further ingredients are added.

&

Serve the chilli with rice or in a warm tortilla, or even on a toasted
English muffin. Minced chicken or lamb can be used instead of the
turkey. Change the spices to suit your own taste, substituting smoked
paprika for the chilli, perhaps, or introducing ground coriander or
cumin. Bring a little garlic into the equation, adding a finely crushed
clove together with the onions.

# Chickpeas and mussels

mussels, tinned chickpeas, onion, harissa paste, bread

Scrub and carefully check **400g of mussels**. Drain **a 400g tin of chickpeas**. Peel and chop **an onion**, then fry it in **a little oil** until pale gold. Add the drained chickpeas to the frying pan and let them heat through.

Drop the mussels into the chickpeas and onion, cover tightly with a lid, and leave to cook for 4 or 5 minutes, until the mussels have opened.

Mix **2 tablespoons of harissa paste** with **2 tablespoons of olive oil** and a little of the liquid that has appeared in the bottom of the mussel cooking pot, and beat to a thin paste with a small whisk. Ladle the mussels into wide bowls, spooning the cooking liquor over them as you go, then splash with the harissa paste. Serve with **plenty of bread** to mop up the juices. Serves 2.

&

Check the mussels carefully, discarding any that are cracked, chipped or refuse to open when tapped hard on the sink. Likewise, discard any that refuse to open after cooking. Make sure the lid is on tight, so that the mussels steam in their own juices.

&

Use clams instead of mussels. Judion beans or cannellini beans can be substituted for the chickpeas. Pesto can also be swapped in instead of the harissa. The whole point is that the dressing should mix a little with the cooking juices in the bowl to give a very small amount of flavoursome broth for you to soak your bread in.

# Lentils with sausage and pecorino

sausages, garlic, vegetable or chicken stock,
brown or green lentils, rocket, pecorino

Warm **a couple of glugs of olive oil** in a deepish casserole, then add **6 fat, herby sausages** and brown them evenly on all sides. Peel and finely slice **2 cloves of garlic**, add to the pan, and cook for a minute or two until they turn pale gold. Pour in **1 litre of vegetable or chicken stock** and bring to the boil. Tip in **400g of small brown or green lentils** (such as Puy), let the stock return to the boil, then lower the heat and leave to simmer, partially covered with a lid, for about 35–40 minutes, until the lentils are tender but just short of soft. Correct the seasoning with salt and black pepper.

Blitz **50g of rocket leaves** and **75g of pecorino** together in a food processor until you have coarse green and white crumbs. Spoon the lentils and sausages on to deep plates, then scatter the rocket and pecorino over the top, letting the cheese soften slightly with the heat of the lentils. Enough for 2.

&

I suggest checking the lentils every 5 minutes throughout their cooking time. Lentils vary in size, variety and, it has to be said, age, and take vastly different times to approach tenderness. I prefer to salt them towards the end of the cooking time, as occasionally an early salting seems to toughen them, as it can other dried pulses.

&

This recipe can be adapted to include thin strips of belly pork instead of sausages. Cut the pork into pencil-thick strips, cook briefly to crisp the fat, then continue as above.

# Chicken, sausage and butter bean broth

chicken breasts, sausages, shallots, chicken stock,
tinned butter beans, parsley

Cut **2 bone-in chicken breasts** in half, to give four pieces, then season them with salt and pepper. Warm **a slice of butter** and **a glug of oil** in a large saucepan or casserole, then add the chicken pieces and brown them lightly and as evenly as you can. Remove them, then add **4 plump, herby butcher's sausages**, each cut into three pieces, to the pan. Let the sausages colour on all sides, then lift them out and add to the chicken. Roughly chop **3 shallots** and let them cook in the pan, with a little more butter or oil if necessary, until they are soft and golden. Return the chicken and sausages to the pan. Pour in **1 litre of hot chicken stock**, bring to the boil, then lower the heat and simmer the broth for 20 minutes.

   Add **a drained 400g tin of butter beans** to the pan and continue cooking for 5 minutes. Add **a handful of chopped parsley** and serve. Enough for 2.

## &

This is a quick, midweek version of a classic chicken, sausage and bean casserole. If you prefer, add a second tin of beans, a tin of chopped tomatoes and some thyme and garlic. Then, once it has come to the boil, transfer to the oven and let it cook for a good hour or more at 160°C/Gas 3. It will taste even better when reheated the following day.

## &

Make this more about the beans by doubling the quantity, adding large cubes of pancetta instead of sausage, and stirring in a couple of spoonfuls of basil pesto just before serving.

# Lamb with spiced parsnip mash

parsnips, butter, lamb steaks, ground cumin, curry powder,
lemon, mint

Peel **800g of parsnips**, cut them into large pieces, then boil or steam
them for 15 minutes, or until they are soft enough to mash. Put the
cooked parsnips into the bowl of a food processor or mixer, add **50g
of butter**, a little salt and a generous grinding of black pepper, then
process or mash to a smooth purée. Scrape into a mixing bowl and
keep warm.

Warm **a thick slice of butter or 2 tablespoons of olive oil** in a
shallow pan. Season **4 lamb chump steaks, each weighing roughly
250g**, and cook them in the butter or oil, over a high heat. When
they are brown outside but still pink within, remove them to a warm
plate and cover to keep warm.

Add **1 teaspoon of ground cumin** and **2 teaspoons of curry
powder** (your own blend or favourite brand) to the pan and let
them cook for a minute. Add **the juice of a lemon** and let it sizzle
and foam with the butter or oil and spices. Chop **a small handful
of mint** and stir it into the juices, then check the seasoning. Stir the
spiced pan juices lightly into the parsnip purée.

Divide the parsnip mash between four warm plates and place the
rested lamb steaks on top. Serves 4.

&

This spiced butter works well with mashed potatoes or swede. Use
boneless pork steaks instead of lamb. This is a fast midweek supper,
so I use a branded curry powder, but you could mix your own and
keep it in a tightly stoppered jar out of sunlight.

# Wet polenta and winter greens

polenta, double cream, butter, Parmesan, winter greens,
beetroot leaves, chard

Put **half a litre of water** on to boil in a deep, high-sided pan. As
it boils, rain in **125g of fine, quick-cooking polenta**. Season very
generously with salt and bring to the boil. As it thickens, pour in
**75ml of warmed double cream** and **50g of butter**. Grate **35g of
Parmesan** and stir it into the cooking polenta. Have ready about
**180g of washed winter greens**, such as kale, beetroot leaves or
thin-stemmed chard. Tear or slice these into manageable lengths.
Steam the greens for a minute or two. Drain carefully, then serve
them with the cooked polenta and more grated Parmesan. Serves 2.

&

As polenta cooks, it bubbles up like a volcano. Take great care, as the
splashes will scald you. Keep the heat moderate and stir regularly
with a wooden spoon, taking care to stir right into the corners of the
pan. It is worth remembering that the longer you cook your polenta
the firmer it will get.

&

The texture of polenta is a personal thing, and I like mine soft, verging
on the soupy; others prefer it to have more of a cakey consistency.
The above ratio of polenta to water makes a stiffish one. Add more
cream, butter or even hot water, as you wish, to make it softer. Chop
and change the greens with whatever you have available or what is in
season: broccoli is wonderful with polenta, as is cavolo nero.

# Pumpkin seed cod

pumpkin seeds, dill, cod fillet, Dijon mustard

In a food processor, reduce **75g of pumpkin seeds** and **25g of dill fronds and stems** to a coarse crumb-like texture. Mix together with **2 tablespoons of olive oil**.

Place **2 pieces of cod, each weighing about 250g and cut from the thick end of the fillet**, in a baking dish. Spread the top of each piece of fish with a thin film of **mild Dijon mustard** (a level teaspoon on each will probably be enough), then pat the dill and pumpkin seed mixture over the mustard on each piece. Generously trickle a little more olive oil over the fish and bake in a preheated oven at 180°C/Gas 4 for between 12 and 15 minutes. The fish should be lightly done, the crust a deep green-gold. Serves 2.

&

Pumpkin seeds can burn quite easily, so moisten the surface of each prepared piece of fish with a little olive oil before you put the dish in the oven. Be sure to cook the fish only until the flakes can be gently pulled apart from one another with a fork. Accompany the fish slices with some lightly cooked spring greens or steamed spinach.

&

It's important to use a fish that comes in good thick steaks. You want to be sure to avoid the oilier fishes, such as salmon or mackerel, as these don't seem to work nearly so well with the dill and pumpkin seed crust. If dill isn't your thing, swap it for parsley or, even better I think, a mixture of half parsley and half tarragon.

# Baked eggs with kale and Taleggio

kale, cavolo nero, eggs, Taleggio, pumpkin seeds

Put a pan of water on to boil. Set the oven at 200°C/Gas 6. Wash and lightly shred **125g of mixed greens, such as kale and cavolo nero**. Add the greens to the boiling water, leave for a minute, then immediately remove and refresh in a colander under cold, running water. Gently squeeze most of the water out of the greens and set aside.

Beat **6 eggs** in a large mixing bowl, then add the shredded greens and season generously with salt and pepper. Warm **2 tablespoons of olive oil** in a non-stick 22cm pan, then, as bubbles start to appear, pour in the egg and greens mixture. Leave to cook over a moderate heat for 2 minutes. Tear or slice **150g of Taleggio, or another soft, easily melting cheese**, and place on the surface of the eggs and greens. Scatter over **3 tablespoons of chopped pumpkin seeds** and bake in the preheated oven for 12 minutes, until the eggs are lightly set and the cheese is oozing. Serves 2.

&

The eggs should be only lightly set. Cook the egg and greens mixture only until you feel it is just firm enough to slice. It will feel soft and lightly springy. It is essential that the greens are not too wet when they go into the egg mixture, so make sure to gently squeeze any excess water out of them, using your hands.

# Celeriac and blood orange salad

blood oranges, lemon, capers, grapefruit, yoghurt, celeriac, nigella seeds

Make the dressing for the oranges by slicing **a blood orange** and **a lemon** in half and squeezing their juice into a small bowl. If your **capers – you'll need 12** – are salted or stored in brine, rinse them then add to the juices. Capers in olive oil can be added as they are, without rinsing. Season with three or four turns of black pepper, then pour in **3 tablespoons of olive oil** and combine lightly with a fork or small whisk. Taste and stir in a little salt, if necessary. Your dressing should be bright, sharp and slightly salty.

To make the salad, remove the peel from **3 small blood oranges** and **a grapefruit**. The easiest way is to remove a small slice from both top and bottom with a very sharp knife, place the fruit, cut side down, on a chopping board, then slice away the peel, cutting downwards, following the shape of the fruit. Cut each orange and grapefruit into about six thin slices, placing each in the dressing as you go, then set aside in a cool place.

Make the dressing for the celeriac by putting **200g of yoghurt** into a large mixing bowl, then beating in **3 tablespoons of olive oil** with a fork, seasoning with salt and pepper. Peel **a celeriac** – it should weigh about 200g after peeling – then grate, electronically or by hand, into matchstick-thick shreds. If you grate too finely, the result will be wet; too thickly and the salad will be too crunchy to eat. Fold the celeriac into the yoghurt dressing.

To serve, arrange the slices of orange and grapefruit on a serving dish or individual plates, pile the dressed celeriac in the centre, then spoon the orange dressing over the fruit. Scatter **a few nigella seeds**, lightly toasted in a dry pan for a minute or two, over the celeriac. Serves 2.

# Crab, broccoli and yuzu broth

thin-stemmed broccoli, vegetable stock, lemon grass, chilli, spring onions, light miso paste, yuzu juice, crabmeat, coriander leaves

Bring a large, deep pan of water to the boil, salt it lightly, add **200g of thin-stemmed broccoli** and cook for 3–4 minutes, until tender. If you prefer, you can steam it. Drain and refresh in cold water.

Pour **1 litre of vegetable stock** into a saucepan and set it over a moderate heat. Using a heavy weight, such as a rolling pin, crush **a little lemon grass**, splintering the stalks to help it flavour the broth. Add it to the vegetable stock. Finely chop **a large red chilli**, removing the seeds if you wish. Cut **2 spring onions** into tiny rounds, then add, together with the chilli, to the broth. Bring the liquid to the boil, then stir in **a tablespoon of light miso paste** and **2 teaspoons or more of yuzu juice**.

Remove the lemon grass stalks from the broth, add the cooked broccoli, let it heat through for a minute or two, then ladle into two large, deep soup bowls.

Divide **100g of white crabmeat** between the bowls, add a few coriander leaves and serve. Serves 2.

&

Once you have added the miso paste, keep the broth at a simmer. Start with a tablespoon of paste, adding more to taste. Don't be tempted to add the crabmeat too early. It will overcook. The cool crabmeat and hot broth is a delightful contrast.

&

Should you not wish to use crab, then scallops, sliced and briefly grilled, would be good, as would any lightly cooked white fish. If you don't have access to yuzu (available at major supermarkets and Japanese grocery shops), you could use a shot of lime juice instead.

# Lamb stuffed sweet potato

sweet potatoes, minced lamb, onion, hot red chilli, mint

Wipe the skins of **4 medium to large sweet potatoes**, then bake them for about an hour at 180°C/Gas 4.

While the potatoes are baking, pour **a thin film of olive oil** into a non-stick frying pan over a high heat, then add **400g of minced lamb** in a thin layer. Let the lamb brown on the underside, then break it up and let the rest of it brown evenly, stirring from time to time. When the mince has browned appetisingly, transfer it to a mixing bowl. Peel and thinly slice **a medium-sized onion** and let it colour lightly in the pan, adding a little more oil if necessary. Finely chop **a small red chilli** and stir it into the onion. As soon as the chilli is soft, tip everything in with the lamb and season with salt, pepper and **a little chopped mint**.

When the potatoes are tender right the way through, remove them from the oven, put them on a chopping board, take a long slice from the top of each – to form a lid – and set aside. Using a teaspoon, scoop the flesh from each potato into a mixing bowl to leave four hollow shells, then put them into a roasting tin. Mix the meat, potato and onion, then pile it back into the potato shells. Put any remaining mixture alongside in the tin. Place the lids on top and bake for 15–20 minutes, till thoroughly hot. Serves 2–4.

**&**

The skin of the sweet potato is thin and fragile. Bake the potatoes only until they are tender, and handle them carefully when scraping the flesh out of the skins so that they do not tear. Keep testing the potatoes as they bake, and catch them before they collapse. I find that medium-sized ones take about 45 minutes to bake.

**&**

Spice the filling up a bit with ground cumin, coriander, a little nutmeg and some garlic, added as the onion is softening. Minced pork is good here, too, in place of the lamb, seasoned with garlic, Parmesan, chopped pancetta and dried oregano.

# Index

531

538